PRAISE FOR *ROLL-UP*

"I have sought out many books on M&A, but this is the only one I have found specific to the utility industry and is immediately useful in a pragmatic way before, during, and after a deal . . . This book contains decades of knowledge and anecdotal experience from the utility M&A expert of our generation."

—Mark Lantrip, former CEO, Southern Company Services

"*Roll-Up* gives a fascinating account of utility sector consolidation from someone who was in the room where it all happened."

—Steve Fleishman, managing director, senior utilities and midstream analyst, Wolfe Research

"Over the course of his career, Tom Flaherty was at the table—advising the industry's best when the stakes were high. His new book sheds important light on a sector that is more vital than ever to the American economy."

—Gale Klappa, executive chairman, WEC Energy

"A comprehensive look at utility consolidation over the past three decades with valuable guidance for managing shareholder risk, navigating the complex regulatory approval process, and identifying and capturing value through successful execution and implementation of the transaction. You could not have a more experienced guide than Tom Flaherty to take you through the labyrinth of issues that must be navigated to successfully merge two utility companies."

—Bill Lamb, senior counsel, Baker Botts

"This book ties together the history, process, and personalities of the massive consolidation of the utility industry over the last thirty years. So much of this M&A, which has shaped the current utility industry, continues to provide lasting benefits to all stakeholders. Over decades of working together, I have witnessed Tom Flaherty's skills and insights, which helped shape the utility industry we know today... few people have had the impact on the utility industry that Tom has."

—Jeff Holzschuh, chairman, Institutional Securities Group, Morgan Stanley

"As utilities faced competition, mergers were seen as a way to become, or stay, a low-cost provider. Tom Flaherty was always involved in estimating savings and guiding the implementation of the transaction, and whenever a merger or acquisition was considered, he was your first call."

—Dick Kelly, former CEO, Xcel Energy

"Tom Flaherty's participation in the depth of detail has given him unmatched insight into utility M&A. One is hard pressed to find another player seated at the table in so many utility combinations. The maturity of the industry and its commensurate lack of top-line growth has caused its leaders to look to M&A to contain costs and alleviate price pressures for customers. Tom is in a unique position to tell these stories and to distinguish among them."

—Mark Ruelle, chairman, Evergy

"Tom Flaherty is the dean of utility M&A consulting and was involved in the creation of many of today's most important companies. His insights and experiences will be valuable for both industry-focused and general readers."

—Joseph Sauvage, chairman of Global Power Group, Citi

"It is absolutely imperative that any leader considering and evaluating M&A opportunities understands how to unlock the deal's intended value. In *Roll-Up*, Tom Flaherty takes you inside the challenges executives face when addressing these critical issues. *Roll-Up* goes beyond the traditional play-by-play of a merger. Tom uses his decades of expertise to dive deeper and examine the types of strategy, drivers, and actions within the utility space that have created the modern era of our industry."

—**Tom Fanning,** CEO, Southern Company

"*Roll-Up* captures the rationale behind the utility industry's M&A historical transactions and the logic for further consolidation. *Roll-Up* is a must-read for anyone interested in the history of the utility industry and its future direction."

—**Jim Torgerson,** former CEO, Avangrid

"No individual other than Tom Flaherty has the experience, knowledge, and insight to write a book such as this. Tom has been involved in more utility merger transactions than any living individual, and I have had the pleasure of working with him on many of those transactions and consistently have admired his contributions. Anyone who needs to understand the 'hows' and 'whys' of utility mergers should look no further than this excellent and comprehensive book. Filled with both history and important insights, it is a must-have resource for utility executives, their advisors, and regulators."

—**Mike Naeve,** former FERC commissioner and head of the Skadden energy practice

"As the utility industry heads for further consolidation, this book provides the roadmap to successful execution. Tom Flaherty's disciplined approach to merger integration, navigating regulatory approvals, synergy optimization, and creating value is a tried and true formula for success."

—**James Judge,** executive chairman, Eversource Energy

"The significant transformation of the utility industry over the years has been truly remarkable. Learnings from the past, skillfully chronicled in this book, indicate how profound change and progress lie ahead. Informed by over 25 years of direct involvement in most utility mergers and acquisitions, and enhanced by the views of prominent executives and professionals, Tom Flaherty has produced a notable work that provides key insights into the past and future of utility consolidations. A must-read for investors, utility executives, academics, and governmental officials."

—**Erle Nye,** former CEO, TXU Corp.

"This is a no-nonsense, fact-filled dissection of how utilities join forces. The book is required reading to attain regulatory approval for a merger or acquisition. I have worked on a number of deals, and it is a testament to Tom Flaherty's credibility that both utilities jointly engage him to deliver on synergies that drive shareholder value."

—**Bob Irvin,** executive director, Joules Accelerator

"When I have listed the 10 most influential individuals in the energy and utilities industry over the past quarter century, this book's author, Tom Flaherty, inevitably makes that list. There can be no better commentator on the history and dynamics of the industry's M&A. If you are involved in the energy and utility industry M&A in any way, or are impacted by it, this book is a must-read."

—**Steve Mitnick,** executive editor, Public Utilities Fortnightly

Roll-Up

The Past, Present, and Future of Utilities Consolidation

THOMAS J. FLAHERTY

This publication is designed to provide accurate and authoritative information in regard to the subject matter covered. It is sold with the understanding that the publisher and author are not engaged in rendering legal, accounting, or other professional services. Nothing herein shall create an attorney-client relationship, and nothing herein shall constitute legal advice or a solicitation to offer legal advice. If legal advice or other expert assistance is required, the services of a competent professional should be sought.

Published by Greenleaf Book Group Press
Austin, Texas
www.gbgpress.com

Distributed by Greenleaf Book Group

For ordering information or special discounts for bulk purchases, please contact Greenleaf Book Group at PO Box 91869, Austin, TX 78709, 512.891.6100.

Design and composition by Greenleaf Book Group and Lindsay Starr
Cover design by Greenleaf Book Group and Lindsay Starr

Publisher's Cataloging-in-Publication data is available.

Print ISBN: 978-1-62634-927-8

eBook ISBN: 978-1-62634-928-5

Part of the Tree Neutral® program, which offsets the number of trees consumed in the production and printing of this book by taking proactive steps, such as planting trees in direct proportion to the number of trees used: www.treeneutral.com

Printed in the United States of America on acid-free paper

22 23 24 25 26 27 10 9 8 7 6 5 4 3 2 1

First Edition

To Robyn, Leah, and Carter . . . eternally grateful for your love and support

CONTENTS

ACKNOWLEDGMENTS

The modern era of U.S. utility mergers and acquisitions (M&A) has stretched more than 25 years and triggered large-scale consolidation of a highly home-grown and fragmented industry. To achieve the successful combination of multiple electric and natural gas companies took the concerted efforts of utilities senior leadership, as well as advice from a range of experts from the investment banking, rating agencies, legal, and consulting professions.

While directly participating as a consulting advisor in most of the utility combination transactions occurring since 1995, the experiences and perspectives from numerous executives and advisors are irreplaceable and provide insightful observations to complement my own views regarding market drivers, utility aspirations, transaction complexities, and future motivations.

The contemporaneous industry history, market backdrop, transaction strategies, and post-close activities captured and addressed in this book have been greatly enriched through participation in its development by several of the most seasoned, respected, and thoughtful executives and professionals comprising the U.S. utility sector and its advisory groups. These individuals represent many of the most visible participants in the U.S. utility consolidation landscape across the last several decades.

These executives and professionals need little introduction as they are well known, and natural inclusions in any discussion of utility M&A

in the U.S. I am appreciative of all the current or former chief executive officers (CEOs) and talented professionals that made themselves available for interview and review of this manuscript. All these individuals have had—and in several cases continue to have—illustrious careers, and their experiences and insights capture a treasure trove of invaluable perspectives and insights from which all readers will benefit.

Specific thanks to the following chairmen or CEOs for their insights and candor provided during interviews for this book and their friendship over many years: Tom Fanning from Southern Company; Jim Judge from Eversource Energy; Dick Kelly from Xcel Energy; Gale Klappa of WEC Energy; Erle Nye of TXU Corp.; Mark Ruelle from Evergy; and Jim Torgerson of Avangrid. It was a distinctive pleasure to work with you and observe your leadership and transactional acumen in action.

Many thanks are also provided to several luminaries from the advisory sector: Steve Fleishman of Wolfe Research; Jeff Holzschuh from Morgan Stanley; Bill Lamb of Baker Botts; and Joe Sauvage from Citi. Your collaboration across a host of utility merger and acquisition transactions is deeply appreciated and personally valued.

Additional thanks to Mark Lantrip from Southern Company, Mike Naeve of Skadden, and Bob Irvin at Joules Accelerator for their kind words and M&A collaboration over the years.

I was also fortunate to work with numerous other utility industry CEOs, senior executives, investment bankers, attorneys, and analysts on various utility M&A assignments that contributed to industry consolidation and shaping my perspectives. To all these individuals, I am grateful for the many collaborations that occurred.

I am also extremely grateful for the invaluable support from the staff at the Edison Electric Institute in compiling a historical time series of key financial metrics to enable consistent data analysis and presentation.

Finally, it's important to recognize the many former partners and colleagues that I worked with on utility M&A assignments over the course of my consulting career. Your contributions were vital to what we accomplished as a team and instrumental to the consulting success we enjoyed.

PREFACE

The archetype for power and gas utilities in the United States has dramatically evolved from its conception in the 19th century—not only is it immense in scale, it is diverse in role, versatile in structure, and unique in operations. These characteristics have enabled the U.S. utilities sector to evolve from an analog, centralized, and standardized business model to one that is digital, distributed, and personalized, all while the industry is rapidly decarbonizing.

The amount of change the industry has undergone—not just since its inception 200 years ago, but in the last 50, 25, and even 10 years—is vast. These changes have facilitated the evolution from widespread local ownership to narrow ownership by a few large companies, to broad ownership by regional entities, and finally to expanding ownership by super-regional companies. Fuel supply sources, power supply mix, transmission grid expanse, network operations intelligence, and customer experience models have been equally reshaped across these time frames.

Unlike utilities, most industries in the U.S. have a high degree of concentration; that is, a few large firms comprise most of a particular industry because it facilitates competitiveness and innovation. These industries have either been reshaped to meet competitive realities or recreated by emerging technologies, enabling tailored offerings and opening up new avenues to go-to-market. Comparatively, the utilities industry lags behind other industries in the extent of change which has occurred over a similar time frame.

From a rather random and disjointed beginning in the U.S. in the 19th century characterized by small, localized companies focused on providing services to city blocks, neighborhoods, and discrete facilities, the utilities industry expanded into more than 6,000 providers of early utility services, including electricity, natural gas, water, transit, and even ice. The easy entry into the utility marketplace itself paved the way for both scrupulous and unscrupulous owners and financiers to build, buy, or broker assets, companies, and systems almost on demand. This of course led to the creation of multiple holding companies, each owning dozens or even hundreds of individual utilities of all shapes and sizes, and in various islands or clusters of locational operation.

As one would expect, the levels of self-dealing, layered financing, stacked corporate structures, greedy behaviors, pricing abuses, and complicated governance eventually attracted attention from federal and state authorities, ultimately creating a day of reckoning over the purpose, role, alignment, and structure of the utilities industry. The call for stricter financial guidelines, greater regulation, and sensible industry restructuring ultimately caused the federal government to intercede and change the permissible structure, composition, policies, practices, and direction of the U.S. investor-owned utilities industry.

With the eventual enactment of the Public Utilities Holding Company Act in 1935, radical restructuring of the hundreds of holding companies and thousands of operating companies began, depending on the time frame, lasting until almost 1960. From hundreds of loosely aligned holding companies, a dozen registered holding companies eventually emerged, subject to direct oversight by the Securities and Exchange Commission (SEC). Accordingly, the SEC codified a series of strictures, requirements, and guidelines for how these holding companies and their related operating companies could function as public utilities providing services for the greater public good.

Most Americans do not know the history of the utilities industry, and how it has consolidated and evolved into what it is today. After all, utilities are very much taken for granted, in that consumers tend not to think about them until the power goes out and the convenience and comfort of heating, lighting, and cooling is lost—even if only temporarily. And while the history of the utilities industry is a fascinating study itself, in fact, leading to a Hollywood movie (*The Current War*) about its development and personalities, it does not naturally draw the average reader or consumer like it does certain types of strategy, finance, engineering, and policy professionals.

It surprised me that so little attention had been given to how the industry evolved to its current state in the modern era, particularly the drivers and actions in different periods over these 25 years. Certainly, there have been numerous articles, presentations, and speeches about utility industry mergers and acquisitions (M&A), but a gap still exists in presenting a comprehensive viewpoint that moves beyond specific transaction events to the challenges executive management faces when addressing their boards of directors rating agencies, and regulators. The gap also extends to navigating the critical issues related to identifying and quantifying value, succeeding with the regulatory approval process, and ensuring effective integration produces the value the deal was predicated upon.

There is much still to be learned from the actions of the utilities industry over the last 25 years of the modern era of M&A and its resulting contraction in the number of electric and natural gas providers. My perspective derives from more than 45 years of working in all elements of the utility industry—electric, gas, telecommunications, and water—as well as all layers of providers, federal agencies, state authorities, investor-owned companies, cooperatives, municipalities, private equity, infrastructure funds, and other investors at both the

U.S. and international levels, with more than 30 of those years focused on U.S. utility M&A.

While many utilities have executed M&A transactions, companies certainly don't pursue consolidation every day. Institutional memory fades and externalities change. Other companies have never undertaken a deal, and managements that have completed a combination may not necessarily still be in place.

This book is intended to inform M&A practitioners, observers, and interested bystanders about the history of consolidation, describe the changing motivations for combinations, provide hands-on perspective on successful transaction execution and outcomes, and establish a hypothesis about what could happen next in the modern era of utility M&A.

To enrich the discussion within the book, I conducted interviews with 11 current or former chief executive officers, investment bankers, attorneys, and ratings analysts to provide introspection and commentary on their own experiences with consolidation in the modern era from 1995 to 2020, both domestically and internationally, and through the five cycles defined for assessment. These essential contributors provide perspectives from those individuals that made the tough decisions about whether to pursue a transaction, those that provided constant advice to management, those that crafted merger agreements, and those that evaluated the logic of a transaction and the potential for successful outcomes. This perspective adds to my own as a consultant involved in various strategic, financial, regulatory, and post-close aspects of the vast majority of U.S. utilities stock transactions greater than $1 billion since the late 1980s.

This book follows a natural course from the original highly fragmented U.S. industry structure, through the development of industry views on consolidation and participation, and finally to the drivers and events occurring in each of the defined cycles. It then addresses deal execution, beginning with the topic of how value is derived from a transaction to the challenges related to gaining board of directors and regulatory approval, and on to how utilities can ensure that value anticipated is value produced. Since the past is not a complete indicator of the future, the book discusses the current nature of business simplification and portfolio rationalization, which will likely continue in an evolving form, and takes a look over the horizon at how future transactions might evolve beyond those seen today.

A Fragmented Industry (Chapter One) describes how the structure and regulation of the utilities industry pre-and post-1935 lead to the market overlay that existed in 1995, and the factors affecting whether and how consolidation could be framed given prevailing constraints and market evolution.

Natural Opportunities (Chapter Two) discusses how different externalities contributed to the rationale and need for consolidation, particularly about gaining scale and capturing value. These factors contributed to changes in the focus on where to transact, as well as the parties participating in utilities industry M&A.

Modern Era of M&A (1995–2020) (Chapter Three) presents a multi-period look at the drivers affecting pursuit of M&A in each period and how they played into management considerations. Each section identifies key transactions, transaction premium levels, regulatory approval timelines, and industry contraction within each period, as well as unique deal types.

Maverick Actions (Chapter Four) recognizes that not all mergers and acquisitions between or among utilities entities are traditional; that is, straightforward and predictable. The chapter identifies the range of non-traditional transactions that have occurred over time and that create high interest when these unique events occur.

Value Sources (Chapter Five) addresses how value is derived from a transaction and the contributors to building value to buyers and combining utilities when executed. This chapter also covers the often overlooked costs associated with deal pursuit and the levels of synergies typically obtained by utilities from transaction execution.

Hurdles and Outcomes (Chapter Six) describes how utilities successfully navigate the requirements to obtain internal and external approvals to undertake and complete a transaction. It also describes the risks associated with undertaking a transaction and how to ensure shareholders are appropriately compensated.

Successful Execution (Chapter Seven) discusses how companies can think about planning, structuring, and executing a post-close integration process which culminates in Day 1 readiness and continuous value capture. The chapter also differentiates full utility integration transactions from non-regulated, international, or cross-sector deals, where a lighter touch is often more applicable.

Return to Restructuring (Chapter Eight) addresses the recent number of utilities pursuing portfolio rationalization, that is, the sale, sell-down, or carve-out of current businesses and assets. It also reflects on the external influences that are driving companies to address their current level of carbon emissions and the effects this has on future business positioning and composition.

Future Direction (Chapter Nine) offers a potential glimpse into the future over the direction and nature of utilities industry M&A and the types of transactions that could result. It also considers the nature of risk and outcomes that could support or hinder continued utilities consolidation and how these elements could be mitigated.

This book provides factual presentation and insight, as well as external perspective and foresight from those that have directly participated through the modern era of utility M&A. The seasoned utility executive and professional will recognize much of the history and drivers affecting M&A, while gaining additional insight into areas where they may not directly participate, but affect the success of their companies or clients. A novice to utility industry M&A can rapidly gain a thorough perspective on a continually evolving sector and a better appreciation of how today's utilities came to their current state and, more importantly, where they may be headed and how motivations for the new energy transition affect company readiness strategies.

The U.S. utilities industry has been steadily repositioning by consolidating itself over the last 25 years (1995-2020) from over 150 companies to fewer than 50 tradable entities (the company is wholly acquirable in the stock market) today. This dramatic reduction has occurred despite a range of uncontrollable externalities, like economic recessions, governmental mandates, technological advances, and regulatory proscriptions, as well as company strategic desires to scale up for future growth and competition, to reach the industry's current state of play

To move to this level of fewer than 50 tradable U.S. utilities, companies have had to navigate a range of deal life-cycle challenges related to merger or acquisition partner identification, strategic, financial, and operational diligence, bid price negotiation, federal and state regulatory commission approval, and post-close integration of the two combining companies.

Compared to other industries, the track record of the U.S. utilities industry has been solid and exemplary—most transactions have closed; regulatory commitments and conditions have not been onerous; value expectations have been realized, and combining companies have been ready to align and operate on day 1.

There are no particularly limiting reasons why U.S. utility industry consolidation will not continue to occur, either in number or scope. The industry is far from becoming too big or difficult to regulate, and benefits to customers continue to be produced and enjoyed. The nature of transactions is always changing, so rationales, scopes, structures, participants, pricing, and regulation will continue to evolve and make for more interesting study of merger motivations, mechanics, and outcomes.

While the industry has been actively on a road to further consolidation, the model to guide the new energy transition is still emerging. Absolute industry direction is uncertain, but the alignment of market drivers suggests that U.S. utilities will remain active in mergers and acquisitions and continue to use these transactions as a fundamental growth strategy.

CHAPTER 1

A FRAGMENTED INDUSTRY

Today's U.S. power and gas utilities industry is the product of more than 200 years of formation, evolution, and transformation, as well as wave after wave of governmental, financial, regulatory, and technology cycles and upheavals. These cycles have forged the parameters of the current utility industry model and the paradigm in which it operates. And now the current model frames the context for how power and gas utilities view continued evolution toward their future roles, strategies, and opportunities for successful market outcomes.

At a glance, the U.S. utility model is far more complicated than it appears, and undoubtedly more complicated than it should be. It is multitiered, multisegmented, and multifaceted in its structure, composition, and regulation. The utilities industry is also largely taken for granted—energy for power, motion, lighting, cooking, heating, and cooling is expected to be available on demand—and it is generally of low daily interest to most power and gas consumers until service is no longer available.

This low visibility belies the high criticality of the sector to the American economy and consumer lifestyle—a vibrant utilities sector is fundamental to development of industrial applications, technological innovation, and infrastructure resilience.

Since the late 19th century, electrification of the U.S. has been foundational to the development of the country. From the large Eastern cities to the Upper Midwest to the great West and the rural South, the availability of abundant electricity has fostered three American industry technological revolutions, such as high-volume process production, high-intensity manufacturing, and high-precision computing assembly), which galvanized sustained economic development. Even earlier, in the early 1800s, natural gas utilities were formed in the U.S. in both Baltimore and Philadelphia for streetlighting and gas distribution, respectively.

The early attractiveness of the utilities industry in the 1800s was buoyed by the unconstrained ability to stand up new electric or gas companies and systems almost overnight to meet emerging needs for fundamental premise, building, and factory consumption. Quickly, savvy industrialists and/or financiers determined that owning one or more utilities was a sure bet for financial success.

The reasoning was clear: customer demand was insatiable; full electrification and gas delivery were decades away, and all existing and new plants, grids, and networks (pipes or wires) were essentially monopolistic. Why not own as many as you could?

And why not pursue ubiquitous electrification or expanded gas delivery where possible, whether from existing sources or for new uses, to leverage existing and new investments for growth?

Utility M&A was birthed in this earlier environment and continues today, although the evolution of the industry has assured that monopoly behaviors that existed in its early days cannot continue today given the number of alternative generation entrants, merchant transmission builders, non-utility equipment interconnectors, and competitive retail energy suppliers throughout the U.S. Today, top-line growth through increased electric or gas demand is viewed as a virtue empowered by new technologies and supported by customer preferences.

To put this attractiveness in empirical terms, U.S. electricity consumption grew from under six million kWhs in 1900 to approximately 75 million kWhs in 1925, 290,000 million kWhs in 1950, 1,750,000 million kWhs in 1975, 3,400,000 million kWhs in 2000, and 3,800,000 million kWhs in 2019 (most recent available data).[1,2] This growth reflects the extension of the national customer base, industrialization of the economy, expansion of electricity uses, intensity of electricity consumption, and alternative fuel displacement, for example, heat pumps for natural gas. Growth in natural gas delivery has had its challenges over the last few decades, as consumption has been heavily impacted through energy efficiency enhancements or electric conversions.

The power sector is now poised for another step-change in electrification and growth as it deploys new technologies to increase infrastructure resilience and reduce carbon emissions. The promise of replacing existing combustion engine vehicles and commercial equipment with a mix of electric passenger cars, light-duty vans, ancillary rolling stock, medium- and heavy-duty trucks, mass transit, and heavy-duty excavation and farming equipment paints a clear picture of an increasingly robust level of electric demand over the upcoming decades. The gas sector can also potentially look to natural gas vehicles and more propane conversion for the future, although on a smaller scale than for electric utilities.

While electric demand has been centered on single-family homes, multi-family dwellings, commercial office buildings, industrial facilities, and government installations, this view will now be supplemented by deployment of charging stations and adoption of electric transport and light- and heavy-function equipment at ports, military bases, airports, rail stations, and remote work sites.

Depending on the charger type, local consumption, and household devices, a single home Level-3 charging installation (rapid charging) is expected to generate incremental electric consumption close to the equivalent to the residence itself in some locales. And when charging parks are installed at corporate, mall, store, hotel, apartment, or stadium sites, substantial additional load will be created.

Additionally, electrification build-out to engage non-traditional entities and convert traditional customers suggests an opportunity and need for companies to be able to act seamlessly across cities, states, and regions to avoid an uneven customer experience. This future explosion in electric consumption enhances the growth and attractiveness of the power sector by offering new sources for electricity demand which make access to customers even more valuable. In some parts of the country, gas is still a substitute for propane and oil to provide growth from enhanced demand.

Why do increased electrification or gas substitution matter with respect to the future of utilities sector M&A? Because each are core to a utility's organic growth and to strengthening the financial capacity of companies to solidify parallel inorganic growth platforms.

Too many utilities still do not have the necessary capabilities or scale to adequately respond to evolving business, delivery, or technology needs. Meeting the needs of future customers places a premium on positioning, agility, and speed, which translates into business model evolution and operating model enhancement. These outcomes are more naturally catalyzed through inorganic rather than organic means. Such requirements naturally point to M&A as a catalyst for acceleration of growth and enhanced market positioning.

The ability to take advantage of this future demand surge depends on how utilities position themselves to meet the market in natural, adjacent, and proximate markets. Practical and artificial challenges existed in the past that constrained the ability to naturally grow within existing service territories. Inorganic growth has been fundamental to unlocking additional value specifically related to how the industry has been owned and operated for most of the 20th century.

Structural Alignment

The electric segment of the U.S. utility industry has been highly vertically integrated for more than 120 years. In contrast, most upstream natural gas exploration, refining, and production has been separated from downstream transportation and distribution for local distribution companies (LDCs). Particularly after the passage of the Public Utility Holding Company Act (PUHCA), and the realignment of holding companies, the electric industry was viewed as a permanent natural monopoly due to natural functional alignment, fungible asset financing, vertical product value, and/or the absence of policies to the contrary.

As a natural monopoly, the electric utilities industry was believed to most appropriately exist without competition to facilitate access to capital for preservation of the public interest, and to avoid duplication in parallel local systems for similar purpose.

The vertically integrated value chain for the electric sector comprises eight elements spanning upstream fuels development through downstream customer engagement, sales, and services. The vertical gas utility value chain looks similar, although the processes of exploration, refining, and production are upstream activities and usually outside the utilities sector, while midstream transportation could be provided by either independent pipelines or integrated pipelines as part of a utility.

Each value chain element plays a unique role in delivering services to customers and each has a level of investment scale that fits its purpose and design. Generation has historically been the largest component of value within the electric value chain due to the scale of capital requirements for large central generation stations and the level of non-commodity revenues. Transmission has historically been between 10 and 20 percent of total investment, depending on the region of the country, with distribution now seizing an increasing portion of total capital spend as large-scale power supply projects have dissipated in the face of less capital-intensive renewables projects.

For decades, these electric and gas value chains remained largely unchanged. But in the mid-1990s, electric utilities began to face the potential that competition could be introduced into a natural monopoly. The notion that a vertically integrated utility precluded its customers from any choice of supplier became a rallying cry for policy development or legislative enactment to unbundle the electric sector.

Power supply became the first casualty of unbundling of the value chain as few natural structural impediments were observed by regulators and legislators to the provision of supply commodities from any builder of peaking, mid-merit, or baseload generation assets. With separation of generation, customers theoretically would be able to find their own supplier(s) as needed, for example, independent power producers (IPPs), and if they could not, then incumbent utilities would take on default supply responsibility.

On why mergers were attractive to Eversource Energy and its predecessor companies in this environment, Executive Chairman Jim Judge offered:

> The result of deregulation and unbundling was to shrink the number of utility holding companies by more than half. As companies saw this outcome unfold and accelerate in the mid-1990s, it became clear rebuilding our scale was needed to continue to survive and become really good at operating our business, which means keeping prices low and delivering high performance to customers.

Moving to an environment where the electric or gas commodity was sold through retail electric providers (REPs) meant that the long-standing utility direct relationship with customers would no longer occur around energy supply or consumption billing, and only continue for commodity delivery and reliability-related issues. These decisions were made well before the emergence of disruptive technologies and would turn out to create future gaps in meeting an expanded set of customer needs.

With generation and retail determined to be competitive services, attention then turned to electric transmission and distribution. These functions were more likely to be bundled because of grid design and voltage step-down interfaces. In essence, while anyone could provide power supply from local or dispersed generation sources, providing transmission and distribution services would be uneconomic to build in parallel and would create significant diseconomies.

However, these considerations also evolved as the Federal Energy Regulatory Commission (FERC) introduced new thinking about broad and transparent generation markets needing assurance that power supply could seamlessly be moved across states, and within and across regions.

Seven Regional Transmission Organizations (RTOs) and/or Independent System Operators (ISOs) were stood up to provide coordinated dispatch, transmission planning, and grid optimization activities. In addition, several transmission systems—such as those of utilities in Michigan and Wisconsin—were sold separately to new operators, or transferred to an independent entity outside of the transmission-owning utilities, to oversee operations.

The notion of merchant transmission evolved, which created the opportunity for incumbents and entrants to compete over new transmission lines if they could demonstrate these additions to be economically viable as grid additions for renewables interconnection, line decongestion, or economic supply.

An integrated distribution network had never been seriously believed to be anything other than a natural monopoly due to the economics of parallel building and/or stranding of network facilities, complexities of interconnection and optimization of disparate networks, and further disengagement from the customer. However, evolution and miniaturization of technologies now suggests that micro-grids and other islanded systems are effective, if only as localized solutions.

The disaggregation of certain generation, transmission, and retail businesses fundamentally changed the purpose and role of utilities.

The grid remains integrated, though it is no longer controlled locally by each utility as power supply and transmission decisions can be made by RTOs/ISOs (collaborating with IPPs, incumbents, and state regulators) and REPs maintain a primary interface with customers in fully competitive states.

Incumbent utilities—whether still vertically integrated or functionally unbundled—have become specialists in the operation of their fleets, grids, and/or networks. Deep capabilities need to exist in their legacy businesses to ensure that service levels are perpetually maintained, costs are effectively managed, and customers are fully satisfied. All these objectives suggest that optimization can be better achieved with sufficient scale and targeted but purposeful growth strategies.

Consequently, both electric and gas utilities have utilized the outcomes of disaggregation as a basis for their market strategies. And both electric and gas utilities have recognized that specialization requires deep capabilities to ensure continued business performance and, where relevant, a positive and supportive customer experience.

The need for deep capabilities has pushed utilities to think more expansively about scale and the need to both bulk up for strength and optimize for efficiency, which has led many companies to M&A to enhance business flexibility and operations optimization.

When discussing the motivations for earlier U.S. utility M&A, Tom Fanning, the CEO of Southern Company, identified a couple of primary drivers:

> It was all about scale. Companies pursuing mergers generally considered their positioning against two elements. First, how did externalities affect the future business. Second, how could business risk from market presence and return levels be optimized through value uplift across owned segments and assets. Portfolio theory emphasizes scale, and earnings per share growth is linked to impacts from available sources or actions. To create real earnings impacts, companies needed to think bigger to

pursue a merger or acquisition. A small transaction adds small earnings growth, but a larger deal provides more sustainable value potential. Utilities recognized they would be better off with a larger platform as, at a minimum, it provided greater degrees of freedom.

A Balkanized Landscape

History has left us with five core levels of ownership—federal, quasi-governmental authorities, investors, municipalities, and cooperatives—within the primary utility ownership groups. But even these five owner categories do not accurately reflect unique elements of the sector as investors can include hedge funds, infrastructure funds, and venture capital, and governmental authorities can be regional, statewide, or sub-regional.

Further, the structure of utilities can vary and multiple permutations exist: generation and transmission; generation or transmission only; generation, transmission, and distribution; transmission and distribution; transmission or distribution only; or a fully integrated portfolio of all the above. And retail can be matched with several of these structural entities depending on the local market model. These ownership models reflect legacy corporate structures, as well as the impacts of mandated unbundling, opportunistic carve-out, and long-serving regulatory models.

A casual glance at a national map illustrates a highly fragmented landscape has existed since the industry's inception, through holding company disaggregation and into the highly consolidated present. More than 3,000 private and public utilities existed in 1900, comprising multiple combinations of electric, gas, water, coke, dam, trolley, and even ice offerings, and this grew to approximately 6,500 by 1920, before declining to just over 4,400 by 1928.[3]

Over the time frame from 1995 to 2020, the scale of the utilities industry substantially expanded in market capitalization, while contracting in the number of holding companies or utilities. The number of operating companies generally remains unchanged since local operations reflect the identity of the incumbent utility rather than the holding company.

While thousands of operating companies existed in the early 20th century, a comparative modicum still exists today, with the decline largely representing situations where the smallest entities collapsed into other local companies to simplify the industry landscape once holding companies were restructured.

While investor-owned power and gas utility holding companies number 50 today, an approximate 2,000 municipalities, 900 cooperatives, five federal power administrations, and 200 state power agencies or authorities also continue to exist and provide services to customers in the U.S.[4] And although not widely recognized, approximately 170,000 water and wastewater systems operate across many different

Figure 1: Utilities Sector Composition

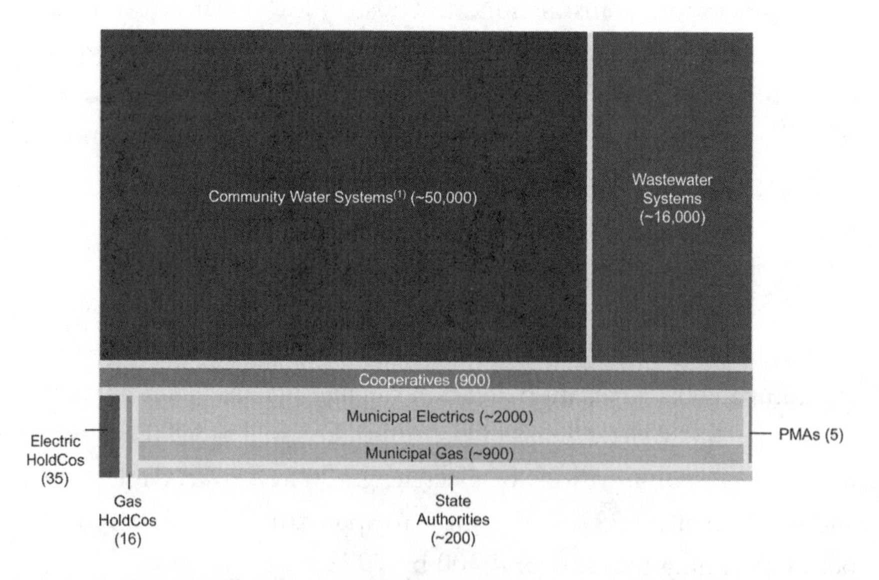

types of governmental models, such as government authorities, municipalities, water districts, irrigation systems, and even trailer parks.[5] All of these sectors have lent themselves to some level of consolidation in recent decades.

The high number of all these entities reflects the low barriers to early industry entry, rapid electrification and gas distribution, industrial fuel needs, competitive technologies, metropolitan partitioning, suburban spread, rural growth, general western and southern expansion, and specialized or localized needs. The number of utilities also paralleled existing constraints in generation and transmission technologies, the clustering of populations, and the entrepreneurial activities of engineers and investors.

The number of small, disconnected, and unique utilities and loads initially created electric or gas islands which then grew into clusters and were the forerunners of networked systems. This patchwork network of entrepreneurs, neighborhoods, municipalities, financial institutions, and industrials framed the subsequent development and continuity of localized utilities, which continues today.

While the Balkanized nature of the U.S. utility industry was an impediment to an efficient grid for decades, it was also a prime catalyst for growth when utilities concluded that consolidation was long overdue to improve regional system operations and enable customer benefits to be produced. But legal and agency statutes inhibited much consolidation for several decades in the 1900s, due to constraining artifacts and standards that quickly became out of step with industry structural and operating realities. It later became crystal clear that structural and ownership limitations crafted in the 1900s had little to do with market realities of 1995.

These constraints needed to be resolved, remedied, or relieved to enable consolidation to effectively occur across the U.S. with circumstances so different from state to state and region to region.

PUHCA Impacts

Since its inception, the utilities industry has experienced both continuous consolidation among investor-owned companies, as well as dramatic disaggregation by way of PUHCA's application. The passage of PUHCA was a watershed event for utilities, affecting both the electric and natural gas sectors, although gas to a far lesser degree. Oversight for this law was established with the Securities and Exchange Commission (SEC) as the lead regulatory agency to administer PUHCA.

In 1932, before PUHCA was enacted, three holding companies controlled one-half of the utility industry, with one owning 130 utilities, and eight electric holding companies controlling almost 75 percent of the investor-owned utility business. For gas distribution companies, 11 systems controlled 80 percent of pipeline miles in the U.S.[6,7]

After the passage of PUHCA in 1935, the SEC instigated a formal restructuring effort to get more companies to register as holding companies and to divest operating companies that were not part of a single integrated system. In 1938, as it started its restructuring program, the SEC had caused 144 companies to register as holding companies, created 51 separate utility systems, and established 524 holding companies and 1,524 sub-holding companies, and many applications for registration or exemption were in process.[8]

From a utility holding company perspective, the number of entities peaked at above 200 by 1930, ultimately dropping to 18 in the 1950s, and to 12 by the time the SEC completed its restructuring of the industry in the late 1950s.[9] The result of this multi-decade PUHCA-related restructuring was a reconstitution of the footprint of the industry into new clusters of individual holding companies and utilities with a cleaner ownership model and more logical integrated systems.

Further operating company consolidation occurred during the SEC's almost three-decade restructuring effort, with more small

Figure 2: Pre- and Post-PUHCA Holding Companies(1)

Pre-PUHCA Holding Company		Subsidiaries(1)	States	Population (Millions)
International Paper & Power	▪ Hydro-Electric System	31	7	3.8
United Corp.	▪ Columbia Gas & Electric	50	8	NA
	▪ Niagara Hudson Power	36	1	2.8
Electric Bond & Share	▪ American Gas & Electric	13	9	3.0
	▪ American Power & Light	26	13	3.5
	▪ Electric Power & Light	32	12	4.1
	▪ Lehigh Power Securities	3	1	NA
	▪ National Power & Light	10	6	3.5
Associated Gas & Electric Co.	▪ Associated Gas & Electric	34	20	5.0
Investment Companies	▪ North American Co.	35	8	5.0
	▪ Pacific Lighting	8	1	3.1
Equity Corp.	▪ Standard Gas & Electric	14	20	6.0
Stone & Webster Engineers	▪ Commonwealth & Southern	12	11	9.2
	▪ Public Service Company	23	11	2.2
	▪ United Gas Improvement	56	4	5.5
Electric Power Associates	▪ American Water Works & Electric	105	16	2.4
Cities Service Company	▪ Cities Service	184	22	4.5
United Light & Power	▪ United Light & Power	53	13	5.2
Utilities Power & Light	▪ Utilities Power & Light	48	18	2.1
Middle West Corp.	▪ Middle West Utilities	40	15	3.3

Post-PUHCA Holding Companies(2)

- Allegheny Power System
- American Electric Power
- Central and South West
- Columbia Gas System
- Consolidated Natural Gas
- Eastern Utilities Associates
- General Public Utilities
- Middle South Utilities
- National Fuel Gas
- New England Electric System
- Northeast Utilities System
- Southern Company

1) Includes second-tier sub-holding companies and traditional operating companies
2) Reflects Securities & Exchange Commission restructuring process conclusion in 1958
3) Sources: Public Utilities Fortnightly "Financial News and Comment" 1935, pp.210-212; 24th Annual Report of the Securities and Exchange Commission, pp.107-110

company rationalization occurring and almost 2,000 operating companies contracting to just over 300 entities with assets above $12 billion by 1948. In addition, more than $12 billion (then current dollars) in assets were divested by the end of the 1940s.[10]

The impact of PUHCA post-enactment became significant in the assessment of subsequent transactions by the SEC and, to a lesser extent, state regulators. Since PUHCA was initially passed to stem abuses from inappropriate financial structures, non-arm's-length transactions, and corporate behaviors, multiple restrictions were enacted within its four corners. PUHCA was intended to avoid a repetition of prior problems and defined structural constraints to multi-state and multi-business utilities as well as adherence to ownership constraints and execution actions and facilitated state regulatory oversight.

These restrictions addressed: contiguous territory, capital structure, security offerings, business composition, unregulated scale, affiliate interests, cross-subsidization, operating integration, and ownership limitations, among other issues. The inability of existing holding companies to satisfy PUHCA constraints related to overall ownership, business composition, and unregulated activities precipitated mass dissolution of holding companies and mass divestment of operating companies and unrelated businesses.

In the aftermath of PUHCA passage, old engineering-based holding companies such as EBASCO, Stone & Webster Engineers, and private holding companies such as Commonwealth & Southern, United Light & Power, Associated Gas & Electric, Cities Service, etc., which owned the bulk of the U.S. utilities sector, were broken up and their holdings reestablished into nine new electric utility holding companies like Southern Company, American Electric Power, and Middle South Utilities and three new gas holding companies for Consolidated Natural Gas, Columbia Gas System, and National Fuel Gas.[11]

These entities became the new mega-utilities, several of which still exist close to their original post-divestment form. PUHCA gave both clarity to industry structure, as well as regulatory models needed to oversee a restructured industry removed from unique ownership pyramids and institutional relationships.

Electric and gas operations were separated at the holding company level and single state or contiguous state utilities were established. Given the geographic areas, Balkanization of the sector, and natural progression of the industry, companies operating in adjacent or proximate areas were obvious opportunities for combination. And as the consolidation wave reemerged in the mid-1990s, the first place to look for a partner was where familiarity already existed and discrete systems and grids could be optimized.

The SEC was not initially friendly toward early utility mergers, stressing tight application of existing PUHCA constraints and causing transactions to be avoided or dropped for fear of an inability to cure SEC strictures or meet its policies. In addition, the SEC and state regulatory agency jurisdictional contests could create a belief that the eventual cures, for example, divestments, could destroy value within the merging companies.

Bill Lamb, senior counsel with Baker Botts, provided additional background on why requirements were evolving:

> By the early 1980s, the SEC thought the utilities industry had markedly evolved from circumstances existing at the passage of PUHCA in 1935—companies were more secure, state regulation was effective, financial markets were more transparent, and there were fewer multi-state holding companies. At the same time, the utilities industry was highly fragmented and ripe for reconsolidating, particularly with unbundling of integrated companies being pursued in several states. While the chairman of the SEC believed PUHCA had outlived its usefulness, the agency could not unilaterally modify it without direction from Congress.

He went on to talk more about how the SEC addressed application of PUHCA beginning in the 1980s through the early 2000s:

> The SEC viewed PUHCA reform was necessary, if not outright repeal. But in the absence of action by Congress, which was complicated to obtain, it determined it could apply its discretion in interpretation and application within the bounds of the existing statute. The SEC began to look at the industry and emerging transactions with an eye toward gradual relaxation of its requirements in areas like territory contiguity and system integration. While the SEC did not fully drop PUHCA application, it took a more discretionary approach to application and provided more leeway to qualifying for an exemption, so it did not unnecessarily impede consolidation.

Given PUHCA's restrictions on utilities consolidation, the approval timelines for federal-level approvals were often extended. For example, several early transactions, like Washington Water Power and Sierra Pacific Power and American Electric Power and Central and South

West, endured approval periods of 24 months or more, with the first transaction subsequently terminated after FERC review was extended.[12]

Over time, the SEC subsequently relaxed its precedents on multistate and multi-business utilities—even before the replacement of PUHCA in 2005—which ignited a wave of subsequent transactions, some markedly different to the structural policies that preceded these prior decisions.

Bill Lamb from Baker Botts shared more insights on the specific actions the SEC took that increased the flexibility of utilities in pursuing mergers:

> The SEC centered its merger review on three key structural constraints: whether a company needed to be registered or considered to be exempt from registration; whether a single integrated system or an unconnected system would exist; and the nature and relatedness of non-core businesses. The SEC applied its standard tests to these questions, assessing the underlying facts, circumstances, and potential mitigations in each area, gradually providing flexibility to applicants. The SEC ultimately relaxed its prohibition on combined gas and electric systems within a single registered holding company, so for the first time in decades, registered electric holding companies could own gas distribution systems.

Technology Evolution

It has been averred that more change will occur to the utilities industry in the next 10 years than has occurred in the last 50 years. If the last three years are any indicator, this expectation will turn out to not just be true, but a foretelling of how different the utilities industry could look by 2030.

The pace of change is rapid and accelerating and a reflection of how fast disruptive technologies are being embraced by large commercial and industrial customers. These technologies are affecting end-to-end utility and customer interactions, as well as relationships from customer expectations to incumbent roles to business models to technology deployment to value propositions. U.S. utilities are now on a path toward more technology adoption and willingness to innovate, even if still behind their competitors and customers.

Grid-level technologies for power supply are rapidly improving asset performance levels, as well as offering at-the-site capacity supplements. Several front-of-the-meter innovative and disruptive technologies have been adopted for advanced network management related to grid planning, interconnection, and optimization platforms, as well as direct operational enhancement. And behind-the-meter technologies are proliferating to provide greater energy consumption insights and control features, as well as site and premise transport electrification support.

The message from technology adoption is not that utilities need to continually enhance their technological savvy and value of adoption—this should naturally intensify and proliferate. Rather, the theme is that utilities are being pushed to reinvigorate their purpose and role with respect to customers, particularly how they envision preserving and enhancing the value of the customer relationship.

Technology deployment leveraging advances in batteries, virtual power plants, micro-grids, charging infrastructure, demand flexibility, micro-turbines, Internet of Things, home hubs, distributed energy resources, artificial intelligence, and/or domotics is contributing to an evolution in the role utilities see for themselves in the future. More importantly, these advances are creating a picture of the future grid, network, and behind-the-meter capabilities necessary to ensure utilities market success.

Several leading U.S. utilities (and mega-oil companies) have also begun to study the future of hydrogen and the impact it can have on the environment and utility businesses. Hydrogen is viewed as being particularly relevant to enabling greater renewables through storage, as well as aiding in the reduction of carbon emissions as a cleaner source of power supply, and may provide the means for nuclear units to develop new revenue streams.

Hydrogen as a source of production or storage has been more actively studied, tested, and deployed in Asia and Europe than in the U.S. However, it is a primary technology evolution focus of multiple dimensions of all economies, given the versatility in production source, that is, green (electrolysis from renewables), gray (from natural gas), blue (carbon capture from coal production), and brown (from conventional coal) without carbon capture, and in potential application.

While hydrogen economics and use cases are rapidly improving, the future of the hydrogen story is only being framed in 2021 and will take another decade or more to become a table stake in energy production at scale. It is not clear the range of roles that U.S. utilities will take in this search for a more environmentally friendly supply source, but its application to renewables storage may have the most near-term benefit to the sector.

These technology advances serve as a continuing catalyst to sector reshaping, but utilities are still behind the technology adoption curve. Advancement of new technologies means utilities need to reimagine their roles with customers, and to do that they need to become far more technologically savvy than they are today. To succeed, utilities need to think like non-traditional market entrants and as entrepreneurs singularly focused on demonstrating the ability to optimize the value of their grids and networks for customers.

Utilities are making progress on these emerging technology challenges. A number have established internal venture capital funds to identify, understand, and evaluate new technologies. Even more have joined external venture capital funds to stretch their technology investment funding, collaborate with other utilities, and create a window into multiple learning laboratories.

The industry now finds itself positioned for its next stage of structural advancement to meet these changed circumstances from deployment of innovative and disruptive technologies. The rapid advancement of offerings and evolution in expectations is leading to a technology *push* and a customer *pull* environment.

The advanced landscape enabled by these new technologies will create a new playing field for why M&A may occur and where it may flourish. The ability to effectively serve the expanding needs of customers makes access to knowledge, experience, technologies, and offerings a priority for tomorrow's utilities. And organic development is a slow and painful way to obtain this positioning—inorganic activity will be a necessary element to bringing needed capabilities to bear on behalf of customers.

Positioning Challenges

The dynamics noted earlier are causing utilities to rethink where to play, how to play, and how to win. Determining the right answers will depend on how utilities envision their future. Are they operators? Are they providers? Are they enablers? Are they optimizers? Or are they catalysts?

After more than 200 years of industry evolution, the industry is positioning for its next stage of advancement. It has approached another inflection point—will it follow a path of cautious experimentation, or will it aggressively lead from the front on adoption and deployment?

The future path to be selected will be a critical determinant of how U.S. utilities strategically position to meet market challenges and satisfy shareholder needs for growth. Currently, many U.S. utilities expect approximately 5-7 percent compound annual earnings growth rates, with some estimating 6-8 percent, or slightly higher.

These growth rates typically envision 1-1.5 percent from organic demand growth (excluding post-pandemic recovery) and 2-2.5 percent from cost management, with the remainder representing the typical growth wedge, or undefined need, which can only come from inorganic activity. A growth wedge of 2-3 percent in incremental earnings is significant and cannot be filled by small actions—it requires a more substantial event or a series of events to drive sustainable earnings addition.

The need to continually fill the earnings commitment at these levels will lead utilities to pursue merger or acquisition transactions or other types of inorganic events such as co-investment, joint ventures, etc. While higher demand and/or customer growth and tight management of costs below inflation levels are core to earnings growth, achieving overall commitments takes something extra in the form of an unconventional event.

The industry has weathered multiple upheavals in policy, regulation, technology, financing, and competition. Preparing for the next 10 years of evolution will make the difference whether utilities enjoy a revitalized market leadership position, or whether they fall behind competitor strategy execution and customer value expectations.

Of more relevance is how utilities take note of external market challenges and their impact on market positioning and success. Too many utilities are not adequately equipped to meet the real strategic, financial, operational, technology, and customer challenges that they will face in the future as stand-alone companies.

External industry challenges have usually precipitated the stages of consolidation that have occurred in the modern era. There is no reason to assume these challenges will not continue to engage utility managements in considering their most viable strategic directions. These considerations will undoubtedly lead companies to conclude that further consolidation can be an effective element of the growth strategy and a catalyst for enhanced market positioning and competitive readiness.

M&A will be one of the primary drivers that ensures the ongoing journey of utilities toward a future of enhanced capabilities, strength, reach, and competitiveness has many years to run. Through use of M&A, the U.S. utilities industry can be positioned to fill capabilities gaps, build enhanced competitiveness, preserve financial flexibility, create incremental value, and leverage institutional brand to further support growth.

NATURAL OPPORTUNITIES

Utility industry analysts and observers typically attribute M&A occurrence to one or more of several factors: massive regulatory changes; significant industry fragmentation; disparate financial positions; executive leadership voids; troubled company situations; or insufficient competitive scale. And, on some occasions, combinations occurred simply because an unexpected opportunity presented itself that was too good to pass up.

These *soft drivers* (broad industry motivations) can be catalysts for a transaction, but are often viewed as more situational than fundamental. The U.S. utility sector has been extremely diffused geographically with wide variability in absolute scale—which are two *hard drivers* (critical company motivations) for M&A potential. These drivers are particularly relevant given how incumbent utilities have thought about post-M&A conditions like financial affordability, integration ease, and value outcomes.

There are not always specific rationales behind the origination and pursuit of deals. Merger transactions may be pursued by a local company simply because the nearby landscape is changing as aggressive out-of-market companies enter combinations with adjacent or proximate companies, which may be more natural partners to the local utility seeking a partner. These events have caused managements to seek partners out of concern that if no action is taken, they could be left with unattractive options, or no options at all except outright sale.

These considerations led to the realization that all companies are potentially affected by industry momentum for consolidation. Utilities have colloquially been grouped into three descriptive categories: *vultures* (large and aggressive); *bait* (mid-sized and attractive); or *roadkill* (small and bite-sized). Where a company falls along this spectrum may start with size, but it also reflects how a company is perceived by its peers, particularly aggressive suitors, and interested partners in general.

The primary focus of U.S. utilities industry consolidation has been on horizontal mergers such as aggregation of companies, versus vertical mergers, which are the integration of upstream and downstream value chain elements, although numerous convergence transactions have occurred. Depending on the time period, multiple assets have changed hands between owners, but these transactions are not at the center of this discussion.

With external momentum building for industry consolidation, U.S. utility managements were forced to consider the efficacy of M&A transactions, even if not a preferred choice, and assess several foundational industry-level questions:

- Could U.S. or global changes drive consolidation?
- What global growth models provide learning experiences to U.S. utilities?

- Would the U.S. utility industry experience the same pace of change as other markets?
- Is there a case for continued U.S. utility fragmentation?
- Are there external influences that will drive U.S. industry consolidation?
- Do real differences exist between utility and industrial M&A?
- What is the value of scale to utilities?
- Can scale be a competitive differentiator?
- Is high concentration an inevitable utility industry outcome?
- What is the risk of inaction to utilities?

Push and Pull

The motivation for consolidation has also been influenced by investment banker *push* and board of directors *pull*. As would be expected, the investment banking community identified early how fragmented the electric and gas utilities sectors were, particularly compared to other industries like telecommunications, pharmaceuticals, hospitals, banks, etc., with small numbers of competitors comprising large shares of the market in scale and competitiveness. By contrast, the five largest U.S. utility companies comprised only 28 percent of the total market capitalization of the sector in 2000 (which has increased to 42 percent of the total sector in 2020), with NextEra Energy itself comprising 16 percent of total market capitalization.[1]

Discussing the drivers for early industry consolidation, Chairman Jeff Holzschuh of the Institutional Securities Group at Morgan Stanley remarked:

> In the mid-1990s, utilities completed a sustained capital spend cycle over 10–15 years and faced the potential for select market competition and functional unbundling. Companies needed to evaluate their current asset base to assess shareholder value and decide which parts made sense to hold, and which might be more valuable to another entity. If deregulation would cause divestment and the current portfolio to shrink, leading to different returns between asset classes, utilities needed to understand which segment—power supply or delivery—best positioned them to strategically grow and compete. With this decision, companies knew they had to build more scale.

Investment bankers recognized that utilities consolidation was long overdue in the U.S. with a deep pool of candidates, high variability in scale, stark differences in financial strength, and broad diversity in competitive positioning. The mid-1990s utilities market environment was ripe for consolidation if it simply followed the pattern of other previously fragmented industries like banking, health systems, insurance, and airlines. Ed Tirello from Deutsche Bank boldly predicted that the roughly 150 utilities (holding companies and stand-alone companies) existing in 1987 could rapidly shrink to only 50 within five years. His prediction was directionally correct, but ambitiously fast.

At the board of directors level, interest in industry and neighborhood actions has always been a subject of the strategic agenda of boards. As transactions occurred, directors took notice and questioned managements on the potential implications to their companies and the value of M&A to their future strategic positioning.

In some cases, interest extended beyond that and boards began to vocalize the need for management to fully evaluate the merits of M&A

to not be caught flat-footed or miss an opportunity that could change the face and future of the company. They also counseled managements to approach M&A cautiously and not sacrifice their current strategy through expensive bids that could handicap the future balance sheet.

With these external events occurring and catalyzing internal board interests, utility managements recognized they would have to be engaged in the debate about M&A efficacy, whether or not they thought it was timely or even necessary. This realization led to a reshuffling of strategic priorities to address whether M&A was a possibility, an eventuality, or a foregone conclusion.

Pursuit of Scale

The modern era of M&A emanates from a search for sufficient scale to weather externalities like policy shifts, and strength to provide flexibility against risks like competition. The need for additional scale was laid bare in the mid-1990s when the sentiment for a competitive power industry began to take shape and gain traction.

As the specter of increased competition emerged in the early 1990s in California and other states, following United Kingdom utility privatization in that same time period, the electric industry was forced to take note of the potential for significant structural upheaval. California's Yellow Book, which laid out principles, objectives, and paths to electric industry restructuring, provided a roadmap subsequently followed by select states for how to create competition in segments like generation and retail.[2]

With a fledgling IPP generation model poised for market participation, the future was clear: generation unbundling would create either new competitors or result in power assets being divested and transferred into the hands of existing or new IPPs. Retail customer divestment would soon follow.

Dick Kelly, the retired CEO from Xcel Energy, remembered the drivers creating the push for consolidation:

> We saw the hand writing that competition would occur and lead to consolidation. We had high growth in Colorado, but knew greater scale could add business flexibility, balance sheet strength, and diversity in weather, rates, and assets. Since PUHCA was a limiter to broad expansion at the time, we prioritized close regional options and valued companies with compatible plants, available market interconnections, and higher growth.

The Yellow Book invigorated the stand-up of IPPs and the creation of multi-region generating asset portfolios as these competitors rapidly scaled up in the following years. The transfer or sale of these assets shrank the level of U.S. investor-owned utility generation and initiated a plethora of short- and long-term contracts from these plants, particularly baseload plants, like nuclear units.

In addition, the Yellow Book called for creating an unregulated retail segment outside of the integrated core value chain, which largely separated utilities from their customers for the first time in their history. In some cases, the retail businesses were sold to new providers, while in others they were part of a joint generation and retail unbundling model. As would be expected, the creation of these new IPPs and retailers precipitated more asset and portfolio swaps, as well as sales of retail sales books, and drove rapid and significant consolidation in two new sectors within just a few years.

This stand-up of essentially new market segments caused incumbents to rethink the market model necessary to ensure their long-term survival and success. With the industry moving toward functional specialization, such as operating generating assets, competing in physical and financial markets, or delivery of commodities to customers, companies recognized that standing pat was not likely to preserve their entities or provide new strategic advantage.

Erle Nye, the retired CEO of TXU, provided insights on early readiness for transactions:

> We just completed our two nuclear units, stabilizing TXU to where we could consider growing the business. Momentum existed in the U.S. for electric competition, and we prepared for that eventuality. We had a solid service territory, were blessed with strong growth, were good operators, with a rich set of available options in and around Texas. We desired to be an even better company, feeling we could transfer our success formula to an acquiree. We looked at many companies, addressing relative success, earnings accretion and growth, regulatory reputation, market position, relationship strength, risk exposure, synergies potential, and social issue compatibility.

Given the wide dispersion in native customers among U.S. utilities, companies have been acutely aware that inorganically adding millions of customers (versus organically adding thousands) was the fastest means to achieve a critical mass that could be further accessed for new products and services, as well as attaining financial and operating economies of scale that enhance sustainable financial performance.

The succeeding time periods changed utility owner perceptions of the industrial logic of owning certain types of assets and customers. But more than anything else, the search for opportunities to grow in large, unique moves, versus small annual increments, has been a foundation of M&A logic.

Growing Significance

From 1995 through 2020 (the modern era), the financial scale of the industry dramatically increased. The total value of investor-owned electric net plant grew from just under $400 billion to more than $1 trillion and market capitalization grew from approximately $240 billion to over $900 billion ($800 billion excluding combination companies whose predominant business is in natural gas in two or more scale metrics).[3] Just between 2015 and 2020 alone, capital investment for investor-owned electric utilities increased by over $600 billion, with over $100 billion in new capital annually.[4]

The LDC sector exhibited significant growth as well, spending over $75 billion in capital between 2015 and 2020, which increased net plant in service from approximately $40 billion in 1995 to over $140 billion in 2020.[5] And similarly, LDC market capitalization grew from approximately $3 billion in 1995 to over $40 billion in 2020 (and $120 billion when including combination companies that are predominantly gas in two or more metrics).[6]

These market capitalization levels reflect adjustments to general utility sector classifications to acknowledge the relative scale of each of the respective business segments of these combined electric and gas companies (NiSource, Black Hills Corp., Sempra Energy, CenterPoint Energy, and WEC Energy) on business elements like customers, plant-in-service or rate base, capital expenditures, and operating income.

Figure 3: Growth in Utility Scale

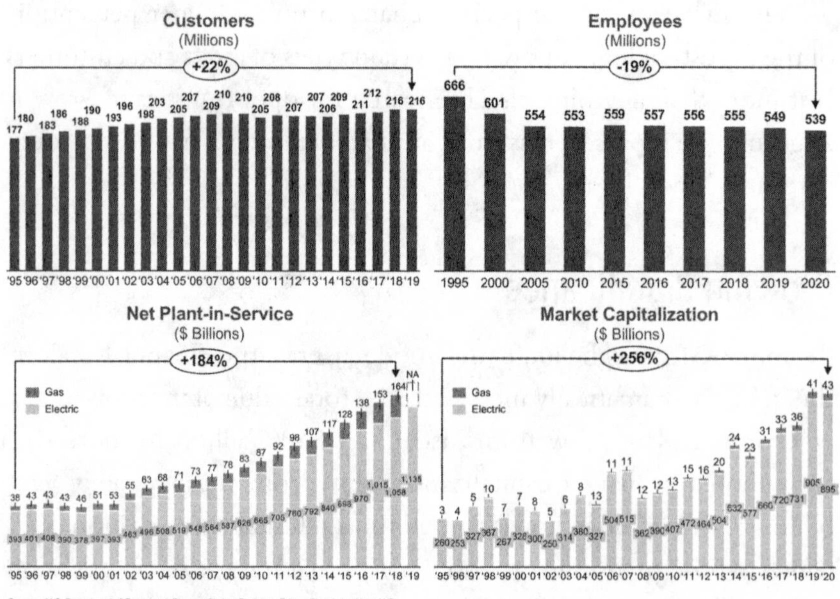

Sources: U.S. Department of Commerce, Bureau of Labor Statistics; Edison Electric Institute; U.S. Department of Energy, Energy Information Administration;; S&P Capital IQ Pro

Asset investment over this 25-year period ramped up for new generation, new transmission, gas main replacement, carbon emission related spend, network modernization, new renewables, and natural system growth. This significant investment, along with more adept operating management, increased financial returns, created improved investor sentiment, and enhanced market value, all of which made transaction pursuit and execution more possible.

The scale of the investor-owned segment of the electric utilities industry demonstrates just how tilted the current playing field is between potential buyers and sellers. In 1995, Southern Company, the largest utility in the U.S. at that time, had a market capitalization of $15 billion, or 6 percent of total electric industry market capitalization of approximately $260 billion.[7] It took until 2000 for Duke Energy and Southern Company to become the first utilities to top $20 billion in market capitalization, which combined equaled 13 percent of total market capitalization of approximately $300 billion at the time.[8]

Fast-forward to the end of 2020 and over 40 percent of the tradable electric companies had market capitalization greater than $20 billion and the single largest utility, NextEra Energy, topped $150 billion in market value of a total predominantly electric industry market capitalization greater than $800 billion.[9]

Gas utilities are led by Sempra Energy with a market capitalization of almost $37 billion of a total predominantly LDC industry market capitalization of approximately $125 billion.[10] Between electric and LDC sector utilities, 17 companies were greater than $20 billion in market capitalization at the end of 2020.[11]

More importantly, the dichotomy between the largest and smallest companies is stark. Of the 33 tradable electrics, 10, or about 30 percent of the sector, are below $5 billion in market cap, creating an industry characterized more by titans than medium or small-scale companies.[12] The reverse is true for the gas sector, where just two of the 16 tradable gas LDCs comprise a combined market capitalization in excess of $67 billion, which is approximately 53 percent of the total sector, with the remaining 14 companies in aggregate less than half of the market capitalization of the two largest sector entities.[13]

Figure 4: Market Capitalization Shifts

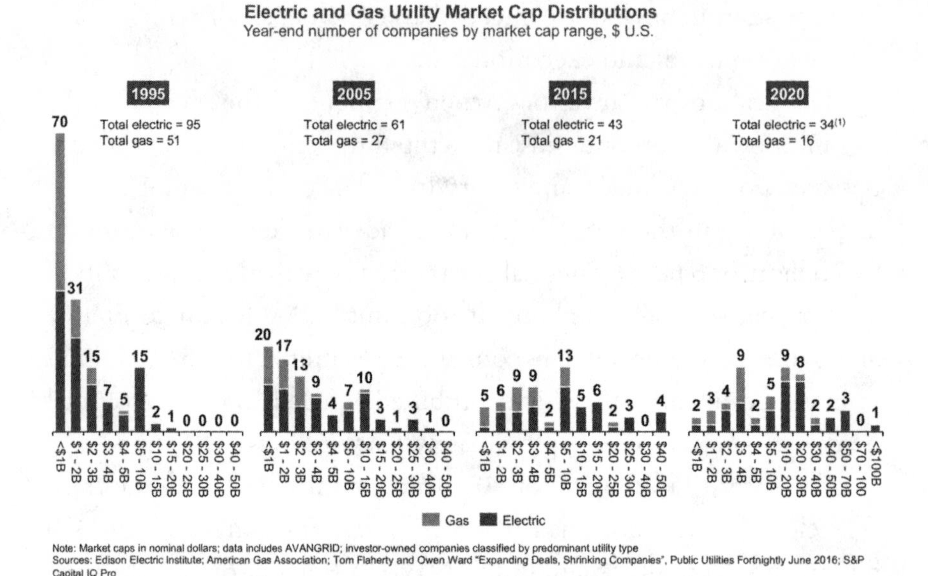

Scale expansion is also true when measured by customers. Several companies like Exelon, Southern Company, Duke Energy, and Sempra Energy approach or exceed 10 million customers.[14] Past growth in company scale through transactions has illustrated the value of scale to participants. Future deals may further change the scale landscape.

At the other end of the scale curve, investor-owned electric customers can fall below 110,000 and below 60,000 for similar gas companies.[15] While more bite-size, companies at the other end of the barbell from the titans also face the same challenges of future competitiveness and financial strength, and can be candidates for acquisition.

Of interest, the scale of public power entities varies widely. For example, the largest municipal electric is the Los Angeles Department of Power and Water, with more than 1.6 million electric customers, while numerous municipal electric departments have fewer than 1,000 customers.[16] Few municipal gas LDCs exist, with PGW at more than 500,000 customers and the rest with very few customers.[17] Among cooperatives, Pedernales Electric Cooperative is the largest at approximately 350,000 customers, with the average cooperative consisting of fewer than 25,000 customers.[18] For water entities, American Water Work serves more than 3,500,000 customers, while more than 29,000 local water utility providers serve fewer than 500 customers.[19, 20]

In the decades prior to 1995, the industry had not been regularly engaged in significant large-scale M&A activity, except in the decades immediately following PUHCA's 1935 enactment when holding company restructuring combinations or divestments led to broad roll-ups and disaggregations, which were utilized to rationalize the scale and scope of sellers and acquirors. Nonetheless, some small, local entity rationalization continued through the 1980s, which continued to move the U.S. utilities sector down the consolidation path.

Figure 5: Tradable Utilities Industry Contraction

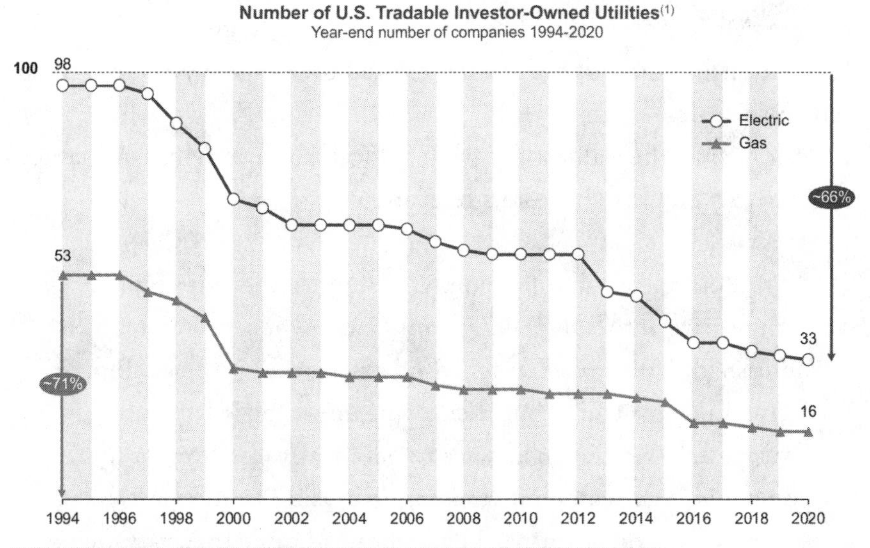

At the beginning of 1995, the utilities sector had shrunk to slightly fewer than 100 tradable entities, with the natural gas sector at fewer than 55 tradable entities. By the end of 2020, 33 tradable electrics and 16 tradable natural gas distribution entities remained.

Value of Scale

Given the emerging external challenges for more market competition and functional bundling, utilities knew the scale they possessed prior to these state movements could very well be diminished with the divestment or separation of an asset class or segment. Thus, it was clear that if companies wanted to preserve benefits from their prior scale level, they would need to re-bulk their businesses to replace the size being displaced.

When companies considered how to re-grow, organic means naturally fell far short of inorganic options, particularly during the mid-1990s to early 2000s eras when new capital spend was not robust. Inorganic means like mergers or acquisitions became the obvious path to faster business repositioning, even if the role of the utility was narrowing. More importantly, the level of existing fragmentation in the U.S. meant multiple opportunities existed to seek merger partners to replenish scale.

Addressing the value of scale, Jeff Holzschuh at Morgan Stanley provided several insights on its relevance:

> At the outset of consolidation, U.S. utilities did not emphasize turning size into value—that came later when power markets flourished and utilities watched others increase in scale. Bigger seemed better at first, but then companies realized they had to leverage scale in the right ways to gain real value from it. Some companies were adept at realizing this value from lower costs, seamless operations, financial flexibility, and capital access. Others

were not. When transactions started to create larger companies, U.S. utilities realized scale could be differentiating strategically and competitively.

An early mantra among utilities in considering a deal was that "bigger was better." This rationale had its limitations and soon evolved into "better was better," which implied that it was not just scale that mattered but knowing how to leverage size that would enable more value to be realized. But what did "better" really mean and how could scale be leveraged? And should value of scale be an outcome management attains by acting intelligently and aggressively at what it does best?

AVANGRID's retired CEO, Jim Torgerson, addressed the question of how he evaluated the value of scale:

> In the early days, I don't believe companies recognized the value of scale. But it was inevitable the utilities industry would have to continue to keep its prices to customers low and the best way to do that was through consolidation. This led to more deals to continue to build scale and use synergies to keep rates low.

Utilities naturally believed synergies were not just one reason for doing a deal, but the means for replenishing earnings levels, growing the earnings base, and further instilling a cost management discipline. Companies also knew that the time frame for realizing value was immediate for synergies capture, while other benefits from scale were neither quick nor certain.

Unsurprisingly, utilities focused on capturing synergies for their short-term and long-term value to earnings and business strength. Of course, synergies were the logical way to avoid earnings dilution, recover financing and integration costs, contribute to cash flows, and reward shareholders for the risk they assumed from the transaction.

And utilities believed they were up to the challenge of capturing synergies since managing costs is among the easiest ways to add to earnings, as well as a core element of their operating prowess.

Given this focus on synergies, utilities did not have to immediately answer the question of how a company could capture the full value of scale, which was fortunate since most utilities did not have an answer for that when they undertook early transactions.

The value of scale—never mind how to capture it—was largely undefined and open to both interpretation and ambiguity. Could it be observed and measured, or was it intangible and experienced?

With respect to the value of scale to utilities, Managing Director Steve Fleishman from Wolfe Research stated:

> The concept of increasing scale made sense, particularly for small and mid-sized companies, where capabilities depth was key to survival. Scale helps in areas like nuclear and transmission infrastructure, but utilities are local businesses and scale here does not change anything. Utilities are good at capturing synergies to convert them to value for shareholders and customers. The best acquirors optimize scale, like perfecting operating models to provide high engagement with customers. Others are less successful with the value of scale because they don't think beyond synergies to creating platforms to leverage in subsequent transactions.

Answering the earlier question required utilities to think about value through a different lens than previously used—one that focused on the long term over the near term, positioning over outcomes, and value over synergies. This required utilities to exercise imagination about what could be accomplished through greater scale and think beyond the obvious that was easier to grasp.

A lack of enterprise imagination is what has usually led to unoptimized outcomes. Costs might be reduced, but business positioning has not been advanced. Utilities needed then—and still need now—to be able to think through what the value of scale is and how it can be harnessed to drive outcomes like expanded market valuation or enhanced customer positioning.

If utilities fully think through the benefits of scale, they will realize they manifest themselves throughout the business, particularly in strategy, growth, market, financial, and operational areas. Each can produce benefit to the enterprise when considered and pursued.

Erle Nye from TXU addressed his views on what the value of scale meant:

> On balance, winners do well and the capable do better. Scale matters when it can be converted into value, not just assumed to be beneficial. Scale is valuable when other factors fall in line, like strong management, responsive regulatory treatment, balance sheet flexibility, operating excellence, and adaptive culture. These items provide the ingredients for success when scale is expanded, but aligning strategies, adopting common goals, and building an effective operating model are better determinants of success than simply thinking bigger is better. I used to always think being big has risks, but being small has more.

While the maxim that "bigger is better" is not wrong, "better is better" is even more valuable to a company. The inherent value of scale appears to truly lie in the flexibility size provides. Flexibility allows companies to weather uncertainties, preserve options, capitalize on opportunities, build strength, and mitigate risks.

Having a certain level of scale expands the access to deal flow that a company can enjoy and may have been foreclosed in the absence of size. More investment banks will cover a company, and more sellers realize the capabilities a larger utility can bring to an opportunity, leading to more visibility of addressable industry divestment or separation situations.

Scale also enables the elevation of the size of opportunities that a utility can consider. The level of scale a company brings to an inorganic opportunity is typically supported by a stronger balance sheet and financing capability when significant investments or commitments are required beyond the level the unmerged companies may have had capability to pursue.

The value of scale is also demonstrated with respect to how strategic options can be evaluated and executed. Scale is a benefit, both when a broad range of options exist for consideration, as well as when choices can be exercised about specific, high-priority moves to advantage the market position of the business.

A valuable illustration of the value scale relates to the clout that a large company has in the market, either competitively or legislatively. Certainly, scale benefits market, competitive, and customer positioning through the ability to successfully meet the nascent or emerging needs of the market and change market perception of individual company go-to-market capabilities and offerings.

Perhaps more interesting is the value of scale in the political domain. A company operating in two states merging with another company operating in two proximate states increases both presence and influence. Rather than each utility having visibility to four members of the U.S. Senate, the combined company now has a presence with eight members of the U.S. Senate, and a similar expanded level of increase in relationships with members of the U.S. House of Representatives. Since policy design is often the catalyst for industry evolution, possessing an expanded legislative voice can only pay dividends to a combined company.

While all these benefits of scale are valuable, they fall short of its maximum value. The value of scale is most significant when it can create real optimization within the business through a leverageable platform applicable to recurring enterprise strategic, corporate, and inorganic moves. This platform would ensure the operating model is immutable, the organization is tailored, the infrastructure is in place, the processes are architected, the culture is embedded, the incentives are aligned, and philosophies are sacrosanct.

With this philosophy of leveraging scale as a differentiator embedded, a utility has the ability to build and apply a portable and scalable platform that can simplify the level of effort related to integration decision-making, quickly assimilate new mergers or acquisitions, and create real advantage in the financial and competitive markets. Having a recognized prowess for integration and creating visible value from a transaction leads to differentiation within the financial community and a higher valuation premium for execution aptitude, particularly if the level of economies of scale can continually be clearly demonstrated in visible performance metrics.

The goal of every business that transacts is to optimize itself and simplify the process for bringing new mergers or acquisitions into its core business. These outcomes are enabled by a platform that enables utilities to move beyond episodic synergies to sustained core value creation, and beyond "bigness" as measured by size, to advantage that is measured by capabilities strength within the business and leveraged throughout a company's strategy and operations.

Tom Fanning from Southern Company commented on the importance utilities initially placed on the value of scale to the business:

> Companies executing mergers did not always appreciate the value of scale available from a deal because they did not bring the right perspective on its future importance. Consequently, transactions frequently did not take advantage of a larger platform through simplified operating models, common standards, greater operating flexibility, stronger cash flows and balance sheets, or lower costs that impact financial contribution.

Moving utility recognition of the value of scale beyond its present spotty level requires that management treats each strategic event or transaction as a meaningful source of sustainable value to the business, and the next building block in attaining the full value of scale.

The utilities industry has been extremely good at capturing the synergies that emerge from a transaction. But the real challenge to surmount and advantage to gain occurs when meaningful value is captured across multiple strategic, financial, and operational fronts and converted into sustained market advantage that can propel a utility toward optimization of its overall future business.

Capturing Scale

Utilities have gained considerable experience at achieving estimated synergies, and have produced better realization outcomes than their counterparts in industrial or commercial product sectors, simply because utilities focus on narrower cost sources, while competitive companies typically pursue both new revenues and lower total costs.

But the larger question of whether the full value of scale has been realized remains open. This is harder to both conceive and manage and usually requires more than a few years to assess. The full value of scale is apparent when attributes like simplification, standardization, and optimization are visibly acknowledged by third parties, not just assumed to be in place by management.

The value of scale is unlikely to be readily apparent through a single transaction unless it substantially changes the size of the entity, such as occurs with the creation of a mega-utility. It is more likely to be observed in the actions and results of serial acquirors that adopt a platform-based and integrated optimization mindset to the business over more common abilities to rapidly integrate and produce synergies estimates.

If utilities determine that their future success will be influenced by the ability to gain sufficient business and market size, then these companies will need to ensure they know how to achieve the benefits of scale strategically, structurally, financially, operationally, and culturally.

That quickly translates into understanding where economies of scale would most naturally exist and how they could be captured effectively, efficiently, and perpetually.

In many industries it is easy to see pure economies of scale in unit costs, total costs, resource levels, etc. However, this has not necessarily been the case in the utilities sector, at least in clear, ubiquitous metrics. And while this logic underlies almost every M&A transaction, companies tend to think first about operating effectiveness over cost efficiency derived from scale.

On the topic of scale, Executive Chairman Gale Klappa of WEC Energy provided perspective on the industry's ability to capture value through consolidation:

> The industry understands the value that scale provides, but it hasn't been universally captured through all transactions. Perspectives vary across companies regarding what scale means, how it is captured, and then how it is leveraged. Companies have captured their synergies, where available, and given greater attention to operating cost management, but that is not the only important outcome. It is of real value to build a top-to-bottom competitive mindset.

Certainly, there is a general belief that the largest companies enjoy benefits from the ability to utilize resources more effectively over a larger base of customers, assets, or employees. And there is empirical evidence that illustrates the benefits of scale in unit metrics, although not always consistently.

An analyst would naturally expect that being larger equates to being more efficient, and that unit costs, such as discrete activity costs, would decline as scale increases. But that is not necessarily the case. Not all large companies fall naturally along a declining scale curve.

Since the U.S. utility industry is dichotomous in nature, that is, different in size, composition, dispersion, operating models, etc., numerous factors can affect the absolute (and therefore relative) cost of operations. In fact, large differences can be observed in utility cost performance, for example, bottom-of-first-quartile non-generation operation and maintenance costs. O&M costs were just over $300/customer in a recent analysis, while bottom-of-third-quartile costs were approximately $450/customer.[21] The gap between the best performers and those around the average continues to widen and illustrates the opportunity for more efficient operating costs—something that a utility merger or acquisition naturally provides.

Figure 6: Electric Industry Operating Performance

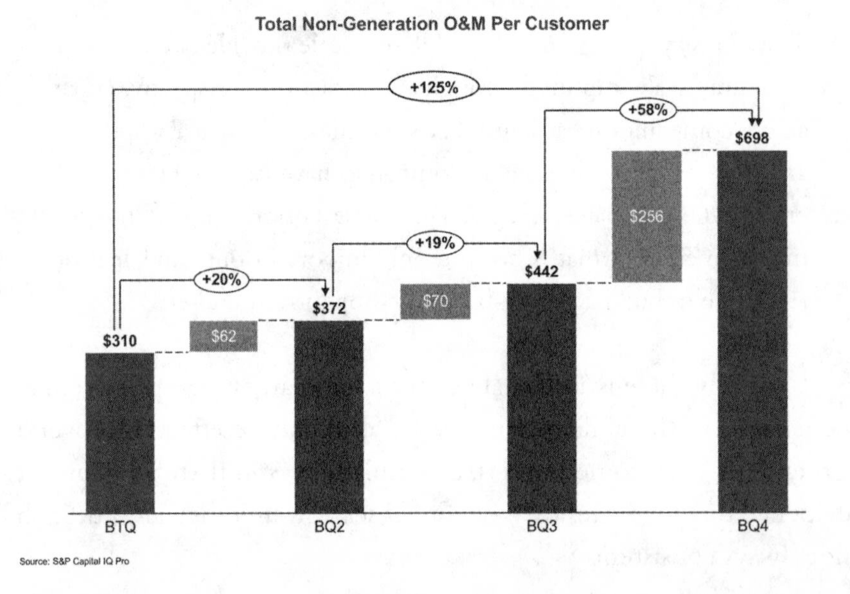

With respect to whether the value of scale is appreciated and captured by U.S. utilities, Jim Judge of Eversource Energy believes experience is mixed:

> Being bigger does not mean better, it only yields better outcomes when companies know how to leverage scale. It becomes valuable

when it is translated into value to customers. We turned our prior merger experience with producing synergies and leveraging best practices into much lower costs to our customers because of how we approach integration. Not every company that executed a merger integrates like we do, and this can be a limiting factor to fully benefiting from scale.

Given these relative cost differences, here is where M&A can be a vital equalizer in reducing O&M costs and enabling more scale economies to be realized. If other large, low-cost companies can figure out how to streamline inherent costs, then the results of a combination should enable most acquiring or merging companies to easily do the same, since the components of company costs are largely the same in substance.

Several factors can influence how successful a company can be in capturing and demonstrating economies of scale and operating synergies from a transaction:

- **Operating model**: An operating model defines *how* a company delivers services and through *which* structures. But choices of philosophy, for example, centralized or decentralized, can vary, and reflect management views of which models such as service companies, hosted organizations, or dispersed roles best fit their organization's characteristics.

- **Relative scale**: As indicated, the size of U.S. utilities widely varies, which affects the ability of companies to realize available operating economies. A multi-million customer company will be far more likely to achieve lower costs to serve customers than one with a million customers, all other things being equal.

- **Relative proximity**: The adjacency of two utilities enables synergies areas like field operations, capital investment, facilities sharing, etc., that are not available to companies separated across regional geographies, where joint operations are limited, and operational line-of-sight is harder to achieve.

- **Integration execution**: The ability to realize economies of scale in a merger is directly impacted by how aggressively the merging parties think about how to capture traditional synergies and reduce unit costs most related to scale of the new business, such as combined transaction volumes.

- **Regulatory actions**: Federal or state commissions can impact the ability to achieve operating and financial economies if restrictions on actions or conditions are implemented, such as requirements for staffing levels and locations, performance targets, asymmetrical savings sharing, etc., which sub-optimize operating efficiencies.

A common lament of several merged companies has been that they are not sure they are fully capturing the value of scale, meaning they have neither optimized their size, infrastructure, and capabilities to create significant and durable efficiencies, nor embedded an innovative and competitive culture to drive performance. This is particularly true among serial acquirors that do not religiously follow a well-defined and aggressive consolidation template that emphasizes standardization, simplicity, and optimization, and eschews structural, process, and individual accommodations made for peripheral, non-economic reasons.

Jeff Holzschuh from Morgan Stanley summarized his perspective on how successful utilities have been at capturing the value of scale:

> Achieving the value of scale is difficult and mixed success has been achieved over the last 25 years. Realizing value from scale requires acquiring or merging utilities to have an unambiguous

> view of their future operating model and how they intend to run the business at its optimum level. While the concept of capturing scale is not difficult to argue, the ability to consistently make future decisions and actions in a manner that emphasizes continuous high performance and leverages an aggressive integration model is harder to accomplish.

Most utilities that have executed transactions are focused on the instant deal more than market positioning and optimization of a business where the outlines have yet to emerge. Consequently, few companies can be said to have mastered the art of full value of scale attainment. However, several utilities, like Eversource Energy, Exelon, and WEC Energy, illustrate evidence of this mindset and have had the chance to follow a model through multiple transactions.

Tom Fanning, the CEO from Southern Company, offered his insights on the experience of US utilities on fully realizing the value of scale:

> The experience of U.S. utilities in capturing the value of scale is mixed—some companies created platforms to optimize how the business was operated. Others leaned into recognizing utilities are a local business and owning this kind of company necessitates trade-offs between localization and optimization. When companies did not emphasize objectives like simplification, standardization, and optimization, it often was because they valued the positioning of their local brand differently than traditional holding companies, where centralization often dominated. Different success models exist, and distinctive choices can be adopted to accomplish specific ownership objectives.

Any structural model theoretically can work, but some offer a far better line of sight into *where and how* costs are incurred. Thus, how a company has managed itself in the past and thinks about how it could align in the future heavily influences the ability to either extend or create new or existing economies.

International Flavor

While the U.S. utilities landscape has consistently produced opportunities for consolidation over the modern era, similar opportunities arose in a select number of countries in Europe, South America, and Australasia. In fact, the progression in regulatory policy toward more open markets for power and gas competition has its roots in the UK. Here is where the concept that functional unbundling or vertical disintegration could create attractive and sustainable market segments that could compete outside the legacy vertically integrated structure gained traction.

As the U.S. utility industry began its consolidation era in 1995, the UK had already announced and executed its privatization and

Figure 7: United Kingdom Privatization

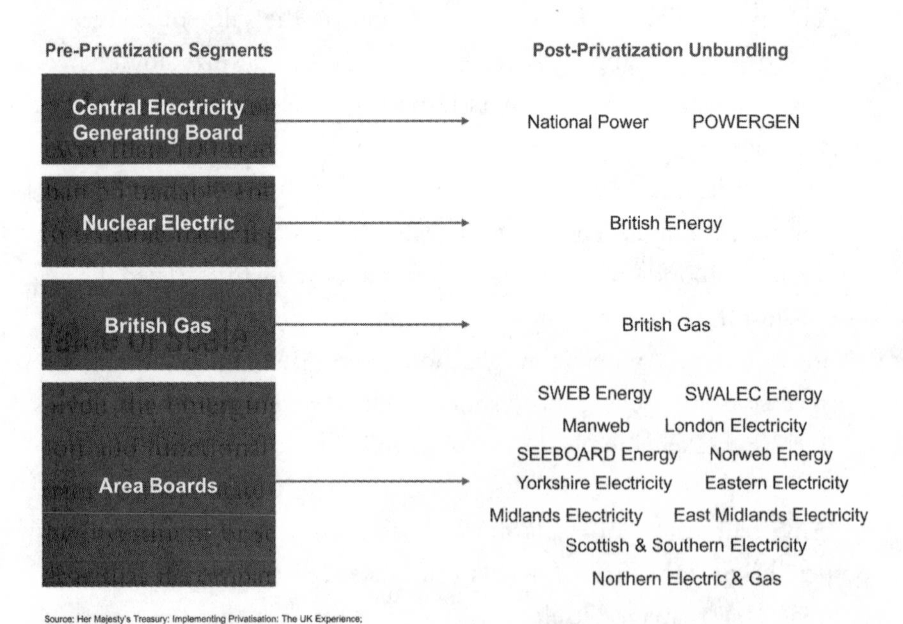

functional unbundling program in the early 1990s, with new entities created for generation such as National Power, PowerGen, and Nuclear Electric, a new grid company called NationalGrid, and multiple new retail companies initiated by new competitors, both from the UK and elsewhere in Europe. In 1991, 12 Regional Electric Companies (RECs) were floated and stood up focusing on local network operations throughout the UK, with Australia following in 1995.[22]

Gale Klappa, of WEC Energy, spoke about early interest in gaining an international presence while at Southern Company during its moves into Europe:

> The late 1990s ushered in a different era for U.S. utilities. Several years of global deregulation had occurred, and U.S. utility models were already changing. Experience in competitive markets and alternative regulation would be important to our future. We sought market knowledge and earnings diversity, which the UK environment provided through a differently incented regulatory model and a window into competitive marketing and scale, giving us expertise we could take back home. We were so committed to success we sent four full-time executives to be part of the UK's learning laboratory, then subsequently entered Germany to gain a different market view.

As a group, U.S. companies did not originally consider international acquisitions to be of high interest. After all, deals in the U.S. were already hard and would be even more complex in a foreign market and regulatory environment. But by 1987, UtiliCorp United had already become the first utility in the U.S. to make a foreign acquisition when it purchased the small West Kootenay Power & Light entity, which preceded several foreign transactions in Europe and Australasia initiated into the early 2000s.

But a new attitude about international acquisitions quickly morphed, as bankers aggressively marketed entities in the UK, Australia, and New Zealand (along with Argentina, Chile, Venezuela, and others). Managements reasoned that the early starts of these separated companies working within restructured competitive environments on unbundled bases would be advantageous to understanding how competitive energy and stand-alone network markets worked in practice, before such possible eventuality occurred in the U.S. And if a foreign acquisition were to be considered, where would make more sense than an English-speaking country with established markets, rule of law, and governmental transparency?

Erle Nye, former CEO at TXU, commented on his interest in pursuing international acquisitions:

> While we had made several small acquisitions in Texas, our expansion frontiers were not limited. We had an early opportunity to test our readiness for a significant acquisition and evaluate an Australian electricity distributor. After diligence, we found the country to be attractive as an investment destination, and the company to be an affordable candidate. We valued the ability to gain international operating experience, learn about deregulated markets, transfer best practices, and expand the business locally within a short period. Australia affirmed we could parlay this experience into the UK by not just owning a property, but influencing market opening and building a valuable market position and returns.

Once the newly unbundled RECs were created, a massive opportunity for purchase and roll-up presented itself to U.S. and international companies in the UK and Australia. The first actual acquisitions in these countries were made in 1995 by Southern Company in the UK and UtiliCorp United, Inc., in Australia, through structured auction processes. These auctions were not limited to U.S. companies, even though they enjoyed an advantage because of their perceived country stability, well-established financial system, and experienced system operators.

These initial forays were quickly joined by even more U.S.

companies as the proposition for international acquisition had been validated and the number of available RECs was limited in either the UK or Australia. Acquisitions by TXU, Entergy, UtiliCorp United, and AEP (both in the UK and Australia), Dominion Resources, Xcel Energy, Cinergy, GPU, UtiliCorp United, and PPL Resources (all in the UK) quickly followed, with almost all companies later selling their UK and Australia RECs, although PPL Resources acquired several of these RECs to roll up a total of four RECs by 2011, before finally divesting in 2021.

Figure 8: U.S. Utility International Company Acquisitions

	United Kingdom	Australia	New Zealand	Germany	Brazil	Peru	Chile	Mexico	Guatemala	Venezuela	Other
GPU	▨										
Cinergy	▨										
Dominion Energy	▨										
Xcel Energy	▨										
PPL	▨										
TXU Energy	▨	▨									
AEP	▨	▨									
Entergy	▨	▨									
UtiliCorp United	▨	▨	▨								▨
Southern Company	▨			▨							▨
Sempra Energy						▨	▨	▨			
AES					▨					▨	
Duke Energy									▨		

Source: Company websites; news reports; Wikipedia

Dick Kelly of Xcel Energy commented on why an international acquisition was pursued by a predecessor company to Xcel Energy:

> By the mid-1990s, the UK had already privatized its local utilities and was in its early days of open competition. The U.S. was just approaching unbundling business segments and creating new

> models for utility composition. We believed there was something to learn from the UK that could be valuable as we considered our specific path. If we were to undertake an acquisition, we wanted to be sure that it generated cash, protected our earnings, and de-risked our exposure. Fortunately, we found another U.S. partner that felt the same way and we created a joint learning experience about unbundled markets for both of us.

Opportunities for acquisition in Europe also extended beyond the UK. Southern Company entered Germany in 1997 with its acquisition of a stake in Berliner Elektricitatswerke (BEWAG), which was intended to establish a presence in Central Europe. Southern Company ultimately extended its ownership levels to have greater control of BEWAG in the ensuing years, before selling its interests and exiting European utility ownership.

Beyond the forays into Europe, U.S. utilities also ventured into Central America, South America, and the Caribbean, where similar privatization was occurring. Duke Energy acquired the utility in Guatemala and various assets throughout Central and South America, Australia, and New Zealand. UtiliCorp United became the only U.S. company to obtain a presence in New Zealand when it acquired two utilities in 1993 and 1995.

Houston Industries and Dominion Resources both acquired generating assets in Argentina, Sempra Energy acquired properties in Peru, Chile, and Mexico, AES acquired properties in Brazil and Venezuela (and generating assets everywhere), and Southern Company acquired interests in island systems in the Bahamas and Trinidad and Tobago. These acquisitions were opportunistic and intended to further extend the competitive market learning curve and/or test the thesis that American operating expertise could be effectively transferred into the international arena.

As noted above, REC acquisitions were not the only pursuits made by U.S. companies around the world. Unbundling the vertically integrated value chain also led to pursuit of generation portfolios and assets throughout the world, particularly by companies that were aggressively focused on trading in newly established or developing trading markets like the UK, Netherlands, Chile, and throughout Latin America, among other countries.

These international acquisitions generally resulted in U.S. executives being transferred to the UK, Australia, Germany, Netherlands, Argentina, Mexico, and a host of other countries to lead local operations, thus infusing expertise and external market-thinking into prior government-run operating entities. These executives were charged with understanding how network models could develop, implementing established operating processes, and ensuring successful local governmental relationships.

Few U.S. utilities were ever truly global in their market reach and participation. However, CMS Energy and AES became heavily involved in both acquisition and development of power stations in many corners of the globe—so heavily that their annual reports depicted enough country presence flags to resemble a mini-United Nations lobby.

The hold period of these global U.S. acquisitions was mostly short-lived due to significant market dislocation from Enron and other headline business failures. Investor sentiment turned against trading businesses, far-flung portfolios, and risk-inducing strategies. The U.S. utilities ultimately created disposition processes to sell their RECs to other parties, which included German, French, and Chinese companies, or investment funds.

While the U.S. companies were able to successfully exit their network businesses before fully learning the lessons of unbundled network management—that is, being an asset owner, asset manager, or asset operator—they were able to take the benefits of this operating and competitive experience back to the U.S. to enhance their perspectives on asset planning and capital prioritization.

Chairman of Global Power Joe Sauvage at Citi addressed the

motivations for U.S. utilities to pursue transactions abroad, and their relative success:

> Companies seeking growth often strayed from traditional paths when pessimistic about their own current direction. With international markets opening and companies finding it harder to sustain extended power contracts, U.S. companies found large generating fleets irresistible and pursued them globally. The more successful companies made digestible buys with an ability to utilize existing scale to absorb deal risks. When companies further expanded their interests, and evolved beyond contracts into trading, outcomes dramatically changed, and investments soured, leading to numerous bankruptcies. Companies may have made money in the UK and Australia, but that was not true in Latin America.

To indicate that turnabout was fair play, European and Japanese companies then began to explore the U.S. market. These companies were attracted to the stability and growth of the U.S. market and the establishment of a U.S.-based acquisition platform to roll up a heavily fragmented sector.

Jim Torgerson from AVANGRID explained why Iberdrola was so interested in acquisitions in the U.S.:

> With Iberdrola already in the U.S. after its acquisition of Energy East and with its separate renewables business, it saw an opportunity to create a true platform for future growth in the U.S. It understood the market, viewed regulation as reasonable, and could obtain higher multiples for its U.S. businesses by listing the stock than it would if U.S. operations were just embedded in Iberdrola's overall stock valuation.

While much tire kicking was conducted over the late 1990s and early 2000s, the meltdown of the U.S. economy and the merchant generation sector in 2001 from Enron, along with the market's distaste for speculative investments, put many plans on the back burner for years until most foreign entity managements lost interest in U.S. entry through utility stock acquisitions.

Nonetheless, Scottish Power was the first to enter the U.S. in 1998 with its acquisition of PacifiCorp, followed by PowerGen's acquisition of LG&E Energy in 2000 (subsequently sold to E.On in 2003). Iberdrola entered the U.S. in 2008 with the acquisition of Energy East, followed by the 2015 announcement of acquisition of UIL Holdings, and the 2020 agreed offer announcement to PNM Resources. Several Canadian companies also followed suit on utilities acquisitions, with Emera entering the U.S. with its acquisition of Bangor Hydro in 1999, Maine and Maritimes in 2010, and TECO Energy in 2015. Fortis acquired CH Energy in 2012, ITC in 2016, and UNS Energy in 2013. In 2020, ENMAX acquired Emera Maine in a transfer of ownership. Algonquin Power & Utilities made a series of acquisitions in eight U.S states over the years, including in water. With the exception of Scottish Power and E.On, these companies still maintain ownership of almost all of the original companies acquired.

With respect to Energy East, Iberdrola acquired an existing holding company, itself the product of several roll-ups, with a high New England and New York concentration. It has two service companies that provide common services across the regulated utilities, with one also supporting the U.S. renewables business. How PNM Resources will fit into this model given its 2,000-mile distance from Portland, Maine, to Albuquerque, New Mexico, remains to be determined if the transaction is ultimately approved.

Unlike U.S. companies making serial acquisitions, these foreign entities have not developed their transactions around the notions of operating effectiveness and efficiencies. These companies largely intended to leave their acquired companies as separate entities, rather than as part of a quasi-integrated portfolio. In part, this reflects the geographic distance between northeastern Canada and the U.S. entities acquired, as well as differences in country markets.

The lack of synergies emphasis in most foreign utility acquisitions of U.S. utilities also recognizes the need to satisfy certain state regulatory commission concerns for local presence, leadership, and control, and the lack of natural synergies precipitated by significant cross-border locations and distance, for example, Fortis in St. John, Newfoundland, and Emera in Halifax, Nova Scotia, as well as the *ring-fencing* (protections against bankruptcy, or other owner governance or financial actions) of broader portfolio businesses with different risk profiles to a U.S. utility.

But the early international buyers did believe they could teach the Americans a thing or two about efficient operations since they were larger entities than their acquirees. After all, the incentive regulation framework in the UK was well known internationally and reflected a heavy hand over cost levels and growth. If a company could thrive there, then what could deter the same outcome in the U.S.?

It was only after the early period of ownership that some of these companies realized that operating standards were not uniform across countries and even regulatory metrics meant different things between the U.S. and their home country.

Would not processes to ensure answering 80 percent of customer calls within 20-25 seconds be simple to transfer? They would, of course, except when customer call answering meant live customer service representative engagement in the U.S., not just connecting to enter a telephone waiting queue, as it could in Europe at the time.

Financial Sponsors

Interest in the U.S. (and international) utility industry did not only exist among foreign utilities. Private equity and infrastructure funds also took great interest in whether value could be derived from utility company ownership. Energy had not previously been a target for private equity, but industry restructuring offered some attractive sign-posts for potential involvement.

In 1998 there were about six private equity firms with $2 billion in invested capital in the energy sector. In 2007, there were 15-20 firms with more than $30 billion invested in the energy sector, mostly in specific generating assets, such as companies like Kohlberg Kravis Roberts (KKR)and Texas Pacific Group (TPG) in Texas Genco's power assets. [23]

As the electric and gas sectors continued to invest in their businesses, new theses emerged for how to optimize value at utilities. Private equity took its traditional view: take a company private, refresh leadership, continue to invest, hold the line on cost growth, recapitalize appropriately with leverage, and then exit within five years at a premium price.

Numerous private equity firms created teams to survey the U.S. for potential sellers, keying on several characteristics: high-quality assets, high-growth territory, well-regarded customer service, consistent capital expenditures, constrained balance sheets, steady cash flow, market volatility, below-market CEO compensation, quality executive bench strength, reasonable regulatory jurisdiction, or limited existing growth strategy.

The first announced private equity acquisition was from KKR in 2003 into Unisource Energy for $875 million in equity, plus assumption of over $2 billion in debt.[24] KKR and its partners argued that their ownership would provide for increased access to capital and would enhance operational performance, reliability, and safety.

This deal was approved by Unisource Energy's board of directors, but subsequently fell short of state regulatory approval at the Arizona Corporation Commission due to an inability to satisfy the public interest, the potential for excessive debt, undue general partner control, and inadequate bankruptcy protection.

Texas Pacific Group (TPG) proposed an acquisition of Portland General Electric in 2005. This transaction was also rejected by regulators at the Oregon Public Utilities Commission due to concerns about the short-term nature of planned ownership and planned rate increases.

In 2007, the largest ever utilities and pure private equity deal was announced between TXU and a partnership of KKR and TPG for $32 billion in equity and another $12 billion in debt.[25] This deal made it to the finish line in part because the Public Utility Commission of Texas (PUCT) arranged a ring-fencing arrangement to protect the distribution business from potential corporate-level bankruptcy, which could easily happen from IPP risk weaknesses, along with other governance and financial concerns.

After the TXU transaction, the overall economy and stock market experienced a significant and prolonged recession, which affected capital markets. In addition, private equity interest in traditional utilities began to wane as capital expenditures slowed, regulatory scrutiny and disincentives to acquisition expanded, and the leeriness of utility managements to high debt levels and short-term sale arrangements increased. Nonetheless, private equity stayed active in the power generation sector through acquisitions, divestments, and swaps.

But the demise of private equity in utilities did not mean that other financial sponsors were not interested in utilities. Internationally, private funds had been established with a long-term view to ownership versus the short hold periods of private equity. These funds focused on transmission and distribution businesses (infrastructure) and were designed to provide stability in ownership and investment to ameliorate state regulatory objections to private equity's perceived penchant for harvesting value for investors through adverse consequences from customers.

These infrastructure funds for utilities had been initiated and perfected in the UK, Canada, and Australia before utilization in the U.S. Infrastructure funds for a variety of stable, fixed-asset businesses like turnpikes, ports, bridges, airports, renewables assets, utilities, etc., were becoming common in the U.S. around the early 2000s and viewed as a "friendlier" form of acquisition.

The target of infrastructure funds were assets that possessed certain distinctive characteristics: low volatility, predictable cash flows, continuing cash yields, and inflation protection. These characteristics closely fit the profile of U.S. utilities and the infrastructure fund acquisition model was more seriously considered by utility managements, though never widely embraced.

The first U.S. infrastructure investment fund transaction in power and/or gas utilities was from Macquarie Infrastructure Partners (Macquarie) when it agreed to acquire The Gas Company in Hawaii in 2006 for $238 million.[26] This transaction closed in the same year it was announced and followed the traditional infrastructure model: a long-term hold (10+ years), retained local headquarters, retained management, new investment, increased energy efficiency spend, and rate credits for customers.

Macquarie also used the same general model when it acquired Duquesne Holdings in 2006 for $1.6 billion in equity, plus $1.2 billion in existing debt.[27] This transaction closed in 2007 and did not encounter the high public and regulatory upheaval associated with subsequent private equity deals.

Macquarie subsequently agreed to acquire Puget Energy in 2009 for $3.5 billion in equity, with another $3.2 billion in assumed debt.[28] This transaction required over $100 million in ratepayer credits and more than $5 billion in incremental investment.

In 2014, Macquarie led another investor group in the acquisition of CLECO for $4.7 billion, including $1.3 billion in debt.[29] This transaction created an extensive record during its proceedings and ultimately led to substantial customer rate credits of more than $130 million, well above the $1 million originally proposed in the regulatory approval filing. In this transaction, the Louisiana Public Service Commission was quite skeptical of the proposed future capitalization of CLECO and sharing of potential tax savings, seeking both front-end and continuing benefits for customers.

In 2018, Macquarie subsequently closed the sale of its prior Puget Energy investment with a new sale to two pension funds from Canada and the Netherlands and an off-load of its remaining investment to existing Canadian co-owners in the consortium. The sale reflected Macquarie's desire to end its ownership as its ten-plus-year hold period conclusion approached.

The most recent infrastructure fund transaction deal was the 2020 acquisition of El Paso Electric by Infrastructure Investments Fund (IIF) for $2.8 billion in equity, plus assumed debt of $1.5 billion.[30] This transaction received substantial regulatory scrutiny over the proposed ownership structure, the manner in which decisions would be made, and how operations would be managed, including investment in the El Paso Electric system. As a result, J.P. Morgan (IIF's owning investment bank) agreed to being deemed an affiliate to the holding company established for ownership of El Paso Electric.

While infrastructure fund transactions were once believed to be easier to accomplish than both private equity and utility-to-utility deals, regulatory familiarity and public interest standards have added unexpected complexity to these transactions and slightly diminished enthusiasm in this class of M&A as well, at least for larger target companies.

Non-traditional M&A transactions have been far fewer in number than traditional combinations, but they have offered a glimpse into how other types of buyers think about the long-term prospects of the utilities industry. They also provide an available off-ramp to smaller utilities should they choose to maintain their stand-alone identity.

Key Takeaways

Although the investor-owned utilities industry had not been actively transacting, particularly at a large scale, in several decades, the industry was ripe for consolidation in the mid-1990s. The industry was fragmented; scale disparity existed; competition was becoming inevitable; and individual companies held contrasting views of M&A viability and value.

Too many utilities existed at almost every tier of structure, even after multiple years of pre- and post-PUHCA shakeout. While thousands of pre-PUHCA discrete utilities had contracted to approximately 150 at the investor-owned level by 1995, the number of stand-alone holding companies or utilities were more than a monopoly industry should rightfully support.

The dynamics affecting the industry were not lost on boards of directors and utility executive management. While the coming sea change in industry roles and structure was not yet known, the trends were becoming clearer: the stability of the past would not continue for very much longer.

The size of the overall industry contrasted with the absence of differentiable scale among industry participants. To be sure, there have always been large companies, but U.S. utilities have been relatively small individually, until well into the modern era of U.S. M&A activity. Consequently, the specter of structural dismemberment and heightened competition became a call for more scale within the industry.

The value of scale could be initially observed with respect to certain companies which possessed size, reach, and the ability to convert these characteristics into operating scale economies, by essentially extending an existing acquiror model across the acquiree. But the prowess of U.S. utilities in realizing the full value of scale is much more limited than it should be and constrained more by internal choices than external factors.

The next stage of U.S. utility M&A activity will demand more attention be directed toward capturing the full value of scale to attain market differentiation through the quality of the value playbook being adopted, and the translation of scale into market advantage.

The relative and absolute O&M cost differences among U.S. utilities is stark and serves notice that effective cost management remains to be accomplished and could yield high value to the business. Far more opportunity to streamline costs exists, particularly in larger utilities that have not perfected their operating models or the discipline to imagine the value of scale through a broader lens.

The ability to transact in utility M&A in the U.S. is often the product of stars being properly aligned. But a parallel jump-start to M&A was available from the privatization fever that swept the UK, Australia, and many countries in Latin America. U.S. utilities found open markets and operating environments that welcomed strong balance sheet companies to provide needed capital investment, and high-reputation operators who could transfer decades of reliable operating experience.

Just as U.S. utilities and financial sponsors fearlessly entered the M&A arena, international acquirors saw the North American market as stable, attractive, and addressable, particularly on the heels of significant European disruption and restructuring. Potential acquirors from Canada, Asia, and Western, Central, and Southern Europe all kicked the tires on U.S. companies, with some acting early and others delaying their acquisition interest.

Once the model for U.S. utility acquisition or merger was established, the table was set for private equity to turn its interests to M&A and begin to fashion acquisition strategies that would be appealing to investors, for example, highly levered, performance-based with short hold periods.

Infrastructure funds took a different approach to deal structuring by constructing an acquisition model designed to be friendlier to utility managements and regulatory commissions, that is, collaborative and non-intrusive with long hold periods. Only a handful of financial sponsor deals were ever closed, highlighting how difficult non-traditional ownership has been.

As the doors to U.S. utility M&A had been opened—both domestically and internationally—momentum was ignited for continued and aggressive transaction activity on many industry fronts, following markedly different models for consolidation. The natural outcome of these foundational events was apparent: rapid growth in transactions, step-changes to company size, and large dichotomies in operating costs.

MODERN ERA OF M&A (1995–2020)

The early establishment, consolidation, and disaggregation of the U.S. utilities industry (with emphasis on electric and gas companies) set a course for how the modern era of utilities M&A responded to challenges from policy shifts, regulatory mandates, financial turmoil, structural realignments, and technology evolution.

These early industry structuring and restructuring activities pointed out that industry fragmentation was inefficient, extreme consolidation was ineffective, and utilities needed to think about optimization of operations, whether in the generation, transmission, distribution, or customer functions.

By the time the modern era was underway, utilities were already into a new unbundling phase: power assets were being divested and acquired; transmission assets were being separated; distribution networks were structurally unchanged; customers were being separated; and retail businesses were being created. A framework of specialization was being conceived, such as portfolio operators, grid optimizers, network managers, and retail suppliers, which began to populate the utilities landscape.

The transition away from decades of continuity in state and regulatory policies and competitive boundaries came suddenly and dramatically. Market theses were contravened, policy frameworks were upended, and operational protocols were shattered.

Utilities initially thought they would only have a few years to reflect these market shifts in new strategic priorities, business models, and operating models—and how true this turned out to be. Moving from the status quo of the early 1990s to the restructuring and repositioning of the mid- to late 1990s unleashed a massive shift in the contours of many utilities. Many portfolios were reset to reflect business rationalization and a releveling of market capitalizations from exchanges or acquisitions of underlying assets or companies.

The number, variety, and significance of these prior drivers and conditions led to a wide range of company responses. The actions that managements pursued reflected legacy company philosophies, perspectives, and priorities, which further shaped the rationales for strategic direction and response, generally centering on growth, value, and survivability.

Beginning in 1995, electric and LDC utilities entered a sustained period of consolidation for the next 25 years, which is still continuing. This consolidation reflected the structural forces referenced above, as well as a variety of competitive readiness actions and ongoing externalities that influence management decision-making. This extended period provides a comprehensive view of how management motivations for consolidation have evolved through several industry upheavals and shaped the industry structure existing today.

To be sure, some M&A activity existed in the late 1980s and early 1990s, but the absolute number of meaningful transactions pursued or closed across the industry was limited as few externalities or drivers existed to cause the overall industry to consider consolidation.

Most proposed transactions involved small utilities like West Virginia Power, Lake Superior District Power, Manchester Electric, New Mexico Electric Service, Allied Power & Light, and Chesapeake Light & Power, among more than 30 other companies, and could be called *tuck-ins* or *bolt-ons*, where adjacency simply made operational sense for both entities.[1]

The five periods of consolidation frame an evolutionary period still occurring today as the utilities industry continuously rethinks its market positioning and value models. The five periods start in 1995 and each lasted five years (except 2015-2020 with six years) until the next wave of externalities, shifts, or inflection points occurred in response to how the industry had evolved or investor sentiment had altered.

Figure 9: Cycles of Change

	~1995–1999	~2000–2004	~2005–2009	~2010–2015	~2015–2020
Era	**"Competitiveness and Convergence"**	**"Rationalization and Roll-up"**	**"Reengagement and Opportunism"**	**"Fortification and Positioning"**	**"Simplicity and Growth"**
Key Drivers	▪ Deregulation ▪ Value chain ▪ Prioritization	▪ Recession ▪ Back-to-basics ▪ Private equity	▪ Business models ▪ Infrastructure build ▪ Liquidity challenges	▪ Valuation gaps ▪ Portfolio mix ▪ Cost curve	▪ Currency strength ▪ Disruptive technology ▪ Platform expansion
Attributes	▪ Proximate territories ▪ Control premiums ▪ Extended approvals	▪ Non-regulated realignment ▪ Cash generation focus ▪ Asset value harvesting	▪ Step-out transactions ▪ Market presence 'footprint' ▪ Regulatory aggressiveness	▪ Regional alignment ▪ Scale and strength focus ▪ Capabilities leverage	▪ Scale dispersion ▪ Third-party activism ▪ Risk realignment

Sources: Tom Flaherty and Owen Ward "Expanding Deals, Shrinking Companies", Public Utilities Fortnightly June 2016; Company filings

Given the lack of widespread, contemporaneous utility industry experience with M&A prior to 1995, before entering transaction assessments or pursuits, utilities took stock of their current position, emerging challenges, and competitive risks. They asked themselves questions such as:

- Is M&A a valuable strategic option?
- Will M&A disrupt current strategy execution?
- How do we determine our best merger partners?
- Does our stock currency support a transaction?
- How do rating agencies view our financial integrity?
- Is the regulatory approval process predictable?
- Are we positioned favorably with regulators?
- Is M&A an inevitability for utilities?
- What are the risks of transaction failure?
- If we fail to act, will we become a target?

Addressing these considerations was the first step for many utilities in understanding the benefits and risks of M&A and determining whether early or late market participation would be preferable.

Joe Sauvage at Citi addressed some early drivers and outcomes of U.S. utility M&A:

> Utilities believed scale mattered and provided competitive advantage in the form of greater capital commitment, lower costs, broader capabilities, and deeper talent. Companies also believed they needed to grow to meet future business needs.

Industry cycles often defined the action, like acquisitions in the UK and Australia, or fleets or plants in unbundled geographies. Comparative advantage flowed to the "first mover," with better opportunities available at a better price, even if it was a struggle explaining the deal to the markets. But, sometimes, the best deals went against the grain within the industry.

When the first M&A period of the modern era began in 1995, the number of tradable electric utilities numbered just under 100, and tradable natural gas companies numbered just over 50. As a walk through the years between 1995 and 2020 reveals, an inexorable march was initiated from a highly fragmented industry to a highly consolidated sector more than 60 percent smaller than at the beginning of the modern era of utilities, and still in the process of selective rationalization.

As utilities M&A gained traction, utilities, analysts, investment bankers, and ratings agencies all looked forward to "merger Mondays" when new announcements were typically made. These announcements heralded the beginning and continuation of the consolidation wave, leaving involved investment banks, law firms, and consultants euphoric, while causing those professional firms not involved to ponder how to create the next headline transaction.

Competitiveness and Conversion (1995–1999)

This initial period reflected a burgeoning move toward more competition in the U.S. utility industry. While the UK, Australia, and other countries had already moved to restructured markets, California was the U.S. leader in evaluating and defining what a more competitive and restructured industry could look like.

The California Public Utility Commission's (CPUC) Yellow Book provided initial perspectives on electric sector restructuring in 1993 and was followed by the Blue Book in 1994 that provided for a deeper investigation of the impacts and challenges of restructuring. These two proceedings ultimately led to an order in 1995, which codified CPUC thinking related to competitive wholesale power markets, independent transmission system operations, and customer choice on energy supply and requirements, and called for implementation by 1998.

The upshot of the 1995 CPUC order was to separate most power supply (except nuclear and hydro) from utilities, create an independent system operator (ISO) for California transmission, preserve transmission ownership by utilities, preserve distribution network ownership by utilities, and allow customers to either secure energy supply from non-traditional suppliers, or allow the utility to provide supply where customers elected to obtain energy on a default basis.

The CPUC investigations and orders signaled to the U.S. power sector that market competition would be encouraged by state regulators and functional unbundling or separation would be the selected means by which to achieve it.

With this shot across the industry's bow, it was quickly recognized that the status quo of vertical integration as many companies had known it was over—not in every state, but in enough large and influential states, like New York, Illinois, Pennsylvania, etc., to fundamentally change the future role of markets and utilities. With industry functional unbundling, an already fragmented and scale-diverse industry would be further challenged to create normalcy within a disaggregated value chain and the consolidation game was now on.

When deregulation starts, it tends to gain momentum, spread virally, and create uncertainty. Utilities had to quickly decide where to play along the value chain and what parts to cede to new entrants, owners, or operators. Companies then had to rapidly assess the risks of disaggregated value chain participation and define how to win in selected value chain elements. Thus, utilities needed to assess where necessary capabilities for success existed and where they would have to be developed or acquired to ensure market success.

Many utilities had no choice in determining where to play as their state regulators decided for them what would happen with ownership and participation in generation, transmission, and retail—although more than half the states determined that full vertical integration would still be the structure of choice in many states. But others had the choice of keeping generation, transmission, or distribution and having to determine how more narrowly defined futures could play themselves out. And selected well-positioned companies were challenged to determine how to take advantage of industry disruption to their long-term market success.

Steve Fleishman at Wolfe Research discussed how Wall Street viewed the wave of utility merger transactions during the mid-1990s:

> The first wave of utility mergers was a surprise as industry activity had not been high running up to this time frame. There was hyper-growth in the sector and the framework for assessing proposed transactions was only emerging with so little prior activity. The themes for transactions were thoughtful, for example mergers-of-equals, alignment of compatible companies, and pursuit of convergence were common rationales and conditions of the time. It didn't take long for analysts to see these transactions were taking a long time to close, and federal and state regulators were sometimes in conflict about authority and standards, which caused some transactions to not be pursued or terminated.

After determining where to play, U.S. utilities had to quickly assess their paths to viability, and hopefully to success. Utilities were largely caught flat-footed with respect to separation of assets and customers—how could a 200-year model be so easily discarded? And why would regulators believe that separating utilities from customers was a good idea for customers or utilities?

As utilities considered their future position in an unbundled world, some elements of the future of unbundled companies looked bleak: smaller scale, less financial flexibility, lower asset growth, and foregone customer access.

Utilities quickly rationalized that the solution to smaller scale and weakened financial flexibility was to bulk up through M&A and preserve the ability to remain viable in the near term or leverage existing scale to *roll-up* companies likely to be unable to survive in a disaggregated world and capitalize on new opportunities.

In a future competitive world—particularly where fully integrated companies would continue to exist—companies posited that customers were vital to business purpose and revenue preservation and you could never have too many contact points, relationships, revenue sources, or continuing growth paths. Consequently, utilities sought out more customers through M&A under the premise that securing the right to compete for future products and services would be one way of bolstering and defending the business in a future competitive market.

Companies had to do nothing more than scan the utility landscape to recognize that customer scale could be grown through M&A for either pure electric utilities, combination electric and gas utilities, or just gas utilities. All were sources for additional customers within an existing service territory or in an adjacent or proximate one.

In this first period of M&A, the five utilities in the State of Iowa (Interstate Power, Iowa Electric Light and Power, Iowa Public Service, Iowa Power & Light [Midwest Resources], and Iowa-Illinois Gas & Electric) completed their roll-up into either Alliant or MidAmerican Energy, respectively.

An unusual utility transaction occurred between WPL Holdings, IES Industries, and Interstate Power in 1995. This transaction also caught Wall Street and the industry by surprise. Not only was it an early transaction in the overall industry, but it was more complex than contemporary deals and also affected by MidAmerican Energy's hostile offer for IES Industries. Managements usually believed that a traditional two-way combination was difficult and could not envision how to deal with multiple exchanges of common stock, approval processes, and integrations simultaneously.

However, this three-way transaction signaled that given the right fundamental circumstances—such as geographic proximity and relative size—and the right natural affinities—that is, the personal relationships developed from working across industry issues—a more complicated transaction could be completed. This transaction has been the first and only three-way combination and integration among multiple utilities, at least at the time of a traded company merger announcement.

Other companies, like Energy East, integrated across multiple utilities in New York and Maine years after each transaction had occurred and New England Electric Service combined prior acquisitions in New York and Massachusetts well after completion of these deals.

New England Electric System (later NationalGrid PLC) also started its northeastern *roll-up* of Eastern Utilities Associates and Niagara Mohawk. This was a hallmark of early M&A—significant single state or tight proximity consolidation, which was the simplest approach to avoiding prolonged PUHCA issues at the SEC.

And, Texas Utilities had actually integrated its three stand-alone operating companies (Texas Power & Light, Texas Electric Service, and Dallas Power & Light) in the mid-1980s in an internal three-way combination after decades of operating separately within a closely aligned service territory of Dallas, Ft. Worth, and Central, Western and Eastern Texas.

In particular, the notion of convergence became a favored strategy for M&A, that is, the acquisition of new customers in an overlapping service territory not fully served by a single electric or gas company, or acquisition of electric or gas customers in a competitor's service territory. In essence, a convergence play became the front door into a pre-existing electric or gas adversary's service territory in the event of future competition for customers, as well as a hedge against poaching of current customers by the same or another electric or gas company.

Joe Sauvage from Citi offered his perspective on why convergence deals were pursued:

> There has always been a utility and market debate over the value of cross-over transactions between electrics and LDCs. During high periods of these transactions, like between 1995 and 2000, electrics and LDCs looked to be the opposite of each other. Electrics had lower growth and lower market premiums, while LDCs showed higher growth and higher valuations. There was no market correlation either—pure electrics or gas can trade well, but so could combination companies. And in certain periods, combination companies traded better than single-fuel entities.

Commenting on the potential of industry convergence in the mid-1990s, former CEO Jim Torgerson from AVANGRID also remembered:

> Some companies believed there would definitely be consolidation between electric and gas companies. With overlapping service territories, it was clear significant synergies would be available, and where better to combine than where two companies are already located. There might always be additional options for a transaction, but better to take action today than have your options taken away.

Convergence mergers occurred almost immediately once the competitive market genie was out of the regulatory bottle. Puget Sound Energy and Washington Natural Gas was the first combination to announce a true convergence merger in 1995, with Pacific Enterprises and Enova, Texas Utilities and ENSERCH, and Houston Industries and NorAm Energy all announcing in 1996, with several others following in the ensuing years, like Brooklyn Union Gas and Long Island Lighting in 1998.

In discussing the movement toward convergence occurring in the mid- and late 1990s, former CEO Erle Nye from TXU addressed his motivations to acquire an LDC:

> Other companies focused on acquiring LDCs to complement existing electric businesses, with a view toward future cross-selling. Our Australia experience, where we also bought a gas distribution company overlapping with our electric utility acquisition, did not heavily influence our next acquisition of the local LDC that was also in Dallas, in part because retail markets had yet to open in Texas. But our Australian experience in electric and gas integration, and the legacy businesses the parent holding company of the LDC operated, showed us that synergies could be captured, complementary businesses could be integrated, and asset diversity had value.

All these transactions were characterized by overlapping or adjacent service territories and a desire to grow scale, particularly at the customer level and protect and capture future revenue growth potential.

During this time period, selected U.S. utilities ventured overseas to find acquisition opportunities in newly privatized countries as a means of securing footholds in key countries, supplementing U.S. growth, and projecting global reach. This U.S. and foreign merger and acquisition activity, as well as other de-risking actions and competitive business entry like marketing and trading, boosted electric market capitalizations over the next few years to as high as approximately $300 billion in 1997, an uptick of 40 percent over the beginning of this cycle.[2] LDCs were less impacted since they did not have the same available growth opportunities as did the electrics.

Also in this time frame, the first non-contiguous mergers began to occur. New Centuries Energy and Northern States Power, AEP and Central and South West, and Unicom and PECO Energy, respectively, agreed to combine their businesses, even though the headquarters locations were more than 650 miles apart at the closest, and 900 miles distant for the farthest apart. Particularly relevant is the Unicom and PECO Energy transaction which brought two large nuclear fleets together for the first time.

Early transactions in this period were also characterized by high one-month-ahead price premiums (30-40 percent), whether acquisitions or mergers. After the early flurry of transactions in the first two years, premium levels continued even higher (40-50-plus percent), creating a large and extended carry of goodwill on the balance sheet.[3]

These formative transactions also carried the burden of educating regulators at the federal and state levels on merger logic and competitive impact. They took up to two years to conclude, or ultimately were abandoned, likely due to Federal Energy Regulatory Commission (FERC) conclusions on competitive market impact, or the SEC administering of PUHCA. With more regulatory awareness of the utility M&A phenomenon and certain jurisdictions seeing multiple transactions, the approval time period began to shrink to 14–16 months on average by the end of the period.[4]

Fortunately, merging companies had been successful in both achieving estimated synergies and securing equitable regulatory savings sharing. These outcomes gave comfort to Wall Street that managements could effectively integrate companies and avoid earnings dilution from over-pricing or execution.

Steve Fleishman from Wolfe Research addressed what analysts were looking for when they first heard about proposed transactions:

> I always hoped the announced deal would make us comfortable with its logic, value, and likelihood. The elements of what I generally considered a good deal included clear strategic rationale, accretive earnings in the near-term without adding leverage, attention to balance sheet strengthening, long-term growth, regulatory quality, regulatory approach, social issue solutions, and avoiding the complication of delivering existing core plans. The more information we were given, the better the insight we could develop about the transaction, and the more helpful our assessments were to shareholders.

This first period on modern-era M&A set a tone for future periods. Proposed mergers would be contested; regulatory scrutiny would be high; conditions would be required; and customers would need to measurably benefit. While an energized level of M&A activity existed, many companies were still skeptical of the value of pursuing a merger.

Notwithstanding these considerations, the 1995–1999 period (particularly 1996 and 1999) was the high-water mark for transactions with 60 transactions announced and 48 ultimately completed (some carrying over into 2000), which far exceeded the number of deals completed in any other following period.[5]

Rationalization and Roll-Up (2000-2004)

The movement toward more unbundling and competition in the electric sector continued after 1999, particularly in states like Texas. But the second M&A period also coincided with an economic recession that featured the implosion of Enron in the merchant power space in 2002-2003, among other highly levered businesses, like WorldCom.

With the emerging insights into Enron produced by its spectacular fall from grace and into bankruptcy from a mix of mark-to-market accounting, special-purpose vehicles, and obscure financial reporting, the stock markets turned against the business model of similarly leveraged and trading-based entities. In addition, growth in new generating capacity had hit a wall and the growth model for IPPs collapsed, leading to significant market valuation reductions.

With respect to the next wave of transactions, Steve Fleishman from Wolfe Research provided additional insight on how Wall Street attitudes also changed:

> After more time passed leading into the early 2000s, it became clearer that some negative themes were also emerging. While gaining international presence sounded exciting, it did not fully

deliver on the promise of delivering a deep and portable understanding of market learnings to the U.S. Many utilities were pursuing mergers or acquisitions, which led to over-paying and building long-term financial dead-weight. It was becoming clear that transactions came in clumps and activity surged and waned depending on market circumstances. The power of state regulation was also not appreciated by companies and set some of them back in pursuing merger approvals.

The traditional vertically integrated electric utility sector was less affected than its IPP brethren, but still felt the impacts of the market response to unplanned surprises in growth businesses. To combat credit rating and market valuation reductions from changed investor sentiment, the utility industry began to remarket itself by embracing a *back-to-basics* (a focus on the core business) theme, which meant de-risking the enterprise by deemphasizing or disposing of non-core strategies, assets, and businesses, streamlining organizations and cost structures, and returning to a more compatible corporate purpose.

The back-to-basics strategy simplified the business scope of many utilities, giving them time to repair balance sheets, focus on cash flow, adjust their portfolios, and reorient strategies toward more familiar growth options, like domestic M&A. The rationalization of utility business scope and composition proved to be beneficial to the execution of future M&A strategy for many companies.

As the U.S. utility industry considered its positioning after the M&A frenzy of the previous period, and the abrupt reversal in fortunes from the Enron situation, it recognized several relative truths: industry consolidation was not a short-term fad; transaction execution was difficult, but not insurmountable; regulatory success was never a given, but could be obtained if benefits of the deal were adequately explained; and the nature of attractive partners could rapidly shrink if companies dawdled in assessing how M&A could advantage them.

In the early days of this period (2000–2002), the incidence of

M&A among utilities continued unabated as some companies like FirstEnergy, Energy East, Atmos Energy, New Century Energies, NationalGrid, Western Resources, Ameren, KeySpan Energy, and PEPCO Holdings pursued second transactions, and others like FPL Group, AES, and Northwestern Public Service moved from observing industry consolidation to active engagement (although not always completion). And three international electric utilities—Emera from Canada and RWE and E.On from Germany—made their initial forays into the U.S. with the acquisitions of Bangor–Hydro, American Water Works, and LG&E Energy, respectively.

The 2000–2004 period provides an illustration of how sensitive M&A markets can be to externalities beyond the influence or control of utilities. With the Enron market jolt at the end of 2001, the U.S. utility M&A market quickly slowed down after the first quarter of 2002 as financial markets were not highly receptive to balance sheet use for financing while the industry was in a period of financial stabilization, and as regulatory approval periods created a drag on the certainty of transaction outcomes.

Limited M&A activity carried over to only two announced deals from 2003 to 2004 as utilities were preoccupied with shifting their businesses to a back-to-basics model, which included selling both assets and non-core businesses. However, Duke Energy participated in M&A through other core segments of its overall business, acquiring Westcoast Energy Company to blend with its earlier acquisition of PanEnergy Corp. and expand its natural gas footprint with assets in pipelines and an LDC in Canada.

But the slowdown in real M&A activity during the latter part of the 2000–2004 period did not dampen the overall enthusiasm of utility managements for transactions; it simply reflected the moods of the market and regulators. The financial markets were still reacting to Enron and the demise of the IPP sector, while regulators were not inclined to see utilities pay high premiums in transactions when customers had lost jobs in the recession and financial durability was an open question.

Several of the transactions completed in this period occurred between large companies and smaller entities like Energy East with RGS Energy, KeySpan Energy with Eastern Enterprises, DTE Energy with MCN Energy, and Ameren Energy with CILCORP, thus further reinforcing the *roll-up* logic of serial acquirors. By the end of this cycle, market capitalization of U.S. utilities had grown to almost $400 billion as the overall economy and utility sector recovered from the Enron debacle.[6]

This second period of transactions was characterized by average one-month-ahead price premiums coalescing in the 35-40 percent range whether acquisitions or mergers, with mergers of equals tilting toward similar levels and scale-disparity acquisitions being even higher.[7] On average, premium levels stayed robust in the early portion of this period, but dropped once the recession occurred and utilities recognized that high premiums would exacerbate the difficulty of obtaining regulatory approval.

The second wave of transactions were the beneficiaries of experience gained in transactions from prior period deals. First-wave regulatory commissions had now dealt with numerous transactions, which both informed themselves and other inexperienced jurisdictions on issues and policies. In effect, they provided a general template for dealing with demonstration of the public interest, which also greatly advantaged utility approval case-in-chief development and risk assessment.

The greater the regulatory awareness of other transaction approval decisions nationally, the better an individual state commission could interpret and consider its own prevailing standards. The number of prior transactions and building regulatory commission experience with approval issues—particularly at the FERC level—also shortened the approval time period to 10–12 months, on average, and reaching fewer than seven months in one transaction.[8]

This second period of modern-era M&A affirmed much of the experience of deals in the first period. Approval periods for some transactions could still vary widely, particularly if multiple state jurisdictions and the SEC or FERC were actively engaged. The parties to merger approval proceedings always seemed to increase, setting the stage for arguments not just between the utilities and the state regulatory commission staff, but also among the staff and intervenors over specific concerns or risks.

Fortunately, regulatory commissions in most states continued to be supportive of transactions if a clear demonstration of the public interest could be made. And financial markets had time to view how management performed post-merger with respect to producing the level of benefits claimed in approval filings. However, the Exelon and PSEG and Northwest Natural Gas and Portland General Electric transactions failed to obtain state regulatory commission support and were terminated.

While market premiums in this era started above the 45 percent level, they started declining in later years of this cycle to less than 35 percent, suggesting that high pricing commitments and high levels of goodwill were not likely to be sustained.[9] While large company acquirors of smaller companies could pay higher premiums, these were often more a reflection of affordability and availability than value.

This track record of merging companies producing customer benefits in prior deals and achieving a level of equitable sharing with shareholders also gave comfort to utilities considering potential transactions. Anticipated merger cost savings were being produced and companies did not feel as if they had been unfairly treated by regulatory commissions through the approval process. These outcomes further alleviated the concerns of boards of directors that M&A carried more downside than upside for utilities—whether the acquiror or the acquiree.

By the end of this period, another ten utility transactions had been announced, with eight completed on top of the 48 completed from the prior period.[10] And the SEC had become less stringent in how it interpreted PUHCA and the FERC was more open-minded about measuring potential market competition. This experience base provided continued impetus to future transactions and set the stage for another wave of transactions as the utilities industry continued to shrink.

Reengagement and Opportunism (2005–2009)

By the mid-2000s, the utilities industry was well into its financial health recovery, just in time for another recession between late 2007 and mid-2009. This period still produced the third largest period of M&A and featured a mix of U.S. utility, international utility, and financial sponsor activity. As would be expected, activity was robust at the beginning of the period and extremely limited over 2008 and 2009 when the recession was at its most debilitating point.

The third M&A period in the modern era continued to prove out the experience gained in deal pursuit in the first two periods. Approval periods extended to an average of 15–18 months longer than those observed in the prior 2000-2004 M&A period.[11] Specific deals became larger and more complex, such as Duke Energy and Cinergy, FPL Group and Constellation Energy, and NationalGrid and KeySpan, with infrastructure fund buyers, who were largely unknown to state regulators, also participating actively in this time period. Accordingly, approval time frames extended even as PUHCA was repealed in 2005 and affiliate issues jurisdiction moved to the FERC.

The transactions occurring during this period were characterized by several characteristics. *Step-out* or unique transactions were structured, with new deal parameters eclipsing conventional parameters for ownership, financing mode, and business alignment. Several transactions were propelled by liquidity concerns and hangovers from the merchant power era. Convergence deals also resurfaced as acquirors again pursued customer scale with the hope that more meters to bill would unleash product and service innovation. After several years of market recovery after the Enron situation, utilities were ready to reengage in the M&A space and pursue further consolidation.

Even as the utility industry's focus on a back-to-basics strategy was undertaken to satisfy market leverage and earnings stability concerns, managements remained interested in consolidation and the announcements exceeded those occurring in the prior period.[12]

But managements also were recognizing the transaction landscape was changing and they would need to be actively prepared, if not participating, in M&A. For those companies that had completed multi-state transactions, a focus on operating model redesign, that is, how to align the elements of the business, served to emphasize more service company or shared services centralization, which would then accommodate simpler and faster integration.

Some acquirors during this period, like NationalGrid and Sempra Energy, were serial acquirors and had developed capabilities to identify, assess, structure, bid, approve, and integrate acquisitions. This prior experience was invaluable in understanding regulatory agency requirements and precedents, shortening filing and approval periods, and accelerating time-to-value after closing.

Several announcements in the 2005–2009 period involved smaller company, affordable acquisitions of under $500 million, like Gaz Metro from Canada acquiring Green Mountain Power, MDU Resources acquiring both Cascade Natural Gas and Intermountain Gas, and Sempra Energy acquiring Energy South. Convergence themes were still on the minds of executives as WPS Resources (a combination company) acquired Peoples Energy (an LDC) and the Gaz Metro deal had a Canadian LDC acquiring a U.S. electric company and MDU Resources, a U.S. combination company, acquiring two LDCs.

But M&A deals were becoming increasingly larger. The Duke Energy and Cinergy deal was both large and complex, requiring five state regulatory commissions to approve the transaction. The transaction also combined two vibrant marketing and trading businesses, in addition to the core electric and gas utilities. MidAmerican Energy—Berkshire Hathaway's previously acquired Iowa utility—acquired PacifiCorp, which was a large western U.S. entity with a multi-state footprint well distanced from the new parent's Des Moines headquarters, creating questions about how the acquired utility would continue to be operated within the holding company.

Perhaps the signature deal of this period was the KKR and TPG acquisition of TXU, which only four years earlier had possessed a diverse business of U.S., UK, and Australian utilities, as well as a gas pipeline, a fuels company, a lignite mining company, and an energy retailer. This was the largest leveraged buy-out (LBO) to date at $45 billion, including debt. Two takeaways emerged from this transaction: there are no limits on dealmaker imagination regarding transaction conception and structuring, and there are no constraints to utility deal scale, even for LBOs.

A few other large deals were also proposed in this period that were never completed. Initially, FPL Group and Constellation Energy attempted to merge in 2005, but ultimately terminated their proposed transaction due to regulatory uncertainty over financial issues and timing. This was also a mega-transaction given the competitive businesses of each company, which also demonstrated that long-distance mergers could be attractive and relative headquarters locations were not an impediment to high levels of benefits.

Berkshire Hathaway also bid on Constellation Energy in 2008 when this company was still experiencing cash flow issues. Four months later Constellation Energy subsequently terminated this transaction and accepted an alternative offer from Electricité de France (EDF) for a 49 percent minority ownership stake in its nuclear business. These proposed transactions were opportunistic in that they sought to capitalize on seller financial weaknesses that could unlock substantial future value for the acquiror.

As in earlier years, regulatory commissions in most states continued to be supportive of transactions if a clear demonstration of the public interest could be made. This was not always the case for infrastructure fund deals, like Australia's Babcock and Brown's attempt to acquire Northwestern Public Service. Babcock & Brown was overwhelmingly rebuked by the Montana Public Service Commission on a 5-0 vote, with the governor not so politely stating, "This is a vote that says pack your bags and ride a kangaroo, because you're not going to be in Montana."[13]

This was an unusual, unexpected, and outlier response that reflected local reaction to an international infrastructure fund attempting acquisition of a well-regarded local company in a populist state, with few indicated benefits and numerous unanswered questions—not the ideal alignment of stars.

By this point in time, the mystery of merging companies had been largely dissipated, even though the battles over the level of merger-related benefits and the achievement of equitable savings sharing between customers and shareholders continued. The track record of utilities producing estimated cost savings continued to be good, and boards of directors were becoming comfortable with the process, timeline, and results of pursuing and adjudicating a proposed transaction. By the end of this cycle, market capitalizations were over $400 billion and reflected the impacts of the Great Recession after topping out at approximately $550 billion in 2007.[14]

Transaction pricing also continued to be reflective of structuring deals as mergers of equals or modified mergers of equals, which generally kept premiums in the 20-25 percent range.[15] Reasonable pricing helped to solidify acquiring company financial stability and secure regulatory support for transactions.

However, regulatory commissions were becoming more demanding regarding demonstration of the public interest, particularly through merger synergies. As a result of the earlier 2001 and then recent 2007-2009 recessions and continuing economic sluggishness, regulators were seeking to mitigate adverse impacts to customers and ensure that they adequately shared in available benefits, where possible.

Commissions became more argumentative and more aggressive in seeking asymmetric benefits distribution. In addition, they became highly focused on establishing high numbers of merger approval conditions and commitments which, while not wholly onerous, were very broad in reach and initially unwelcome.

Another 18 utility transactions were announced between 2005 and 2009, with 14 ultimately completed on top of the 56 that were completed for deals announced between 1995 and 2004, which reduced the number of tradable companies by approximately 40 percent over these years.[16] FERC market power issues were also dissipating, in part because of the successful operations of the RTOs and ISOs which had assumed dispatch and transmission responsibilities, thus mitigating FERC concerns over market access and pricing power. Consequently, approval time periods again were approximately 15-18 months across this period.[17]

Although deal activity in the last two years of this period were adversely impacted by the recession, no new impediments emerged to pursuing and concluding a transaction, except the continued shrinkage of attractive and logical targets.

Fortification and Positioning (2010-2014)

The first decade of the new millennium had proven robust with utility M&A activity, and further increased over the succeeding five years. The overall U.S. economy was recovering from the end of the recession in mid-2009; financial markets had returned to normalcy, and business confidence was slowly improving. Similarly, the utilities industry was well into its own recovery as demand returned and capital access was available to most companies that needed it.

In a departure from the past, the electric industry was just entering a new era of wind and solar renewables that had emerged from a collision between carbon emission policies, technology availability, and consumer interest. The advent of renewables as a viable source of supply created a new set of original equipment manufacturers (OEMs), which energized scale production.

The desire for reduced carbon emissions enabled governmental policies on renewables penetration and created an environmental "Governors Cup" of individual state proposals such as an individual state's proclamation of 20 percent of supply from renewables by 2030 being one-upped by a neighboring governor's pronouncement of 25 percent of supply from renewables by 2025, all intended to accelerate a higher level of renewables commitment.

With the elevation of renewables as the climate savior, utilities took notice of the shift in policy and sentiment and began to directly participate in the sector, first by contract and later by development or acquisition of projects. From this point forward, utility strategies were influenced by the fuel composition of the future generation portfolio and M&A considerations included coal generation levels, renewables focus, and carbon reduction commitment.

Within this time period, market capitalizations markedly grew from a level of approximately $435 billion at the beginning of 2010 to over $675 billion at the end of 2014, an increase of around 55 percent over the five-year period.[18] This increased market capitalization reflected overall market recovery, utility industry relative total shareholder return (TSR), an uplift in sustained capital investment, and an overall market growth environment.

These high market capitalizations provided a tailwind to utility M&A strategies over these five years as there were substantial gaps between the largest companies, that is, the roughly one-third of entities over $20 billion, the next one-third of companies between approximately $10 and $20 billion, and the bottom third of entities fewer than $10 billion. These market value disparities provided financial capacity for both strategic and opportunistic transactions and enabled larger and stronger companies to fortify their market positions financially and operationally.

While companies with high market valuations were not always the most efficient performers, the likelihood that scale could be leveraged for operational advantage was not lost on these entities. There had always been substantial variability between quartile performers across utilities, thus leveraging scale to move down the cost curve was a notable driver for many acquirors. With the high degree of industry success in synergies attainment, companies knew that further scale advancement and operating model alignment could further unlock value for customers and shareholders.

The range of utility industry O&M cost levels has always been broad, with differences between and among quartile groups depicting cost-level differences of 50 percent to 100 percent from one quartile to the next. These differences reflect a host of underlying causation factors like scale, location, asset age and mix, bargaining unit contracts, technology position, and operating models, among other reasons.

This period again featured second or third deals by serial acquirors like Duke Energy, Gaz Metro, Fortis, Macquarie, Berkshire Hathaway Energy, Exelon, AES, FirstEnergy, Emera, and Northeast Utilities. These companies had successfully navigated their boards of directors and regulatory waters and had developed workable approaches to structuring a deal and obtaining approvals to close. Some had developed internal M&A playbooks to codify learnings and models for continued use and readiness for opportunistic situations.

These years also produced a period of high M&A activity and featured mostly traditional utility acquiror activity, with selected financial sponsor and international activity. And, given the increasing scale of the industry, the deals continued to grow in enterprise value. Duke Energy and Progress Energy's combination exceeded $32 billion, higher than the FPL Group and Constellation Energy and Exelon and PSEG Enterprises deals, which were both $25 billion or higher, in enterprise value, although this scale did not help either of them close. The KKR–TPG and TXU LBO in 2008 of course approximated $45 billion in enterprise value but was structured as an LBO.

The deals that occurred in this fourth M&A period reflected a wide variety of deal archetypes. Emera, Gaz Metro, and Fortis continued to pursue U.S. regional presence and positioning. Proximity encouraged several deals, like Duke Energy and Progress Energy, Northeast Utilities and NSTAR, Exelon and Constellation Energy, FirstEnergy and Allegheny Energy, Laclede Gas and Missouri Gas Energy (and then EnergySouth), and Wisconsin Energy and Integrys Energy Group.

The lack of proximity (almost 5,000 miles between headquarters) did not faze NextEra Energy with its pursuit of Hawaiian Electric, although that deal was terminated after long delay. Nor did distance constrain Fortis's acquisition of Unisource (more than 3,000 miles distant), TECO Energy's purchase of New Mexico Gas (almost 1,500 miles away), or any of the Canadian utility acquisitions from Nova Scotia or Newfoundland.

Figure 10: Unbounded Reach

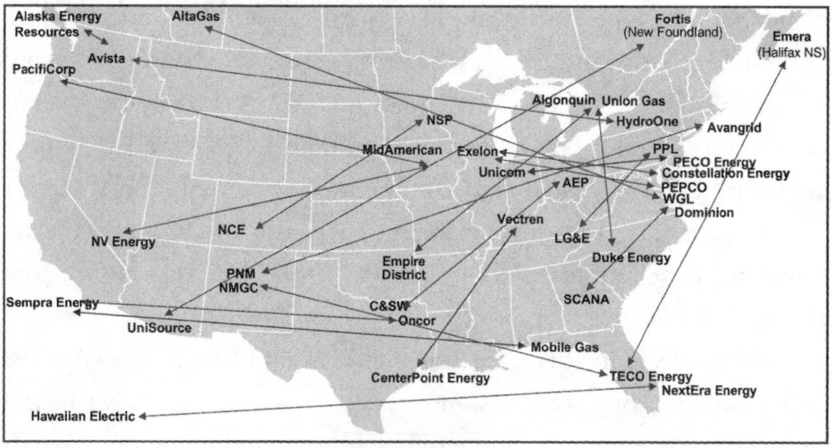

NCE-NSP – 700 miles
AEP-CSW – 900 miles
NextEra – HEI – 5,000 miles
MidAmerican – PacifiCorp – 1,500 miles
Unicom – PECO – 650 miles
Exelon – Constellation – 600 miles
Avista – Alaska Energy Resources – 2,400 miles

PPL – LG&E – 575 miles
MidAmerican – NV Energy – 1,200 miles
Sempra – Mobile Gas – 1,700 miles
HydroOne – Avista – 1,842 miles
Duke – Westcoast Energy / Union Gas – 900 miles
Avangrid – PNM – 1,872 miles
TECO-New Mexico Gas Company – 1,500 miles

Emera – TECO Energy – 1,550 miles
Fortis – UniSource – 3,100 miles
Exelon – PEPCO – 600 miles
Sempra – Oncor – 1,350 miles
CenterPoint – Vectren – 722 miles
AltaGas – WGL – 1,973 miles
Algonquin – Empire District – 916 miles

Sources: Company announcements; excludes European acquisitions; Tom Flaherty "Lessons Learned for Tomorrows Deals: Many Deals Completed, What Have We Learned?", Public Utilities Fortnightly September 2016

Some deals focused on joint competitive capabilities like Exelon and Constellation Energy, while others, like Northeast Utilities and NSTAR, leveraged operational capabilities at one of the entities. Wisconsin Energy and Integrys expanded the overall gas footprint across the upper Midwest, and Laclede Gas, TECO Energy, and PPL Resources made initial deals to assess M&A value and growth potential while increasing business scale and mix.

Large deals at this scale both enhanced financial flexibility and created advantaged regional positioning, particularly as new generation and transmission investment was receiving high interest in this period. The combination of these larger entities also created capabilities foundations that could be applied in the current business to improve operating performance and be further leveraged in subsequent transactions. By the end of 2014, market capitalizations for U.S. electric utilities had reached over $625 billion, while LDCs were approximately $50 billion.[19]

Transaction premiums centered around 15-20 percent (one month ahead) with wide variability as large and complex deals continued. Some significant deals, like Northeast Utilities and NSTAR and Duke Energy and Progress Energy, were built around a low-premium (~5 percent) merger-of-equals model.[20] When below-average transaction pricing was achieved, it substantially helped to solidify acquiring company financial stability and secure regulatory support for transactions—the only problem was most companies were not interested in selling for a low premium to then face lawsuits for foregoing shareholder value.

Several deals in this time frame precipitated high external visibility as regulatory commissions were even more intensely engaged regarding demonstration of the public interest and synergies. With the effects of the 2008-2009 Great Recession still lingering, regulators again sought to mitigate adverse impacts to customers by ensuring that sufficient synergies were distributed to customers, including immediately after close.

Given transaction scale and complexities, approval time frames continued at 15-18 months, consistent with those durations seen over the last several periods of utility M&A.[21] This was not surprising when multiple commissions were involved in transaction approvals and the business issues associated with these larger deals such as enterprise risk and credit quality created questions in regulators' minds over ongoing stability, future rate cases, and investment commitments.

Another 17 utility transactions were announced, with 15 completed on top of the 70 that were completed between 1995 and 2009.[22] Although deal activity since early 2008 had been adversely impacted by the recession into 2010, the number and significance of the deals that did occur illustrated that utilities were not going to stop pursuing strategic or opportunistic combinations.

Simplicity and Growth (2015-2020)

The final M&A period reflects 25 years of consolidation among US activities. At the outset of this period, the electric industry had shrunk by more than 60 percent and the LDC sector by approximately 70 percent. Most of the same rationales for consolidation in 1995 carried through this time period, and there was high similarity in how state regulatory commissions addressed and approved proposed transactions and financial markets evaluated and treated acquirors or merging companies.

Large enterprise value deals (over $10 billion) continued through this period, although no acquisitions above $15 billion occurred within these six years. In some cases, these transactions enabled already large companies, like Dominion Energy, Duke Energy, Southern Company, Eversource Energy, and Sempra Energy, to become even larger in market capitalization scale. At the end of 2020, the market capitalization of the predominantly electric sector was above $800 billion, with predominantly LDCs around $125 billion.[23]

The pace of renewable growth in utility portfolios through acquisitions of existing and contracted projects, as well as greenfield development of new projects, continued to accelerate and reshape existing power supply portfolios. This period characterized the greatest window of total capital investment—growth and infrastructure—the electric utility industry had ever experienced. Every year from 2015 through 2020 (and projected through 2023), more than $100 billion annually was expended on new infrastructure.[24] This spend substantially enhanced market capitalization and provided balance sheet strength to utilities considering M&A.

After two recessions and an extended period of disruption, the strategies of utilities were becoming clearer, with surprisingly less differentiation than would be anticipated. The focus of these strategies—for example, energy sector transition, carbon emissions and renewables, infrastructure resilience, customer centricity, and de-risking the business—looked similar across companies, even if their strategic circumstances were different.

Beginning in 2014 electric utilities became interested in new, disruptive technologies designed for grid and network modernization, optimization, and performance, as well as behind-the-meter information and intelligence. A few companies, like Edison International, Southern Company, Duke Energy, and others, began to utilize M&A in a broader manner than they had previously.

Now, smaller non-regulated acquisitions or joint ventures were executed to enable these companies to learn about these emerging technologies without absorbing excessive risk or expending significant capital to prepare for future competitive markets. And they also began investing in these new technology providers through internal or external venture capital funds to further expand their market horizons, awareness, and readiness.

Companies had realigned their operating models and were now in position to absorb small acquisitions or integrate larger acquisitions much more seamlessly. The realignments that took place at Duke Energy after its merger with Progress Energy, and Iberdrola after its acquisitions of Energy East and UIL Holdings, provided more centralized operating models that simplified the alignment of add-on acquisitions occurring between 2015 and 2020.

Certain companies that had executed early modern-era transactions, for example CenterPoint Energy, Vectren and Southern Company, were reentering the M&A market after an absence and now facing a determination on how best to realign operating models across dispersed service territories and/or parallel business segments. A focus on the dynamics of the new energy transition began to permeate utility thinking on how to leverage M&A to enhance competitive capabilities and experience.

One-month-ahead transaction premiums for traditional utility deals varied widely (from 10 percent to above 70 percent) but centered around 25-30 percent as the mix of buyers was broad, potential targets were scarce, and a few auction processes created deeper competitive pools.[25] In addition, first-time acquirors like NextEra Energy (first actual close) engaged in the market and international acquirors, like HydroOne, Iberdrola, Emera, and Fortis, further made for a frothy market.

The average premium range offered expanded, in part, to reflect acquiror desires to avoid being topped from *go-shop* provisions (agreed post-definitive agreement seller conversations with other potential buyers) in merger agreements. Smaller-scale acquisitions (attempted or completed), like Hawaiian Electric, Westar Resources, Avista, Questar, TECO Energy, PNM Resources, Piedmont Gas, UIL Holdings, Empire District Electric, El Paso Electric, and Gulf Power, reflected the ability to attract both natural buyers and opportunistic acquirors shopping for bargains, and thinned out several utilities with market capitalizations under $5 billion.

Interest in water companies, a sector characterized by small-scale and fragmented providers, also attracted interest from some electric and LDC utilities. While water companies had been looked at over an extended period, the similarity of an infrastructure business to what utilities were used to operating was not lost on managements. Eversource Energy pursued this path in its 2017 acquisition of Aquarion Water Company, its 2018 pursuit of Connecticut Water Service, and in continuing efforts to further consolidate water properties since then. In addition, Northwest Natural Holdings (primarily an LDC) had been rolling up small water companies in the Pacific Northwest and Texas for several years.

Jim Judge of Eversource Energy commented on the attractiveness of water companies:

> We believe water fundamentals are similar to those of electric and gas distribution companies. The same regulation, capital intensity, unions, skill requirements, and customers exist, with far more fragmentation than electric and gas utilities and significant infrastructure and water quality issues to solve. If specific water companies meet our transaction criteria, then we're very adept at operating distribution systems and maintaining lower prices while delivering reliable service.

Regulatory commissions remained actively engaged in merger approval proceedings, particularly where premiums were or appeared high, like in Duke Energy and Piedmont Gas and Southern Company and AGL Resources, or where international utilities or financial sponsors proposed financial or operating models that were considered risky or complex from a regulatory perspective.

Synergies sharing mechanisms again followed historical precedents and allowed for equitable savings sharing, while the number of merger conditions and commitments seemed to plateau in raw numbers as most areas of regulatory concern were widely recognized and traveled from one state commission to another.

One phenomenon that did occur during the end of the prior period and throughout this fifth time frame involved the topic of synergies. Notwithstanding the need to satisfy the public interest through quantifiable customer benefits, several transactions were approved without any demonstration of these cost savings.

For example, in Southern Company and AGL Resources no merger savings were identified or offered, even though the headquarters of both companies were only blocks apart. The lack of merger synergies reflected the operating model to be adopted, where one company would operate a core electric business, while the other would operate a core gas LDC and neither would be operationally integrated with the other, except in limited areas.

In other deals, like Sempra Energy and Oncor Energy and Duke Energy and Piedmont Gas, nominal synergies were proffered, with Oncor Energy being operated as a separate entity due to distance and legal ring-fencing. Piedmont Gas operated as part of North Carolina operations, rather than fully integrating with the broader Duke Energy gas business in the Midwest.

Another interesting phenomenon in the last six years is that transaction approval time frames markedly shrank back to 10 to 12 months from longer durations, even with several high-profile, large-entity, complex operating models, and geographically distributed deals in play.[26] While selected deals had been done in time frames even shorter over the 25-year period, these were more the exception than the rule.

Another 14 utility transactions were announced in this time frame, with 12 completed by mid-2021, on top of the 85 already completed between 1995 and 2014, with the Iberdrola and PNM Resources deal still pending.[27] The number of deals reflected full recovery from the previous recession and a healthy overall economy, with utilities experiencing historically high valuations through most of this time frame. At the end of this cycle, the total market capitalization of the U.S. utility sector had expanded above $900 billion in 2020, from fewer than $200 billion in 1994.[28]

Reach and Concentration

The almost 100 completed U.S. utility transactions occurring over the last 25 years has been impressive, but it obscures some other outcomes about the composition of the current industry that resulted from these deals, namely the number of serial acquirors, the geographic reach of certain companies, the presence of international entities, and the aggregation of operating companies.

As mentioned, several companies have frequently utilized M&A to both jump-start and sustain growth. These companies knew that reaching competitive scale—that is, not pursuing bigger to be better, but rather leveraging bigger to enable flexibility—would be more quickly achieved by leveraging inorganic growth means. This is invaluable in a fixed universe of attractive partner choices, but with a broad array of potential competitors for those few best choices.

Companies like Duke Energy, Exelon, FirstEnergy, AVANGRID, Evergy, Sempra Energy, Berkshire Hathaway Energy, NationalGrid, Ameren, Xcel Energy, and Eversource Energy have accomplished multiple transactions since 1995. And international companies, like Scottish Power, Iberdrola, Emera, Gaz Metro, Alta Gas, and Fortis, have also

Figure 11: Serial Acquirors in the U.S.[1]

Current Entity	1990–1994	1995–1999	2000–2004	2005–2009	2010–2014	2015–2020
FirstEnergy	Ohio Edison		GPU		Allegheny Energy	
Berkshire Hathaway Energy		MidAmerican Energy		PacifiCorp	Sierra Pacific	
Sempra Energy		Pacific Enterprises		Mobile Gas Willmut Gas		InfraREIT Oncor
Exelon		Unicom	Conectiv		Constellation Energy	PEPCO
Duke Energy			Westcoast Energy	Cinergy Pan Energy	Progress Energy	Piedmont Natural Gas
Eversource Energy		COMEnergy			NSTAR	Aquarian Bay State Gas
Evergy		KGE	UtiliCorp United	St. Joseph Light and Power Aquila		Great Plains Energy
Avangrid			Central Maine Power	RGE	Energy East UIL	PNM Resources[2]
NationalGrid		Nantucket Electric Eastern Utilities	Niagara Mohawk	KeySpan		
WEC Energy			Wisconsin Natural Gas	Peoples Energy Aquila	Integrys	
Ameren		CIPSCO	CILCORP Illinois Power			
Spire					Missouri Gas Energy	Willmut Gas Mobile Gas Alagasco
Fortis					UniSource Energy CH Energy Group	ITC
Emera			Bangor Hydro			TECO Maine & Maritimes
Dominion Energy		CNG				Questar SCANA Energy

Sources: Edison Electric Institute; S&P Capital IQ Pro; news reports;
(1) Excludes Algonquin Power and Utilities due to acquisition scale
(2) Pending closure in 2021

participated in the consolidation of U.S. utilities. The growth of these companies has fueled the addition of assets, revenues, customers, etc., that have created substantially greater scale than these companies probably expected to be attainable when they started down the M&A path.

Not surprisingly, executing serial transactions also creates a broad footprint within the U.S., some contiguous, and some broadly dispersed. The footprints of Xcel Energy, FirstEnergy, Berkshire Hathaway Energy, Sempra Energy, and Exelon, among other companies, expanded to include multiple time zones, RTOs/ISOs, regions, and states. The broad reach afforded by prior transactions brings multi-jurisdictional experience, as well as regulatory diversity.

Tom Fanning of Southern Company addressed the subject of serial acquirors within the U.S. utilities industry:

> Portfolio theory would suggest that segments and assets should be allocated to the best owner, which is inconsistent with the serial acquiror model, unless they are also continually harvesting other elements of their portfolio. Not all assets in a portfolio are always valuable over their entire period of ownership. Value rises and falls, and owners need to recognize these shifts and then optimize overall portfolio value through divestment of the underperforming pieces. A serial acquiror strategy can be flawed if it just focuses on segment or asset aggregation. Higher value can be created when an owner embraces earnings growth, return levels, risk management, and cultural alignment alike.

Many transactions were conducted by utilities that were already holding companies as determined under PUHCA, but others created new holding companies not previously existing. Southern Company, AEP, Entergy, Northeast Utilities, and New England Electric System all previously existed as PUHCA holding companies at the beginning of the modern era of U.S. utility M&A. But others, like FirstEnergy, Duke Energy, Berkshire Hathaway Energy, AVANGRID, Xcel Energy, and Eversource Energy established formal holding companies when PUHCA was either still in place or no longer as restrictive.

To illustrate the effect of prior consolidation, just 13 companies now own almost 80 electric operating companies, comprising more than 50 percent of the total electric operating companies within the U.S. The level of operating company concentration for LDCs is far less, since a number of these operating companies were also acquired by electrics.

Figure 12: Electric Operating Company Concentration

Owned Electric Utilities
AEP
Evergy
NationalGrid
FirstEnergy
Duke Energy
Eversource Energy
Berkshire Hathaway Energy
Exelon
Entergy
Avangrid
Xcel Energy
Ameren
Iberdrola
Southern Company

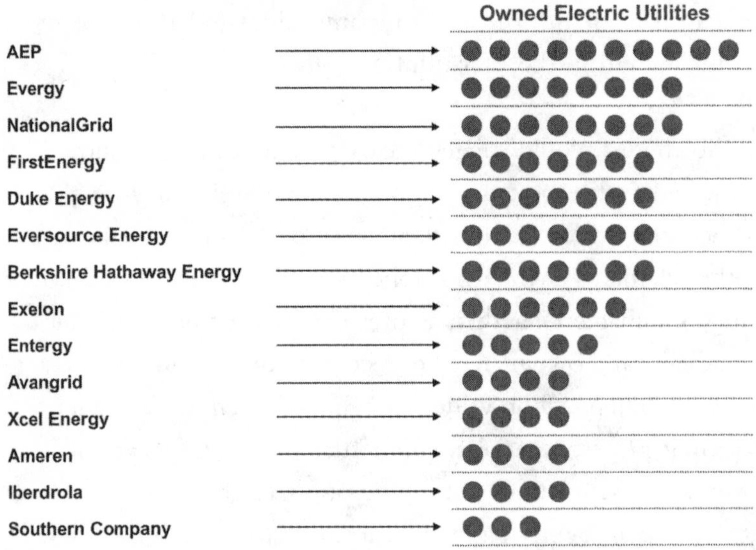

Source: Company websites

The stark contraction in tradable utilities over the last 25 years has dramatically reduced the number of available and attractive targets for acquiror consideration. Many companies with fewer than $5 billion in market capitalization exist, but a number reside in rural areas with low growth, and/or do not appear worth the effort to larger companies given the lack of a strong industrial logic and a minimum eight months to receive regulatory approval.

Key Takeaways

Since 1995, most consolidation transactions have been precipitated by changes in risks from significant policy shifts affecting the utility marketplace, or conventional industrial logic regarding the value of combining similar operations to enhance market positioning and value. But some transactions have been either unnecessarily reactive to market occurrences, essentially following the herd, or merger approval filings were insufficiently supported and lacking the clear demonstration of public interest or absence of market power.

Many early completed consolidation transactions were straight-up stock acquisitions (while more transactions since 2005 have been all cash) between friendly utility partners, and most hostile offer transactions have not been successfully completed, regardless of the currency utilized. Hostiles have experienced a difficult environment for completion and require the stars to be properly aligned for most of these types of transactions to achieve regulatory approval, no matter how supportive investment analysts can be.

The culmination of 25 years of consolidation from 1995 to 2020 has left the U.S. utilities industry in a position of greater strategic strength, financial flexibility, operating stability, and customer accessibility. Shrinking from about 100 tradable electric companies to 33, and from about 50 LDCs to 16, has clearly repainted the U.S. utility landscape, while enabling heightened emphasis on building value for shareholders and customers.

Beyond the inevitable response from local and state governments for hostile offers, there have been few practical constraints to utility M&A as financial markets have been accommodating, regulators are generally supportive, and companies have successfully captured synergies and realigned operating models to integrate operations.

Transaction models have been flexible, and companies use cash, stock, or both for transactions dependent on market trends and acquiree preferences. Merger price premiums have consistently ranged over the period between 20 and 30 percent and have bracketed this range depending on relative P/E ratios and style of transaction, for example, merger-of-equals at 5 to 10 percent, modified merger-of-equals at 10 to 20 percent, or control acquisitions at 20 plus percent.

Regulators have shortened transaction time frames to around 10-12 months from 15–18 months or more in the early days of consolidation. Regulators have allowed utilities to equitably share merger synergies with shareholders, that is, ~50/50, and to retain savings between rate cases or longer, in certain cases, if the appropriate justification is demonstrated. Regulators have also viewed that the logic of merger transactions is far more practical and superior to the notion of *synthetic* or *virtual* mergers that assume contractual arrangements are possible to pursue.

However, regulators have required earlier and higher levels of merger savings to be distributed to customers, including in year one, when no positive net synergies exist. The conditions and commitments adopted in merger regulatory approvals have substantially grown over time but have not turned out to be onerous to effective governance or operations.

Throughout the modern era of utility M&A, managements have effectively navigated the shoals within boards, financial investors, federal and state regulators, state and local governments, and customers to bring announced and completed combinations to fruition and to successful demonstration of value for all parties involved above.

But the conventional transactions that have been predominant throughout this entire period are not the only types of M&A activity that have occurred. Several other types or methods of utility consolidation have also been attempted or argued, some with success, and others that were doomed to fail from inception.

CHAPTER 4

MAVERICK ACTIONS

As the utilities industry evolved over the last 25 years of the modern era, its surrounding environment was also shifting, leading, and affecting the activities of utility companies. Industry dynamics were constantly fluid and causing managements to rethink long-held norms. Value drivers were also shifting as markets evolved and required different types of responses.

The nature and pace of change has caused the utility industry to think beyond the more vanilla type of transaction that characterized much of the observed contraction of existing companies. Companies began to realize that other third parties could be active players in potential transactions—either "uninvited guests" to proposed transactions, or sources for acquisition that were not thought to be previously available in the market.

While these types of non-traditional transactions were not common occurrences, when they did occur, they received high interest in various corners of the M&A community, such as from other utilities, bankers, and attorneys, as well as from different levels of regulators and intervenors. These transactions gave further credence to the notion that the industry could not assume conventional wisdom about consolidation sources would be limited to the simplest form of utility consolidation.

But the occurrence of these unconventional actions was not predictable and would likely be unexpected in timing and unique in form. Consequently, utility managements needed to consider a broader range of potential questions than they had in the past:

- Is the industry evolving past its long-standing structure?
- Are emerging archetypes transitory or permanent?
- Are externalities emerging that create unexpected opportunities?
- How can we position ourselves for unconventional transactions?
- What are the boundaries for potential transaction uniqueness?
- How do we get the board of directors comfortable with unconventional transactions?
- Is the financial community supportive of unique transactions?
- Will unconventional transactions be more difficult to finance?
- How different will regulatory processes look for unconventional opportunities?
- What barriers to unconventional transaction pursuit could emerge?

While the five time-based consolidation periods were all robust in traditional transaction execution, three maverick archetypes emerged that added to the allure of utility M&A—hostile offers, special situations, and auctions. These types of transactions not only brought into play a new category of utility operating owners, but also a different type of rationale for business disposition and a new type of investor and mindset.

Hostile Transactions

Hostile offers were highly unusual in the utilities industry, which was historically more genteel in its public face toward its counterpart companies—certainly more so than aggressive companies in competitive industries like consumer products, manufacturing, financial, and media and entertainment, among others. Since 1995, there have been 14 unsolicited offers to utilities, with almost all of them failing to be achieved.[1]

Figure 13: U.S. Utility Hostile Transactions

Acquiror	Acquiree	Year	Engagement	Terminated
Edison International	San Diego Gas & Electric	1988	• Secured shareholder approval, but CPUC voted not to approve	●
Eastern Utilities	Unitil and Fitchburg Gas & Electric	1989	• Withdrawn, with two targets subsequently combining after transaction termination	●
PacifiCorp	Arizona Public Service	1989	• Withdrawn and replaced with a long-term transmission contract	●
Kansas City Power & Light	Kansas Gas and Electric	1990	• Terminated after KG&E shareholders approved a "white knight' offer from KPL	●
IPALCO Enterprises	PSI Energy	1992	• Terminated after shareholders rejected the offer	●
Western Resources	Kansas City Power & Light	1993	• Secured initial shareholder approval and then re-traded, leading to withdrawal	●
PECO Energy	Pennsylvania Power and Light	1996	• Withdrawn when PPL, market and regulatory reaction was negative	●
MidAmerican Energy	IES Industries	1996	• Withdrawn after IES agreed to a three-way merger with two other utilities	●
WPL Holdings	MGE Energy	1996	• Withdrawn when MGE, market and regulatory reaction was negative	●
CalEnergy Resources	New York State Electric and Gas	1997	• Withdrawn when NYSEG, market and regulatory reaction was negative	●
NiSource	Columbia Gas	1999	• Completed after the Board and shareholders accepted a lower tender	
Gaz Métro	Central Vermont Public Service	2011	• Completed after management and shareholders accepted a revised tender	
Algonquin Power & Utilities	Gas Natural	2014	• Terminated after management and Board rejected multiple sweetened offers	●
Eversource Energy	Connecticut Water	2018	• Terminated after shareholders voted for acquisition by San Jose Water	●

Source: Company announcements; news reports

Hostile offers were usually delivered after the close of business hours and could appear any day. They usually appeared in a letter from the acquiring CEO to either his counterpart or chair of the board of directors of the target company noting the offer price and premium, defining the benefits of combination, and describing social elements of the deal, and were reasonably brief. Over time, these letters became a little softer—a *bear hug*—and more expansive in extolling the merits and value of the proposed offer.

If so timed, the hostile announcement made for surprise Monday morning *Wall Street Journal* headlines and stunned a historically clubby industry not prone to meddling with existing company independence. In part because of the normative industry behavior model, these hostile transaction announcements also shocked local state regulatory agencies involved and affected state and local governments where target company headquarters were located.

Jeff Holzschuh from Morgan Stanley provided insights on the environment surrounding early hostile offers:

> Hostile offers had been occurring in the 1980s, before the transition to competition began in the mid-1990s. When unsolicited offers were made, on top of the shift toward more open markets and portfolio contraction, utilities were forced to recognize the implications of buyers seeking regional scale and buttressing their asset base. Managements knew the most logical transactions were closest to them, which was also of course true for their preferred partners, and limited opportunities would exist to pursue overlapping or proximate companies. While hostile offers were not at the center of U.S. utility consolidation, they caused buyers to think about offensive strategies, and targets to worry about a hostile defense.

When hostile offers were announced, industry stakeholders took immediate notice, target company bankers closed ranks on their clients, reporters found a full-time preoccupation, government officials offered early perceptions, regulators avoided immediate judgements, and non-involved bankers and consultants scurried about for potential *white knights* to counter the hostile or work for the target in fighting the offer itself.

Although much dust gets immediately thrown up in the air, this public interest and enthusiasm did not fully recognize that a proxy solicitation process, acquiror—target engagement, regulatory filings, and public relations campaigns—do not immediately occur, nor is the hostile offer likely to be quickly resolved.

Many bankers, lawyers, consultants, and accountants tend to comment that "there's nothing like a hostile," which essentially means that a lot of work needs to be done and large sums of money will be spent by the acquiror, target, and potential alternate companies on litigation, proxy fights, advertising, bid analysis, options assessment, and expert advisors, among many other spend areas. And, given the potential length of a proxy fight, the flow of fees could extend for up to a year. Hence, much effort was directed toward joining other professional firms in securing a seat at the table.

These hostile offers usually occurred after some type of prior attempted dialogue—formal or informal—over target willingness to engage in serious discussion when the hostile acquiror had been rebuffed. Some hostile offers did not last long—sometimes as short as three or four weeks. Other times, the hostile process went through an all-out proxy fight and could last the better part of a year.

Hostile offers were usually met with visceral anger by the target company board of directors and CEO, although they still had to give them careful consideration to fulfill their fiduciary duties. In one case, the target company CEO referred to the hostile offer as an "old-fashioned Texas ambush," while others vilified the offer as insufficient, unmerited, and "dead on arrival."

Dick Kelly, formerly from Xcel Energy, spoke about the reality of past hostile transactions:

> CEOs do not like hostile offers within the industry. The industry is highly collaborative and certain behaviors make CEOS uncomfortable in dealing with their peers. More importantly, hostile transactions are expensive to pursue and even more expensive to defend against. They create risks to customers as high premiums can adversely impact customer rates and service once closed. Consequently, neither shareholders or regulators like hostile

transactions either and explains why most hostile offers fail and aren't likely to be widely pursued in the future.

The late 1980s and early 1990s experienced a high number of hostile acquisition announcements as companies considered how to take advantage of opportunistic situations precipitated by financial underperformance and/or regulatory dissatisfaction. Proposed transactions like Southern California Edison and San Diego Gas and Electric (1988), PacifiCorp and Arizona Public Service (1989), Wisconsin Power & Light and Madison Gas & Electric (1989), Eastern Utilities Associates and both Unitil and Fitchburg Gas & Electric (1989), Kansas City Power & Light and Kansas Gas & Electric (1990), IPALCO Enterprises and Public Service Company of Indiana (1992) all occurred before the start of the modern era of utility M&A, perhaps leading to a reawakening about M&A, although few of these transactions were completed.

On the topic of why Kansas Power & Light (KPL) decided to play the role of a *white knight* in Kansas City Power & Light's (KCPL) hostile offer for Kansas Gas and Electric (KGE), Chairman Mark Ruelle of Evergy (a successor company) described the circumstances:

> KGE was having troubles digesting its recent nuclear plant completion and was exposed to high financial risk. KCPL was the plant co-owner with KGE and understood the challenges small nuclear owners faced and the potential for synergies from both companies. We had a new outside CEO and believed we were better geographically aligned with KGE. KCPL's unsolicited offer led us to a counteroffer to preserve our position in the state and unlock synergies with KGE. We believed we had a stronger bid since we offered a superior price, were AA-rated, had completed our baseload construction program, and had constructive regulatory relationships…
>
> When KCPL made its hostile offer, we realized we faced a now-or-never moment—make a counteroffer or risk losing

> future options. We knew many eyes were on this transaction, since unsolicited offers were not the norm, and white knights in the industry even rarer. We recognized a winning bid would be pricy, create a large amount of balance sheet goodwill, and run a risk of blended rates before synergies would justify them. Our road-show focused on a better package of synergies, regulatory plan, and financial capacity compared to KCPL. When we made our second bid for KGE, we had to deliver a compelling offer or risk a series of topping bids. Fortunately, we prevailed and were able to obtain an acceptable regulatory outcome.

These unsolicited offers continued into the 1995–1999 period with PECO Energy offering PPL Resources (1995), Western Resources offering Kansas City Power & Light (1996), MidAmerican Energy pursuing IES Industries (1996), Cal Energy pursuing Energy East (1997), and NiSource offering Columbia Gas (1999), the last of which ultimately was successful.

Hostile offers receded after 2000 as they became continuously harder to successfully complete. However, Gaz Metro offered Vermont Public Service (2011), Gas Natural was offered by Algonquin Power & Utilities (2014), and Eversource offered Connecticut Water (2018), with only the Gaz Metro offer turning out to be successful.

Perhaps the most ambitious and exhausting hostile transaction related to the multi-stage deals surrounding bidding by Western Resources (Western itself a by-product of a hostile transaction response) for Kansas City Power & Light (KCPL) in 1996, after KCPL had agreed to an acquisition by UtiliCorp United. This transaction dragged on for over three years before finally being terminated in 2000 after several repricing negotiations and other simultaneous transaction complexities.

First, also in 1996, Western swapped its Kansas and Oklahoma LDC businesses for a 45 percent interest in ONEOK, an Oklahoma-based LDC. This was an unusual piece of financial engineering for its time and traded a slower-growing set of properties for higher growth potential.

After its original offer, Western subsequently made a parallel hostile offer for security business ADT, later in 1996, with the intent to create cross-selling opportunities for each company as residential and commercial competition ensued.

Ultimately, this bid was dropped after it was topped by Tyco International, with Western then making a controlling offer for Protection One, another security company, in 1997, using the almost $1 billion in proceeds from the sale of the ADT shares it had acquired to reduce its balance sheet debt load and pay for the new security company. The controlling interest in Protection One subsequently drove the stock value of Western to low levels compared to its much higher-offer value for KCPL.

With all these proposed transactions diluting the value of Western's stock, but still determined to conclude the original deal, Western then started over with KCPL by raising its bid price and then creating a new publicly traded entity (Westar) to hold its regulated businesses, with Western still holding the non-regulated home security businesses.

This re-trade of the Western and KCPL deal enabled the attainment of shareholder approvals. However, this revised deal package was not enough to secure regulatory approvals and the deal was ultimately terminated in 2000 due to regulatory uncertainty. Shortly after the end of the KCPL deal, Westar struck a deal to sell its remaining utility operations to PNM Resources to focus on the non-regulated businesses. However, this transaction was also terminated, thus ending a long-running saga of back-to-back transactions and high-profile and creative deals that never came to fruition—a combination of strategic over-reach, financial complexity, and pure bad luck.

Jeff Holzschuh of Morgan Stanley offered insights on the impediments to success of unsolicited offers:

> Hostile deals are hard in any industry, particularly utilities, as political and regulatory pressures affect how these offers are received. More than a dozen hostile offers have occurred in the industry, with few successful. Usually, a high premium underlies the offer, creating a financial challenge to overcome. Winning a proxy fight is difficult as investors are skeptical of recovering high premiums. Hostiles take longer to close and are expensive, providing a target time to prosecute a defense and diminish offer value. Utilities are local and adept at rallying support from shareholders, regulators, and communities. Hostile offers are opportunistic and hard to win without sentiment the offeror is a better operator than the incumbent.

Several other utilities considered pursuit of a hostile when a logical target was overtly uninterested, but most did not go either to the full hostile offer or to the *bear hug* approach, even when the industrial logic for combination was clear and compelling. Unsurprisingly, most early hostile M&A pursuits failed due to regulatory concerns about logic, benefits, policies, jurisdiction, outcomes, or risks. The prior experience of companies pursuing hostile takeovers was a stark reminder to managements that the price of prevailing in these unsolicited offers might not be worth the effort or the subsequent effect on industry reputation, balance sheet, and public goodwill.

Bill Lamb of Baker Botts summed up the history of hostile offers for utilities:

> Hostile offers reappeared in the late 1980s as the era of increased competition began to emerge and companies felt they needed to secure a better competitive position. These offers were never popular and created turmoil with shareholders, local governments, and regulators. Hostile offers disrupted both the bidder and the target, as the issues were already complex and were now placed in a brighter spotlight. Most hostile offers failed, but the few that prevailed had to demonstrate compelling benefits and secure

relationships. Regulated utilities are a local business and this, more than any other reason, caused hostile offers to be rejected.

Special Situations

Not all M&A transactions followed conventional source or structure models—special situations within the industry also contributed to strategic actions by U.S. utilities. These special situations could include operating contracts, bankruptcies, privatizations, and even municipalizations.

The attraction of these special situations is that they did not always require outright acquisition and further leverage of balance sheets since they were often centered around only taking over operations of an entity. The distraction from these special situations is that they involved governmental—and therefore political—entities, which added an additional level of complexity to transaction success. Thus, these opportunities occurred very infrequently for this significant reason. It is extremely hard for governmental entities to let go of utility operating entities they've held for decades, or longer. Unsurprisingly, local citizens tend to demonstrate an affinity with and attachment to these entities.

The Long Island Power Authority (LIPA) is a corporate municipal instrumentality with electric customers in eastern New York. After years of complaints about Long Island service quality, Long Island Lighting was pushed to sell its electric properties in 1998 after it was acquired by Brooklyn Union Gas, with LIPA to assume responsibility for operations.

After seven years of operation by KeySpan, LIPA then extended the responsibility for transmission and distribution operating services (as well as power supply and energy management agreements), with NationalGrid (which had acquired KeySpan). NationalGrid held this Management Services Agreement (MSA) from 2005 to 2013, until it was re-bid and awarded to PSEG at that time for another 10-year period.

This operating services contract is complex, requiring the provider to meet multiple requirements for normal operations, system hardening, customer service, storm planning and restoration, energy efficiency, gas transportation, and power plant repowering, along with cash considerations. This type of transaction was new for U.S. utilities to pursue as service providers, even though many companies themselves maintained agreements with contractors for similar services.

In this case, assets changed hands at the time of the creation of KeySpan and flowed from the incumbent utility to a new owner (LIPA). This was the reverse of conventional utility M&A but signaled that property deals could be structured advantageously for utilities, which ultimately were considered more frequently after 2015. This special situation involved investment banks, law firms, and consultants, and exhibited all the accoutrements of a conventional deal.

A similar unique transaction was considered involving the Tennessee Valley Authority (TVA), one of five power marketing agencies (PMA) administered by the federal government. This transaction was reportedly considered by then-President Barack Obama on the heels of the Great Recession and precipitated by a recognition that TVA's assets had significant value that could be unlocked for Washington, and this PMA was an extremely attractive entity to several proximate U.S. utilities.

This transaction never progressed but was believed to involve the potential privatization of TVA, its sale to another U.S. utility, or creation of an operating services agreement, similar to what existed at LIPA, except structured for generation and transmission facilities.

While the transaction did not come to fruition, it signaled that the art of M&A imagination extended well beyond conventional utility-to-utility consolidation. Over the years, variations on the underlying themes of the special situations above have emerged for assessment, involving situations like the PG&E (restructuring), Puerto Rico Electric Power Authority (operating services), Santee

Cooper (acquisition/operating services), and Jacksonville Electric Authority (acquisition/operating services).

These public power situations are interesting because they are notoriously difficult to navigate and prevail. The level of local politics far surmounts that experienced in traditional utilities M&A transactions, as competing interests at the mayoral, city council, city manager, utilities head, local union, and local taxpayer levels are usually at odds with one another about the need for action and the most appropriate path forward. Statewide and federal entities are even more demanding and challenging. In addition, the ownership models, and therefore the financing and taxation structures, are vastly different between investor-owned utilities and municipalities and are viewed as leading to higher rates under private ownership.

It is worth noting that investor-owned utilities have occasionally acquired municipal utility departments in the past, particularly in water, but the non-water transactions generally occurred decades ago. Recent attempts at acquiring municipal utilities have been checkered, with NextEra Energy successfully taking over the Vero Beach, Florida, operations in 2018 (after a long courtship), but most utilities are rebuffed for the reasons mentioned above.

Also of note is that municipalities have frequently attempted to municipalize local investor-owned utility operations in several states, including Arizona, California, Colorado, and others. Recent attempts have also been made to turn investor-owned utilities into quasi-governmental entities in California and Maine. These situations arise over issues such as management responsiveness, rate levels, environmental concerns, energy efficiency commitment, service quality, and other local matters. Generally, these efforts fail due to asset valuation, financing requirements, and operating capabilities gaps, or complexities in the general political environment and differences in state versus local perspectives on separation and stand-up viability.

This disappointing history, however, does not seem to diminish the antipathy the public can hold for certain local incumbents, which provides continuing interest in pursuing municipalization—or even cooperatization—as environmental, rate-level, and reliability issues aggravate public sentiment.

A final twist on special situations relates to the emergence of activist investors, such as hedge funds, that have emerged as antagonists (in a negative way) or catalysts (in a more positive context) to incumbent utility managements and boards of directors. These activist investors take minority positions in companies they believe are under-valued and/or mismanaged and seek to gain direct influence over utility strategy and priorities.

Steve Fleishman from Wolfe Research addressed the role that activist investors are playing with utilities:

> Activists are an aggressive class of investor. While minority investment can shake incumbent management, the presence of activist investors can cause companies to not become complacent about their enterprise—strategically, financially, or operationally—and focus on producing incremental value to avoid activists appearing. But even if an activist enters the picture, this should not mean that companies need to succumb to undue influence from these entities. The board of directors and management need to continue to own their business plan and pursue a course of action that is just as shareholder friendly as what activists are seeking.

Activist action sends shudders through boards of directors and managements as it signals a major disruption to strategy pursuit and business execution in the short term, as well as the potential for a dramatic shift in ownership and composition in the long term. The announcement of a minority position in a utility causes a board and management to defend themselves against a no confidence vote on the direction and outcomes of current enterprise plans and prospects.

Bill Lamb from Baker Botts also noted that activist investors are becoming more visible, vocal, and influential:

> Activist investors are sophisticated and undaunted by utility norms, are prone to aggressive action, and bring an approach more economically rational than an outright hostile offer for the company. Activist investors focus on eliminating shareholder value destruction and unlocking additional value within the target. Most activists follow a formula that drives utilities to improve cost management, enhance operating performance, deploy more capital, retire inefficient assets, and/or upgrade internal capabilities—and they are very good at it.

In essence, the activist investors believe the ideas or motivations they bring can spur incumbent management to make smarter decisions about the business or asset composition of their portfolios, improve decisions about where to prioritize capital spend, and take more aggressive actions about operating performance. All with the intent to enhance the intrinsic performance and value of the business that will be translated into a windfall in shareholder value to the activist investor.

This investor class can seek immediate representation on the boards of directors and creation and representation on a special committee charged with evaluating alternative courses of action and recommending a new path forward to substantially enhance shareholder value. Some of these paths can include some combination of aggressive cost takeout, sale of the enterprise, disposition of businesses or assets, merger with another utility, reprioritized capital direction, and changes to financing and financial policies.

If target utility management does not sufficiently respond, the potential to wage a proxy solicitation is always there to convince more disaffected shareholders to support new ownership or leadership and significant change to the business. Some of these activist situations are still alive in late-2021, while other companies settled their differences through announced disposition or management actions.

Since 2015, there have been 16 of these activist situations occur spanning both small and large utilities and bridging both electric and

LDCs.[2] Most have captured headlines and turned heads as they represent the latest version of activism in an industry not used to direct action from vigilant investors. Larger companies, such as CenterPoint Energy, Sempra Energy, Duke Energy, FirstEnergy, Evergy, and Pacific Gas & Electric, have had to respond to activist investors, but even small companies like Hawaiian Electric and Southwest Gas have experienced hedge fund or private investor interest.

The history of these activist interventions indicates a subtle progression from advocating for improved operations to increased capital investment to asset sales to business rationalization to portfolio optimization. A recent example at the time of this writing is Elliott Management Corporation's (Elliott) "suggestion" for Duke Energy to carve out its operations and capitalize three separate regional utilities under the theory that the sum-of-the-parts will exceed current total value.

Elliott's proposal anticipates that value from certain larger and faster-growing regional jurisdictions like North and South Carolina and Florida is constrained as part of the overall enterprise, which also includes smaller, lower-growth jurisdictions like Kentucky, Ohio, and Indiana. Thus, segmentation is assumed to unlock and release overall value to existing shareholders simply due to separating existing regions and standing up and capitalizing alternative entities for investors to choose among, without considering individual debt ratings, cash flows, capital requirements, capitalization, dividend policies, regulatory actions, or stand-alone operating costs. In this case, the value of separation is assumed to exceed the value of integration, and the focus on creating unique entities will offset potential diseconomies from diffused operations with reduced scale.

It is not likely that the active engagement of activist investors will dissipate anytime soon. The increasing dichotomy in strategic approaches, management depth, business scale, financial position, operating performance, and regulatory quality all create differentiated positions among U.S. utilities—both electrics and LDCs—where an activist investor can seek to create intervention advantage.

If the U.S. utility industry wants to vaccinate itself against this type of active intervention, then it will need to heed the lessons from the companies above and think like a hedge fund, not just an incumbent utility.

Auctions

Approximately 120 utility electric, LDC merger, or acquisition transactions have been announced since 1994, with almost 100 completed. Several of these transactions have been conducted as auctions, that is, setting a wide parameter of potential bidders rather than a negotiated deal only involving the seller and a single buyer.

The advantage of running an auction process is the ability to obtain participation from multiple bidders in an *indicative stage* (initial bid pricing using limited data) of the process, which can then be extended into conducting a *best and final* (firm bid pricing using more complete data) stage among the most qualified and attractive players (hopefully many). An auction creates a higher level of competition among bidders and could include logical utilities, private equity, infrastructure or sovereign wealth funds, special purpose acquisition companies (SPACs), or even international or unrelated industry acquirors. But while auctions are viewed as increasing potential buyer interest and participation, they have their limitations and frequently leave potential bidders less than satisfied with the process.

As sellers, companies should be focused on obtaining the highest price attainable, consistent with parallel fiduciary objectives of ensuring post-sale operational reliability, quality, and affordability, as well as the ability of the buyer to successfully finance the transaction. Concerns about obtaining all of these outcomes can lead sellers to seek out the *best price* (balancing multiple factors in addition to price) if higher prices may carry more post-close risk to the business going forward.

A negotiated deal between a seller and a potential buyer typically conveys more data and information and enables broader engagement and dialogue between the two parties than in an auction. This more expansive due diligence allows the potential buyer to kick the tires on a potential utility acquisition in a greater level of detail and produce more and deeper insights into the quality of the company, the future needs of the business, and opportunities available to drive more value from ownership. It occurs specifically because both the selling and buying parties are committed to a successful transaction conclusion.

There is a noticeable difference in process and content between a negotiated sale and an auction. Auctions can be more efficient and faster than a drawn-out merger, but they can also be less informative and more frustrating than the traditional option. To be sure, the nature of the auction is fundamentally different, so expectations need to be calibrated to match the option style.

Potential bidders typically run into several key areas of frustration during an auction: a more targeted data room, a sparser confidential information memorandum (CIM), constrained management presentations, narrower incremental data access, and limited dialogue with management beyond the initial session with the seller management team.

Often, sellers believe that running an auction is the best path to success—it's faster, easier to execute, more insightful, and more controllable. And when the field of qualified and interested parties can exceed a dozen or more, then managements feel comfortable that they can realize an attractive acquisition price without the same level of effort as required in full, arm's-length negotiation from the start.

Sellers adopting an auction model often tend to become complacent with the structure and execution of the process and rely on its simplicity and formality more than its extrinsic value. Sellers should be interested in obtaining the best price through the auction process, which means that management's efforts should be highly focused on signaling to potential buyers *where and how* to enhance the level of value capturable by them after close.

When CIMs, management presentations, and incremental data are limited in scope and content, this directly translates into more limited business insight, operating analysis, and value identification by the buyer. It is extremely hard for a potential buyer to sharpen a bid when insufficient transparency is available into sources of underlying value.

Sellers can suggest that potential bidders should rely on their experience and that the field is level for all buyers, but that's not what seller management should want. It should want all potential bidders to have all the information necessary to offer the best price available, not just the price that looks more certain, which will undoubtedly be conservative.

Management can enhance its auction outcome by emphasizing one simple action: think like the potential buyer, not the seller. In other words, management (and its advisors) should put themselves into the buyer's shoes—what would they like to see if the roles were reversed?

Potential buyers can only evaluate what they are provided, and if that is limited, then the evaluation will suffer from an absence of information, leading to an incomplete perspective on the business being acquired, or a decision not to proceed with a bid. Financial forecasts are a tablestake for potential buyer review and analysis. But enterprise strategies, operational plans, infrastructure details, performance metrics, and investment priorities are equally important. And insight into how the business is architected, aligned, and managed sheds even more valuable light on how well it is doing.

A highly undesirable outcome in an auction is a buyer exiting the process because it believes the seller is not serious about its intent or the execution of the process, or that the seller is leaning toward another buyer and only going through the paces with the full buyer field.

For sellers to achieve the best price and most value, and not the *observable price* (metric-based) and fair value, they need to prioritize the provision of expanded operational data and more revealing performance execution. This would include details about business strategies, organization architecture, staffing distribution, facilities locations, cost composition, operating metrics, capital investment, fuel supply, reliability metrics, carbon emissions, energy efficiency, and a host of other discrete elements that provide insight into the current state of the enterprise, how the business works, and where value can be resident.

This additional layer of data and information, whether early in a data room (core to the process), or management presentation (preferred), or later through incremental disclosure (probably too late), is not an overwhelming or expensive internal or external task, particularly compared to the value that can be derived from enabling better buyer evaluation and bid development. Value is foregone forever by too simple and rigid an auction process, and managements need to balance the limited costs (man-hours) of expanded data flows with the conservative decisions (share prices) of constrained bids.

Synthetic Mergers

Intervenors and regulatory commission staffs often like to make a case that merger-like benefits are not justified because they can be realized without executing a merger and incurring mountains of debt, diluting shareholder equity value, or reducing customer savings through synergies sharing. In their minds, utilities can accomplish everything a merger can through contractual arrangements, sharing of information about operations, or more persuasiveness with their regional peers.

The approach they have in mind is the creation of a synthetic or virtual merger between utilities, that is, an arrangement where two or more utilities essentially share information and decision-making to extract joint benefits without any structural change to either utility. While this type of friendly non-merger approach sounds attractive and logical, it is exactly the opposite—it is uninformed and impractical.

The *synthetic* or *virtual* merger approach is grounded in the assumption that what could be effectuated between two (or more) merging companies into a single new entity can easily be replicated through simple cooperation and information exchange, or a contractual arrangement that enables open and non-competitive collaboration—an approach well short of actual integrated combination.

Intervenors and regulatory commission staff often utilize a power purchase agreement as an example, where one utility provides power supply to another, which either fills a capacity gap or avoids future expenditures for new capacity. But the intervenors and staff overlook a simple salient point in this example: this kind of supply agreement is an arm's-length transaction with the selling utility having a clear profit motive in mind from the arrangement. This is not the model utilized by two companies in a merger transaction for a post-close operating environment.

These parties suggest that the common available methods for attaining joint benefits between two (or more) utilities outside a merger transaction are typically: contracts, licenses, joint ventures, partnerships, outsourcing, or the assumed willingness to share information and insights across companies—all these assumed arrangements fall short of what is achieved through a merger.

First, there need to be two willing parties to any formal agreement (contract, license, joint venture, partnership) for it to achieve what intervenors and staff think can be accomplished. And for there to be two willing parties, each party must benefit in an equivalent manner. That is not the case in a simple contract between two utilities when each party usually believes that it brings more to the agreement than the other and has different objectives. More importantly, in a merger, no need for compensation of a party arises because all information, experience, and insight are resident in the combined company for no additional cost.

Second, a license agreement is not about open sharing; it is about structuring a common economic relationship between the parties, which means agreeing on a value to be directly paid for what is provided. Again, a merger does not require compensation between parties or negotiation of terms and conditions on information access, utilization, protection, and/or conveyance.

Third, trying to frame a contractual agreement to replicate a merger falls short, by definition, as only selected elements of the business would lend themselves to consideration, even if the approach were practical. Many elements and related costs of business performance are particular to specific entities and would not need to be shared, or could not be shared, due to confidentiality. In a merger, all elements of the business are shared and there is no extra cost or complexity with aligning interests between or among the parties.

Intervenors and regulatory commission staff like to utilize several specific areas to illustrate *where and how* utilities can accomplish a synthetic or virtual merger. These typically include supply chain, shared services functions, information technology, operating services, and operations, and are considered as useful examples for argument by intervenors and regulatory commission staff.

Achieving joint savings in these areas through a contractual arrangement rather than a merger assumes that relative benefits are close to or equivalent to those from a full combination. Otherwise there would be no point in attempting to justify a synthetic or virtual merger. Each of these areas is briefly addressed below.

- **Supply chain**: Materials and contract service spend is a primary source of savings in all utility mergers. These savings relate to a discrete level of spend and reflect volumes, design differences, price disparities, specific vendors, and special terms and conditions. *A contractual arrangement could not easily address this degree of uniqueness.*

- **Shared services**: The single broadest source of synergies in a merger and the place where most overlap and duplication occur is the corporate center. Reductions in all the same sub-functional areas could not occur in the absence of a merger. *A multi-element contractual arrangement would not be practical to attempt to execute across entities.*

- **Information technology**: Operating expenditures of this function, both capital and O&M, are subject to overlap, duplication, and avoidance. Reductions in several areas would not be available in the absence of a combination. *The need to adopt common platforms and rationalize infrastructure are impediments to use of a contractual arrangement.*

- **Operations support**: These areas parallel corporate shared services and are wholly overlapping and duplicative. They address plant and field back-office functions dependent on asset composition and similarity. *Fundamental operating philosophy differences would likely obviate the potential for an effective contractual agreement.*

- **Operations**: Only portions of these functions or facilities are directly affected in a full combination, since some are already contracted to third parties, and fewer would be available to fully share outside a merger given the nature of work differences. *A contractual agreement would be limited in scope and impact, if negotiable at all.*

From synergies and operational perspectives, contractual arrangements are a poor substitute for full merger synergies—less of the business is affected, benefit levels are severely limited, and agreement complexity is higher—if such an arrangement is even possible.

Intervenors and regulatory commission staff like to assume that all activities can lend themselves to a joint arrangement outside of a merger. But the practical constraints are overwhelming, and this is demonstrated in the lack of such arrangements. In many areas, the ability to even consider a joint contractual arrangement is simply precluded:

- **Strategic activities**: Some activities that lend themselves to merger-related reduction from overlap and duplication—for example, strategic planning—cannot be performed between arm's-length partners because these activities are directed at individual company positioning, not creating competitor advantage.

- **Mutuality of interests**: It is difficult to develop a harmonious view of future business across two independent utilities, such as desired absolute or relative cost position, when the companies are not aligned within a single enterprise view and motivations and incentives to drive common thinking are absent.

- **Underlying uniqueness**: Wide recognition exists that utilities in the U.S. are vastly different in their infrastructure starting positions and business approaches such as information technology, and the ability to agree on common application features, consistent infrastructure, and business support protocols is highly unlikely.

- **Inherent confidentiality**: Certain activities are beyond consideration because the shared information necessary to take advantage of two companies acting together is proprietary to each party or their vendors, and while shared equipment pricing data is fine after a merger, it is prohibited in the absence of a common company.

Utilities have unsuccessfully tried to engineer collaborative sharing arrangements in the past, like Pantellos and Enporion in the supply chain, but they were not sustainable as the utility participants could not universally agree on inclusion across broad materials and contracts categories. Underlying philosophy, priority, design, and risk differences led to the undertaking's collapse. The absence of effective two-party contractual arrangements within the utilities industry, other than for joint generation construction or certain nuclear materials, indicates that the difficulties associated with these models are simply too hard to overcome.

Across the cycles of the modern era of U.S. utility M&A, there have been a range of different transaction models and financing approaches. Utility M&A has been a watercolor of nuanced shades of transaction rationales, types, scales, buyers, and geographies. The cycles have also revealed several different types of motivations to transact, from policies to currency to scarcity to opportunism, causing some transactions to reflect being on offense, with others appearing defensive.

As close industry observers already understand, there is no constraining influence to further consolidation, and the expectation is that the current 33 tradable electric companies and 16 LDCs will continue to consolidate. And it is likely that international and financial sponsor acquirors will still maintain a presence in auctions and special situations. Although numerous convergence deals were struck early in this time frame and continued through the last decade, the recent specter of state governments disfavoring the expansion of gas infrastructure due to carbon emissions could dampen enthusiasm for LDCs—at least by electrics—if not resolved at a national policy level.

What will be most interesting is whether the combination of two mega-companies could occur, which could potentially set the fuse for more of the same transactions and create more significant industry concentration, particularly in super-regional settings.

The last 25 years of utility industry consolidation have been instructive to U.S. companies, as well as all other stakeholders involved in enabling or evaluating M&A. Utility consolidation has not been intermittent or limited; it has been continuous and ubiquitous. M&A has become a fundamental ingredient of how utilities fashion their future.

The number of transactions completed has resulted in both significant contraction of remaining U.S. utilities and the substantial growth of many companies through transactions. Large and mid-sized companies like Exelon, Duke Energy, AEP, Dominion Energy, Southern Company, Sempra Energy, NationalGrid, Xcel

Energy, Ameren Corp., PPL, WEC Energy, Eversource Energy, and FirstEnergy have all become large through deal execution, that is, at or above \$20 billion in market capitalization.

Figure 14: A Glimpse of Scale Growth

Key Takeaways

Over the modern era of M&A, U.S. utilities capitalized on a wave of policy evolution that spurred the industry to pursue safe havens of greater scale, expanded markets, and superior economics. All of these competitive sanctuaries were achieved from a mix of serial M&A and bespoke strategic transactions that enabled companies to optimize their overall business portfolios.

While most of the activity in the U.S. utility industry looked like traditional company-to-company consolidation, the modern era of M&A also was characterized by the continuous pursuit of differentiation and innovative thinking. A number of transactions over the years reflected aggressive actions, like hostile offers, unique deal structures, such as public power takeovers, or seller-friendly activities in the case of auctions.

The utilization of unsolicited offers, that is, hostile transactions, is not a new phenomenon to the modern era of utility M&A, and actually preceded it during the 1980s. While the number of hostile offers is not substantial, they are not random or rare either—many companies have thought about them (directly or quietly), only to decide against this approach for social, financial, or regulatory reasons.

The fact that fewer than 15 hostile or *bear hug* offers have been made (or at least made public) indicates just how complex, time-consuming, and expensive running a successful proxy fight can be. Most of the unsolicited offers failed because the financial and regulatory communities neither saw the logic of the transaction, nor believed the high premiums to be paid were economically justified. In the presence of either reaction, a strong anti-hostile sentiment at the public level would generally signal the hostile offer would have tough sledding to become a reality.

As the history of utility M&A in the modern era progressed, the nature of available consolidation opportunities advanced in tandem. Investor-owned company combinations were the foundation of industry consolidation, but they were joined around the year 2000 by instances where federal and state public power entities were willing to entertain the notion of a sale or an alternative operating agreement. However, while property and asset sales were regular occurrences among all types of owners, these *unicorn* opportunities—that is, large, coveted, and scarce entities—were episodic, rather than common. International privatization provided acquisition opportunities to numerous U.S. utilities in an environment where a firm commitment to a sale existed, unlike other federal or state agencies or municipalities.

It is difficult for a public power entity to decide to part with the decades-long ownership of a business that has well served its constituents. But, in selected cases, the capabilities necessary to serve future customers in a different operating environment may be too thin for success, or operating performance may dictate that new ownership capabilities would enhance customer value.

When outright transfers of ownership were not politically possible, public power entities can turn to an operating contract, where an investor-owned utility would step in and take primary responsibility for day-to-day operations. This is an attractive option to public power, given the depth of resources and capabilities, but even this benefit did not lead to many actual agreements. In the end, parting with operating responsibility was just as difficult as selling the property itself.

Regulatory staffs and intervenors are fond of suggesting this approach as a real alternative to a merger, but these assertions lack a fact foundation and do not reflect the realities of pushing two companies to virtually combine in the absence of sufficient economic justification.

Even with investor-owned utilities, a similar challenge exists in convincing a partner that a *synthetic* merger—that is, a co-agreement to commonly operate without an actual ownership transfer and integration—is a viable alternative as this approach is also fraught with complexity over strategy and data confidentiality, governance and decision-making, selection of operating platforms and processes and, of course, the belief that one or both companies are unique.

The advent of activist investors has further changed the environment for U.S. utility M&A. While none of the activist interventions have yet led to a sale or merger, it has been assessed in most cases as an option to increase shareholder value. But the mere presence of these investors in the stocks of their targets indicates that management can be encouraged to entertain a sale at any time.

So far, activist investors have focused on unlocking enterprise value through some combination of strategy reformulation, capital redeployment, asset shutdown or sale, sharp cost reduction, or business model shift to create value—some the product of reversing myopic management decisions, and some occurring from accelerating the capture of market opportunities. Activist investor Carl Icahn is the latest to seek portfolio rationalization and enhanced board governance as means to enhance utility value in his pursuit of Southwest Gas.

When utilities believe there is inherent value in their business, it is not a prerequisite that they find a single, preferred merger partner and proceed to close a transaction. Rather than align with a partner through a confidential and private process, they can seek to maximize this value by leveraging a process that offers the ability to see the whole market landscape and exercise more discretion and flexibility in partner selection.

The use of an auction process—where a selling entity broadly publicizes its interest in a sale to multiple qualified entities—allows the seller to simultaneously let the bidders create market momentum through indicative and final bid stages of the process. Of late, the scarcity of properties, expansion in financial buyers, and availability of financing have generally helped the seller to achieve its strategic and financial objectives, and sometimes resulted in the continuity of management, in whole or in part, depending on the nature of the buyer. Auctions have greatly enhanced market transparency to the seller and also exposed bidders to how their counterparts consider creating value in utilities, compared to how they have approached it.

The types of maverick transactions described reflect differentiated thinking but are not a substitute for conventional M&A, which usually enjoy the merits of market understanding and support, regulatory familiarity and acceptance, and utility experience and adaptation. The desired result from a maverick transaction is generally focused on achieving a step-change in market position, portfolio composition, and/or operating economies. The downside, however, is that these unconventional transactions typically take substantially longer to accomplish as the complexity of public power ownership transfer, built-in financial market norms, and unique structural and regulatory biases are natural impediments to rapid success.

While utility merger consolidation in any form is not for the faint of heart or impatient, the industry has demonstrated that it can effectively reshape the boundaries of M&A to meet the objectives of policymakers, competitors, and customers when necessities emerge. The utility industry has also proven that it is willing to consider options beyond traditional M&A as a means to release value to shareholders through other creative structural mechanisms.

CHAPTER 5

VALUE SOURCES

Utilities pursue consolidation to preserve or advance their strategic market positioning or to capture opportunities to improve operating effectiveness, enhance revenues, or capture cost efficiencies. Transactions are an effective catalyst for both redefining the contours and scale of a portfolio, as well as reshaping how operating elements can be realigned to enhance organizational agility and performance.

At the start of the modern era of utility M&A, executives were highly skeptical of pursuing transactions as they perceived them to be unnecessary, costly, excessively long, and disruptive to their business, employees, and communities. And pursuing a hostile was anathema to the industry and could paint them as out of step with their peers and public sentiment.

But utilities were also particularly concerned about how the need to capture synergies to support any acquisition price premium would affect their business post-close. They recognized they were taking on a new market risk related to their ability to identify, capture, and retain merger savings and that achieving these anticipated cost impacts would be closely monitored by investment analysts and rating agencies.

Skepticism also carried through to fundamental questions about merger synergies that needed to be answered:

- Are potential synergies real?
- How difficult is synergies capture?
- What business changes are required?
- How would employees be affected?
- How would regulators view job losses?
- How is earnings dilution avoided?
- What regulatory sharing treatment is possible?
- Would Wall Street give credit for synergies capture?
- What happens when synergies sharing ends?
- Is the transaction pain worth the outcome?

At least in the early days, these and other questions gave pause to many managements as executives were cautious of taking on challenges where a clear track record of outcomes did not exist. And they were particularly circumspect about being subject to a regulatory approval process that was not well established and likely to be politicized. So, the end-game—realizing and retaining synergies—was viewed as an uncertain and potentially adverse outcome.

Getting to the point of capturing merger synergies or cost savings from a target combination is obviously dependent on negotiating an acceptable price, securing necessary state regulatory commission approvals, and integrating operations successfully. If none of those predicates are sequentially satisfied, then hoped-for cost savings to supplement stand-alone earnings will never be available.

Thus, utility mergers are a true *chicken or egg* dilemma. Companies negotiate a deal to unlock available synergies, but offering an attractive acquisition premium depends on sufficient synergies to support this price level and demonstrate public benefits.

One way to think about the four critical transaction components (bid prices, merger synergies, regulatory approvals, and integration prowess) is to consider the analogy of designing an automobile: the bid price fuels the transaction engine, while merger synergies create a durable chassis to support operations, the regulatory approval provides the tires to enable the business to move forward, and internal integration prowess ensures that internal features work together to operate at high performance.

Managements have come to recognize that development and quantification of merger synergies is far more art than science. Typical areas of opportunity commonly travel across most transactions, but identifying unique areas and determining the level and timing of synergies extends beyond just filling in the lines. Synergies levels are heavily influenced by circumstances surrounding the transaction—for example, relative scale, composition, and proximity, as well as management prerogative (that is, philosophy, priorities, and aggressiveness)—and depend on substantial judgment and insight.

Regardless, utility managements enjoy a wide and deep pool of potential value and synergies sources throughout the businesses to be combined. They also have the benefit of experience from observing their peers who have already completed one or more combinations.

Value Definition

Although not consistently recognized or valued by utility managements, merger value opportunities are far broader than simple cost savings. The tangible impact to earnings from a merger is easy to discern, but not all value sources are measurable in the same manner. For example, an uplift in the P/E multiple occurs from market recognition of an acquiror's ability to price and execute a transaction and what it does to redefine financial policies like dividend growth.

Figure 15: Positioning the Value Sources

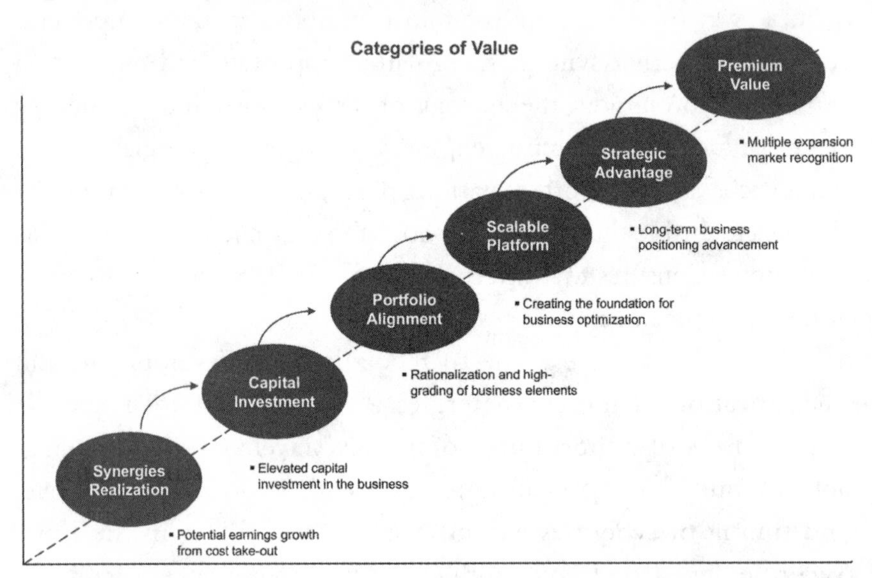

Similarly, the ability to use a transaction as a growth multiplier has value from enabling the utility to punch above its weight and expand portfolio growth opportunities for an acquiror. Finally, the new merged enterprise can elevate how the market views its long-term strategic thinking and execution capabilities, which enhances its execution reputation and market perception and can create a strategy premium.

Utilities pursue combinations with the expectation that they can create substantial incremental value from how they structure and execute a transaction—value that can drop to earnings, add to dividend levels, streamline balance sheet debt, expand capital investment, add incremental revenues, and/or drive a higher P/E multiple and subsequent market capitalization.

Value from a proposed combination typically emerges from creating new or accelerated growth sources, reducing or avoiding costs, optimizing capital deployment, and/or modifying the capital structure, and is derived from unique elements from within and across the combined companies.

The nature of potential value arising through a utility merger transaction spans a range of discrete types and sources: regulated v. non-regulated businesses; revenue v. expense v. capital; corporate v. segment v. functional; one-time v. recurring; and/or immediate v. deferred—a Rubik's Cube of where to identify value.

When addressing how his company positioned synergies in transactions it was involved with, Mark Ruelle from Evergy commented:

> Synergies have been a focal point for regulators, as they may think estimates are high and could potentially carry adverse consequences for service or other local concerns. Over time, companies learned how to compensate for regulatory concerns and focus on community impacts, particularly jobs and service standards. Utilities offer some of the highest-paying and steadiest jobs in small states and cities, and no one likes to see them lost. Like other utilities, we agreed to no involuntary layoffs and emphasized the non-labor components of synergies. We spent quite a bit of time positioning synergies as a critical element in compensating shareholders for the risks borne from a transaction.

Because they affect near-term earnings, the available synergies from a regulated utility merger transaction are vastly more substantial from operational costs savings than incremental revenues, which tend to rise to higher levels when non-regulated retail energy companies combine established customer sales books or can jump-start business start-up in new energy services.

Merger cost savings can be viewed as a permanent reduction or avoidance of costs. Some may be one-time in nature, like avoided capital spend, but most are perpetual, such as reduced positions, streamlined third-party costs, lower unit costs, etc.

Since cost savings areas reflect decisions about how the future business should look and operate, cost-based synergies are a perpetuity and will extend forever. Unless fundamental markets change, or the customer base radically declines, incremental revenue-based synergies will also extend into the future from new products, new services, new offerings, and/or new pricing.

Traditional synergies typically relate to duplication and overlap within the operating and support functions of the consolidating companies, economies of scale that are addressable through higher purchasing leverage within the supply chain, capital avoidance from foregoing similar expenditures, and financing cost reduction from capital structure optimization. Cost-oriented synergies thus result in the combination of one plus one equaling less than two.

Duplication and overlap most logically occur from parallel staffing resources in the corporate center and operating function back-office areas, with field operations hardly affected as basic activity volumes, such as work orders, maintenance requirements, service turn-ons, capital replacement, etc., do not change due to a transaction.

Duplication and overlap may also occur in non-labor-related areas where the focus of spend is on discrete cost types, like insurance, public company, information technology, and employee benefits, among a host of other areas. This category of merger synergies is simpler to achieve compared to economies of scale, as similar financial and operating cost elements are easier to discretely identify and address.

Economies of scale reflect relative comparability of the merging companies and the commonality of the types of expenditures made. When the acquiror is far larger than the acquiree, it can extend its purchasing leverage to the benefit of the smaller company and obtain lower unit costs when total spend levels are reoffered to vendors. If materials procurement and contracting spend is relatively common in scope and similar in scale, then both companies are likely to realize a lower unit cost across all categories of spend as volumes double and it becomes more attractive to vendors to offer pricing breaks.

This category of merger synergies is harder to realize than overlap and duplication where managements control most elements of decision-making, that is, selecting between two position candidates, two groups, two locations, two cost sources, etc. The realization of synergies from economies of scale depends on how effectively the two parties negotiate with vendors or third parties. Hence, available synergies can be foregone without determined negotiation on comparability, quantities, timing, and non-quantifiable terms and conditions.

Capital avoidance is another relevant category of synergies, arising from the ability to forego parallel spend in similar areas like power plants, information technology, operating facilities, or growth investment. These opportunities typically occur when the stand-alone capital investment plans of each company are laid side-by-side and specific projects can be identified that are no longer needed by each company post-close, for example, new customer information system, new call center, new control center, etc.

Most merger synergies are reflected as reductions or avoidance of O&M expense. Capital spend avoidance, however, is reflected as a reduction to the capital budget, as well as a reduction in the revenue requirements (or underlying rate levels) associated with that spend over the operating life of the asset, which is how the customer benefits. Revenue requirements include the annual pre-tax return on investment, depreciation or amortization, property taxes, and other related asset charges.

Reduction in capital spend has the effect of shrinking rate base for the foregone spend. But it can also result in available capital being redistributed to other, higher-value investments. If no redistribution or replacement investment occurs, then customers benefit from reduced revenue requirements.

Changes in capital structure from avoided or rescheduled debt or equity issuances offer the ability to reduce annual financing costs or interest changes, while improvements in cash flows can improve ratings levels which can further reduce interest charges. However, these synergies opportunities can be difficult to distinguish, as financial models often reforecast combined company financials and sweep all cash and capital structure-related activities into non-discrete financial outcomes and mask unique transaction events from specific quantification.

When companies consider identification of potential value from a combination, the intent is to think as broadly as possible about synergies sources and not be constrained by convention, complexity, timing, or lack of imagination. The synergies sources identified should consider how the business that exists today can be reimagined, reconfigured, and enhanced.

While merger synergies are typically pervasive throughout the enterprise, there is no guarantee that identified value sources will be achieved and monetized. Consequently, approaching available merger synergies aggressively, but with a realistic expectation of what can be realized, is a precondition for preparing management estimates of potential revenue, growth, cost savings, and capital spend rationalization.

Jim Torgerson, the retired CEO from AVANGRID, spoke to how he considered synergies in his merger calculus:

> Companies can reduce costs on their own, but not at the same level as through integration of two companies. The deals we pursued had to be accretive to our shareholders and synergies were the way to accomplish that, as overlap and duplication were

> obvious, and economies of scale opportunities were abundant. We gained experience as we progressed through transactions and recognized the risks of attaining synergies were relatively low, particularly as integration experience and understanding was accumulating.

While the specific tests for merger approval will be discussed more in the next section on regulatory processes, the overall standard is the public interest test, which requires that merger benefits to customers be demonstrated. These can include lower combined costs, which lead to lower total rate levels, or environmental commitments, local investment, etc., that provide direct state, community, and customer benefits.

Although there are numerous state-specific requirements, the public interest test provides an overarching umbrella for transaction assessment—either demonstrate a *positive showing* (specific illustration) of customer benefit, or that *no harm* (generic argument) would result from the transaction. As one would expect, a positive showing of merger synergies is far more compelling than a simple showing of no adverse impacts.

Much attention was given to the nature of identified synergies in the early days of utility consolidation and continues today. This topic created significant and contentious argument between applicants, commission staffs, and intervenors over whether identified cost savings were truly merger related. To be construed as merger-related synergies, cost savings would not exist *but for* the existence of the merger—that is, they are *created* by the transaction, and not attainable in the absence of the merger by management action such as implementing new technology, modifying the operating model, offering an early-out plan, etc., which could be done at any time.

This definition has been important in merger approval proceedings as it provides the foundational standard for evaluation of merger synergies within the overall public interest standard. But there are two other ways to think about additional cost savings available to managements to capture overall synergies, those that are *enabled* or accelerated, like technology, and those that are *developed* or could occur without a merger, like transfer of best practices, or comparison of costs across companies.

In practice, certain cost savings arise that are not entirely attributable to a merger or entirely separate from a transaction. A combination of two companies may allow the parties to pursue an entirely new path that the merger has unlocked. For example, a replacement of a core technology system planned for further in the future by either party may now make economic sense to accelerate and benefit both parties.

Additionally, the scale and economics of the business may have changed to where in-house non-core activity performance now makes more sense to receive through a lower-cost third party. Either company could decide to insource or outsource or accelerate or defer actions on its own, but the new post-merger scale now enables those decisions to be revisited from an integrated and larger-scale perspective, even though they are not wholly attributable to the combination.

Sometimes cost savings can occur that have nothing at all to do with the merger. They could be developed outside the transaction itself. For example, operating performance levels or costs can be different between the merging parties. The higher-cost or poorer-performing company could decide at any time to improve its own service cost performance whether a merger transaction existed or not.

These management actions clearly have nothing to do with a merger, and regulatory commissions have not provided much weight to calling those savings merger related. Nonetheless, non-merger-related cost changes are likely to occur during the period after transaction close, and these are just as valuable to companies as traditional merger savings.

All benefits to customers matter, but satisfying the public interest standard is usually best addressed through clear linkage to the specific merger transaction presented before regulator commissions.

Bootstrapping (leveraging other items) non-merger-related benefits into the calculus of the public interest test complicates the approval process and adds unnecessary contention that can be avoided.

Value Demonstration

Once the sources of value can be defined, the next step is to quantify these areas, define the timing of their capture, develop their value, and present the synergies outcomes in a clear and compelling manner that communicates contribution sources, impacts, realization, and related costs to achieve.

Typically, a merger synergies *waterfall* (cumulative compilation) can be constructed to reflect conceptual or real synergies by type and relative value. The easiest way to display synergies is between regulated and non-regulated businesses, with specific components quantified by source. The level of detail provided can be flexible depending on the

Figure 16: Transaction Synergies Build-Up

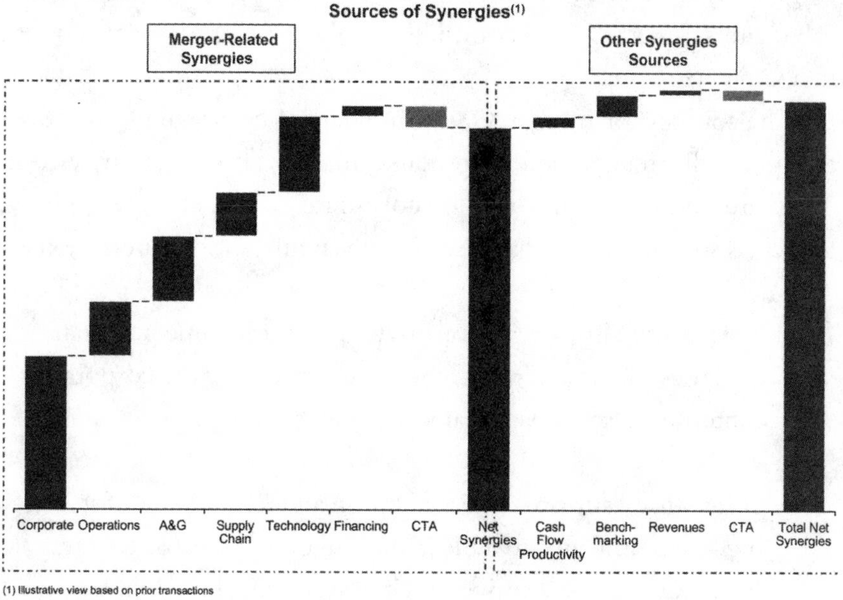

Sources of Synergies(1)

Merger-Related Synergies

Other Synergies Sources

Corporate Operations | A&G | Supply Chain | Technology | Financing | CTA | Net Synergies | Cash Flow Productivity | Bench-marking | Revenues | CTA | Total Net Synergies

(1) Illustrative view based on prior transactions

audience and the purpose. For example, a board-level presentation will focus on broad business segments or areas, while working group and regulatory presentations will identify all areas or types of synergies to add more specificity to where revenues or incremental cost savings will arise.

The level of synergies is typically represented for a multi-year period of at least five years. In earlier periods, this time frame often extended as far as ten years to include the avoidance of capital investment in a new generation plant. When new baseload, mid-merit, or peaking assets were no longer being built due to high reserve margins, this opportunity area diminished or evaporated. Companies then recognized that synergies growth over a longer period without lumpy capital spend did not really affect ongoing cost savings composition and merely reflected the changing value of inflation, thus a ten-year view became less valuable.

At the traditional utility operating cost level, a broad array of cost pools and cost types exist to address for streamlining from overlap, duplication, and/or economies of scale. These operating costs are catalogued by area of the business, like power supply, fuel acquisition, call centers, finance and accounting, supply chain, insurance, benefits, financing costs, etc.

The sources for merger O&M and capital cost savings are broad and generally recognized as available in conventional transactions. They are composed of a mix of corporate and operations sources, as well as specific functional areas where significant cost pools exist.

- **Corporate support**: rationalization and realignment of staffing levels and mix to reflect the ongoing needs of the corporate center (e.g., executives, shared services, etc.)

- **Operations support**: rationalization and realignment of staffing levels and mix to reflect the ongoing needs of business operations (e.g., executives, back office, etc.)

- **Corporate and administrative**: reduction of non-labor administrative and general expenses (e.g., insurance, benefits, boards of directors, professional services, etc.)
- **Supply chain**: negotiation of preferred unit cost pricing for common operating equipment and services vendors (e.g., materials and supplies and contract services)
- **Information technology**: rationalization of the corporate and operating technology environments and infrastructure (e.g., data centers, applications, networks, etc.)
- **Energy supply**: rationalization of portfolio fuels requirement sources, transport, and commodity prices (e.g., coal, natural gas, and nuclear fuel)
- **Power operations**: integration of plant additions (e.g., planned uprates and new builds, and dispatch of owned generation, outside an RTO/ISO)
- **Cash flow productivity**: application of cost savings to higher-yield business pursuits than current business plans (e.g., growth investment over short-term debt avoidance)

The historically largest potential source of synergies used to be the avoidance of parallel power supply options between the two merging utilities. If a baseload plant is displaced through reserve margin management, the full cash capital expenditure and ongoing O&M expense is avoided. Generation dispatch also used to be a significant source of synergies, particularly when summer–winter peak diversity was present. The advent of RTOs/ISOs removed these savings as the role for dispatch transferred from the host utilities to these regional system operators.

The contribution of the above cost savings areas vary widely by element, as they reflect the absolute and relative scale of each cost savings source. One general fallacy in utility M&A synergies quantification is that synergies are overwhelmingly captured through staffing terminations. While job losses from duplication and overlap do occur, smart synergies pursuit and quantification can find more non-labor cost savings than those from labor.

Figure 17: Relative Synergies Decomposition

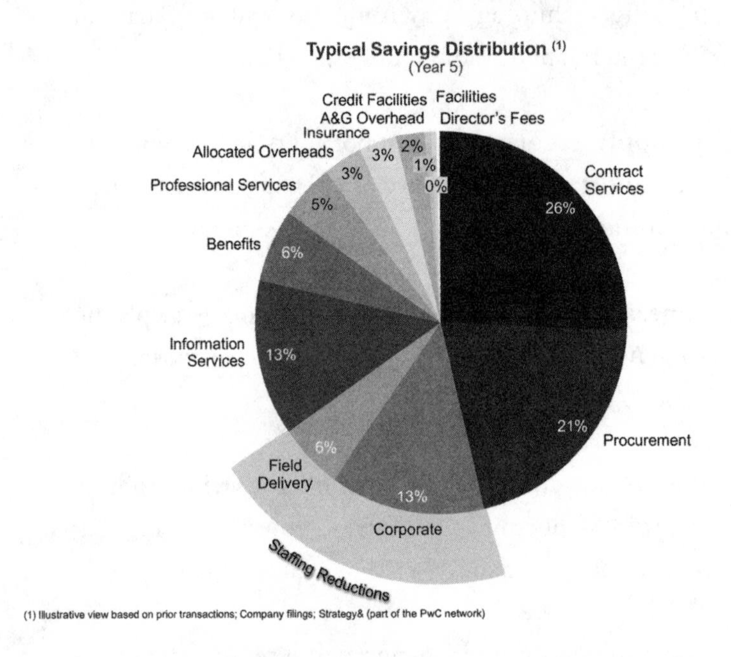

Revenue growth and cost savings are realized in both the regulated and non-regulated business segments. Traditional merger synergies development focuses separately on regulated v. non-regulated sources for several reasons: regulated synergies relate directly to satisfaction of the public interest; non-regulated synergies come from businesses supported by shareholder versus ratepayer funding; and most companies have fledgling or no non-regulated businesses between them to drive synergies.

The incremental revenue category of merger synergies first depends on the comparability of existing businesses. For example, two retail or energy services businesses are likely to identify opportunities to cross-sell, expand geographies, extend product and service offerings, and reprice market offerings to create new revenue streams or levels, where one plus one equals three.

If the businesses are not comparable, as is the case for a generation asset operator and an infrastructure construction company, incremental revenues will be harder to identify and capture given the unique focus of each business, and one plus one may simply equal two.

Interestingly, merging two similar nascent businesses can optimize the value of the two businesses as market timing can be accelerated, existing market position from one entity can be leveraged by the other, and greater focus can be provided to the combined business in establishing new revenue streams not previously available.

Figure 18: Non-Regulated Value Sources

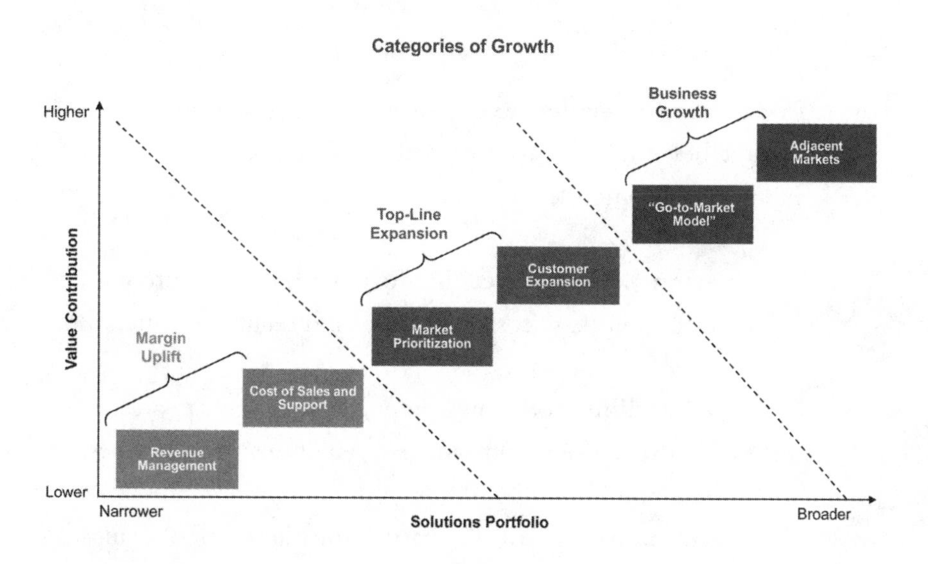

Incremental revenue or market offerings, planned to generate growth and enhance merger-related value, arise from a variety of sources, like acceleration of timing, enhanced market penetration, expanded geographic customers, alternative pricing models, and product bundling, among other sources.

- **Pull-through**: the leverage of existing offerings using cross-selling across discrete customer bases to create new revenues (e.g., energy services)

- **Market expansion**: step-out into adjacent market territories to offer existing and new offerings to create new revenues (e.g., back-up generation)

- **Load development**: creation of new electrification demand from adoption of new offerings (e.g., electric transport charging)

- **Customer high-grading**: rationalization of current customers (i.e., *cutting the tail* to elevate overall contribution) (e.g., margin optimization)

- **Product and service expansion**: taking new offerings to market beyond the current portfolio (e.g., *behind-the-meter* energy management)

- **Origination performance**: improving sales team outcomes and contribution (e.g., costs to acquire and retain customers)

- **Product bundling**: combining products and services to create a more attractive customer offering (e.g., equipment and services)

- **Customer penetration**: increasing the range of offerings embedded in customer operations (e.g., platform expansion)

- **Value uplift**: enhancing the profitability of customer offerings through risk modification (e.g., shared outcomes)

- **Repricing**: defining alternative approaches to individual offerings (e.g., base charge, plus value for service)

- **Entry acceleration**: pull-forward of market introduction and scale-up (e.g., sales timing and resource deployment)

- **Channel expansion**: leverage of incremental paths to the market beyond existing avenues (e.g., partnering)

- **Risk management**: mitigation and avoidance of existing execution risks to "go-to-market" outcomes (e.g., equipment performance)

- **Development spend**: avoidance of planned new business stand-up spend from pre-existing activity (e.g., market studies)

- **Back-office rationalization**: integration of business support functions and infrastructure (e.g., technology applications)

Not all the above opportunity areas are available in every transaction, as they are business dependent, and most utilities do not have a perfect side-by-side match of non-regulated businesses. But in future years, this will not be the case as markets expand, technologies mature, and customer demands broaden.

Non-regulated revenue synergies are becoming more viable today as most utilities are pursuing growth businesses in areas that will be core to the future business. Electric transport, storage, utility scale wind and solar, roof-top solar, distributed energy resources (DERs), demand flexibility, energy services, and behind-the-meter offerings are all believed to be natural fits with the traditional utility service model.

And the wider acceptance and production of hydrogen may have broad impacts on operating costs, reliability, and carbon emissions.

The experience of the U.S. utilities industry has been that cost savings do not need to be achieved on the backs of employees. Rather, available synergies can and should be captured from non-labor sources, even though labor costs can exceed 50 percent of O&M.

Where synergies are available differs from *what* types of synergies are possible, which differs from *how* synergies are realized—all three distinct perspectives are necessary when considering the level of value that can be realized. Nonetheless, the range and diversity of value sources in utilities M&A offer ample areas for evaluation in a traditional utility combination and a strong track record that these value sources can be realized.

Costs to Achieve

The identification and attainment of synergies are a vital element of the value equation. But determining *where to look* for value does not fully address *what it takes* to realize this value. The gross synergies available are not the true value sources—the net synergies are what matter.

The difference between gross and net synergies is the costs to achieve (CTA) these synergies. The CTA reflects the out-of-pocket costs of completing the transaction excluding the premium paid, that is, the costs associated with closing and integrating the transaction to produce the identified and expected value.

Unlike synergies, which start after Day 1 post-close, CTA starts before the transaction is approved and closed. These charges reflect the costs associated with enabling transaction announcement, regulatory approval, and post-close integration. These CTA costs start in year zero (pre-close), and largely extend for three years (though sometimes longer), which is typically consistent with the full integration period when costs to align and combine are being incurred.

In year one, CTA far exceeds achieved synergies as the out-of-pocket cash costs are incurred immediately, while synergies are just ramping up and following the integration process and timeline. By year two, sufficient synergies exist to cover these CTA elements and leave a positive net synergies level.

By the end of year three, integration is essentially concluded and final CTA—usually for integration technology applications and lingering separation activities—is nominal in succeeding years, if incurred at all. At the end of the third year post-close, net synergies are essentially at steady state and continue as escalated into perpetuity, except for asset write-offs, if not already taken.

CTA arises from a host of sources and reflects a mix of labor, non-labor, capital, and financing-related charges:

- **Change-in-control**: reflects the compensation contracts of executives displaced by the transaction and related equity conversion values

- **Separation**: reflects the standard separation agreements with non-executives and the payouts to displaced employees

- **Employee support**: includes small amounts of dedicated expenses to provide office space and job search support for a certain period

- **Retention**: allows for fixed payments to secure availability of targeted critical employees for a specific period of time to ensure resource and capabilities adequacy

- **Relocation**: covers out-of-pocket costs and allowances for employees moving to a new corporate or operating facility for an agreed time period and expense coverage

- **Communications**: recognizes stakeholder engagement and information dissemination on how to access the post-close enterprise and explain business changes

- **Facilities**: costs related to restacking existing facilities to accommodate changes in employee staffing locations and related infrastructure

- **D&O coverage**: provides for continuing coverage protection to existing directors and executives for a defined period

- **Information technology**: reflects infrastructure rationalization, application conversion, and potential unamortized application costs (non-cash)

- **Bridge financing**: covers the costs for obtaining temporary financing and the actual costs of borrowing for these funds

- **Transaction costs**: recognizes costs associated with service providers in support of banking, proxy, legal, and consulting activities to achieve deal announcement

- **Transition costs**: addresses integration costs for internal and external resources and related support activities

CTA are out-of-pocket cash costs that would not be incurred in the absence of the transaction. Thus, they do not relate to ongoing operating activities and are caused by the need to announce, negotiate, approve, close, and integrate a transaction. They are a necessary element of synergies quantification and the accurate calculation and demonstration of net merger benefits. Importantly, merger synergies cannot be realized without expenditure of significant CTA.

Synergies Experience

Companies that pursue utility M&A transactions are used to presenting detailed description and information related to identified merger synergies, including source, rationale, timing, value, costs, and net benefits.

The more descriptive the information, the more compelling the synergies presentation and the less contentious the regulatory approval process. As noted earlier, multi-year presentations have become the norm with regulators as it is only natural for state commissions to inquire about the view of the future, not just the steady state. And regulators also want to understand *when, where, and how* these identified synergies will be attained.

Two demonstrations of synergies have been successfully utilized in prior transactions—the annual net synergies build-up, and the decomposition of CTA. These two simple illustrations—plus the detailed models, sources, rationales, assumptions, and calculations used to support the quantification—provide substantial and valuable insight into merger synergies.

In an annual build-up of merger synergies, cost savings are slow to ramp up despite regulatory and intervenor presumptions and arguments. These reduced cost outcomes take time to be realized even as they continually grow. CTA, on the other hand, occurs during year zero and immediately at close and runs for a few years only. For regulatory decision-making, net synergies are the most critical, even though gross synergies tend to attract more initial attention.

Of equal interest to regulators and intervenors is the decomposition of merger synergies, by source. The specific synergies sources can be rolled up into categories like those described above or disaggregated into specific sources, which provides for greater delineation and comparison. Whether presented at the category or source synergies level, regulators will demand that sufficient quantification be clearly provided and clearly justified.

Despite the quantification presentation requirements described above, regulators also want to know how these synergies compare to those occurring in prior U.S. utility transactions. Fortunately, there is significant experience available within the public domain to understand prior transaction comparative synergies levels and ranges. Given my participation and visibility into most U.S. utilities transactions, these comparisons were developed and maintained from 1995 forward with constant updating.

The information in the accompanying figure reflects a typical comparative chart developed to present in my typical direct or rebuttal testimony to regulatory commissions to place then-current identified transaction synergies into context. The analysis reflected prior transaction work performed and testified to on synergies quantification, and reflected transactions where I possessed hands-on, direct knowledge of the detailed assumptions and quantification.

Usually, the peer set captured initial synergies estimates for the 20 most recent transactions, which provided a current set of typical transactions, except for financial sponsor or international buyer deals, where synergies were not a focal point as state regulatory commissions focused on financial capacity and commitment, and simple rate credits from the new owner. These deals were not synergies based given the structural approaches to ownership and did not give rise to comparative synergies levels existing in traditional transactions.

Compilation of prior utilities transaction synergies results for position reductions in my prior testimony approximated 7 percent, with non-fuel O&M reductions also averaging just over 7 percent. These averages indicated that across the 20 comparative transactions, approximately 7 percent of the total affectable staffing of both companies was calculated—by individually captured sub-functional area—as the reduction level that could be assumed from the merger. The same logic applied to the approximate 7 percent O&M reduction, which reflected all addressable non-fuel O&M costs for both companies at a granular expense level.[1]

Figure 19: Prior Transaction Synergies Impacts

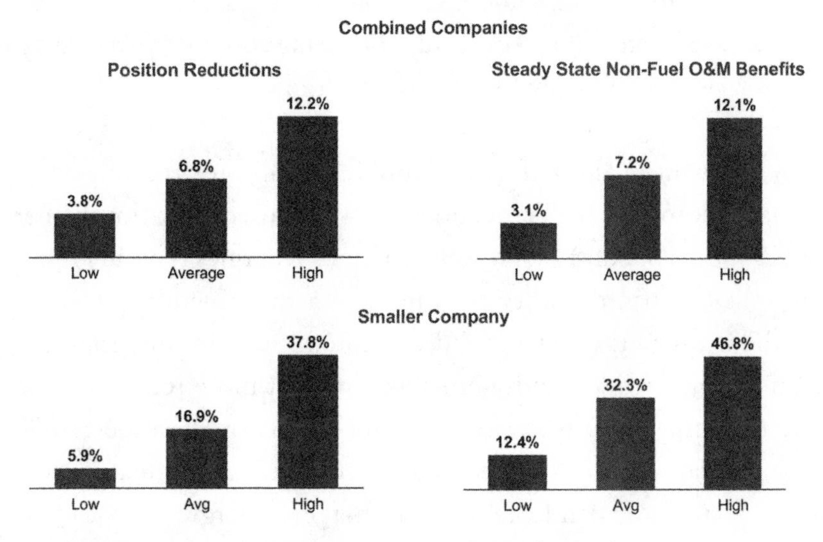

Source: Testimony of Thomas J. Flaherty Before the Kansas Corporation Commission; Company filings; Strategy& (part of the PwC network)

But the underlying analyses indicate significant variability in prior deal synergies ranges reflecting two primary drivers: significant scale differences between the two companies, and meaningful impacts in addressable synergies areas across the companies. For example, an acquiring company could be 2–3 times the smaller company in pure size, which naturally constrains the average compared to two more similarly sized entities. Alternatively, the scale measurement could also reflect the absence of similar business segments, for example, nuclear, natural gas, etc., that could reduce the affectable cost base itself.

Gale Klappa of WEC Energy discussed how important synergies are to achieving the promise of increased shareholder value and lower costs to customers:

> Our perspective is, it's not about budget control, it's about driving efficiency and best practices throughout the enterprise. We want to achieve results that allow us to defer future rate cases. That

> requires a thorough, bottom-up review to identify opportunities and enable focused execution. This approach has been successful and allowed us to reduce day-to-day operating costs by an average of four percent annually for five years in a row.

The amount of the reduction would have an outsized impact to the smaller company if all reductions were measured from this smaller base as a means of contrast. However, merger synergies typically result from both companies rather than just the acquired entity. In a few cases the acquiring company did not intend to fully integrate the acquiree, which made stand-alone measurement more relevant.

The industry and its investment banker advisors have been able to use the data previously prepared to support management or my testimony to understand the level of merger synergies that can be obtained in similar situations. Even in dissimilar transactions, the comparative information can be used to help gauge their level of expectations and guide.

Synergies Attainability

Earlier, it was mentioned that utilities managements have always had a healthy skepticism about synergies, even though the track record of realization is extremely high across all types and sizes of transactions.

One way to increase utility management awareness of synergies attainment risks was to illustrate how the various elements related to one another from a risk of attainment perspective. That is, show management where on a degree of control spectrum a specific source of merger synergies resides. For example, management controls almost all decision elements for staffing reductions, thus it faces little risk to synergies realization.

Alternatively, management incurs more risk in areas where economies of scale exist and third-party negotiations with supply chain vendors and insurance brokers are necessary to effectuate the identified merger synergies. In this case, management needs to be sufficiently knowledgeable about market dynamics, volume timing, and order quantities to be prepared for an aggressive but fair negotiation.

Figure 20: Synergies Risk Attainment

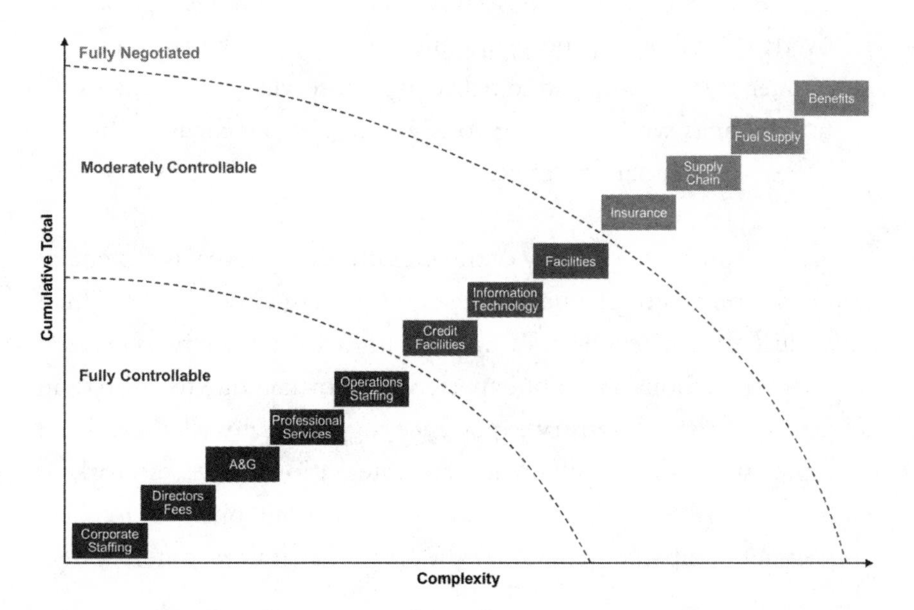

Figure 20 illustrates how managements can assess their relative degree of control over a specific source of synergies. Little risk to expected synergies attainment is borne when management either controls the key elements of the decision or execution process, or there is minor dollar risk exposure from non-synergies realization.

As the figure shows, the level of risk increases as decision control, market conditions, or synergies concentration become more variable or constrained. Risk-adjusting identified synergies is a smart way to assess the impact of adverse outcomes and to direct focus to mitigating these potential occurrences.

Jim Judge from Eversource Energy discussed the importance of synergies realization to the outcomes he has pursued:

> Our board, shareholders, regulators, and customers expect we will deliver value from a transaction—that's our core DNA. If we want equitable regulatory treatment, we need to capture synergies that justify the premium paid, at a minimum. In the transaction creating Eversource Energy, we produced annual reductions to O&M of five percent for five consecutive years, which reflects typical overlap, duplication, and economies of scale, plus best practice transfer. But we also need to deliver on our service commitments to customers while reducing costs, and not let our focus be distracted from either objective.

As mentioned, the history of the U.S. utilities industry is extremely good with respect to planned versus actual synergies realization. While individual category synergies amounts can vary, total synergies realized in prior transactions have not experienced shortfalls due to estimation or execution issues. Industry experience suggests that well-formulated synergies studies and well-structured integration processes work in tandem to enable companies to avoid adverse outcomes and enable combining companies to capture the level of estimated synergies.

Key Takeaways

Available synergies play a critical role throughout the transaction process, but their value extends beyond stages of the deal into the impacts on multiple aspects of the enterprise. Standing back from a focus on synergies development mechanics, numerous reminders emerge regarding synergies benefits and determining how to approach defining, quantifying, and presenting these cost savings and revenue benefits.

- The north star for a transaction defines where a combined company hopes to be at integration end. *A strategic mindset expands the view of the art of the possible.*

- Operating model design drives the development of available synergies. *This model establishes where and how two companies align and work.*

- Synergies extend across the entire enterprise from many sources, forms, and types. *Cost savings do not need to be heavily achieved at the expense of the employee base.*

- Synergies provide a significant impact to baseline cost structures. *A similar reduction impact to enterprise costs is difficult to replicate through business-as-usual actions.*

- Utilities have been successful at realizing expected synergies. *Integration teams are good at achieving targets, making the risk of non-attainment minimal.*

- The corporate center produces the most visible and concentrated source of synergies, *but business operations affect a larger addressable volume of total spend.*

- Synergies realization is achieved over time as integration activities conclude. *Positive savings exist, but are substantially outweighed by costs to achieve in year one.*

- Costs to achieve are necessary for synergies realization to occur and will be substantial. *These out-of-pocket costs should be managed in the same manner as synergies.*

- Top-line revenue and margin growth will become increasingly valuable as the business matures. *An emphasis should be placed on commercializing key offering elements.*

- Synergies play a central role throughout the life cycle of the transaction. *The savings provide an end-to-end link to Wall Street, regulators, and integration team focus.*

The U.S. utilities industry has brought increasingly careful diligence to the identification, quantification, and demonstration of merger synergies since the advent of the modern era of M&A. This diligence has paid off as the industry has an exemplary track record of both demonstrating sufficient total benefits to satisfy the public interest, as well as achieving merger synergies.

Synergies are available throughout the business in utility transactions, in the same manner they are for industrial or consumer companies. Incremental revenues, reduced costs, avoided capital expenditures, and reduced financing costs are all available to pursue, with some more likely to be available than others depending on the composition of the transacting party businesses.

The single most important factor to drive these synergies throughout the enterprise is the operating model which defines business and functional alignment and rationalization. Categories of synergies comprise the entire enterprise, specific business segments or units, discrete functional areas, unique cost types, and targeted capital investment. Synergies begin to occur at close of the transaction, ramp up over three years, and extend into perpetuity as they escalate year-to-year from steady state.

In a typical utility M&A transaction, more than 12 incremental revenue sources and 25 discrete cost types can be identified as synergies sources, depending on the nature of the two merging companies. In addition, almost 20 specific functions and more than 100 unique sub-functions can be utilized to define where staffing savings can exist, depending on business scope and structural circumstances. Typically, the corporate center is the largest source for these synergies since it houses more overlapping functions and positions than in field operations support and is where A&G expenses are incurred.

Merger synergies have typically approximated 7 percent of existing combined and addressable staffing and O&M expense, depending on relative scale, relative baseline, business composition, general proximity, and integration philosophy. Disparate scale transactions, that is, combining small and large companies, may correspond to approximately 3 - 4 percent of O&M expenses on these same measures, and generally reflect affectable base constraints to synergies, not a logic shortfall.

The industry's track record on synergies attainment reflects the ability to control and manage the execution risk related to achieving cost savings. A healthy portion of typical identified merger synergies are within the control of utility managements, with higher attainment risk related to negotiated economies of scale or differences in cost pool structures, like in benefits. Revenues are far more variable than costs and carry a lower degree of attainment likelihood given the vagaries of markets and lower inherent experience in origination, pricing, and margin management.

CTA, which reflects out-of-pocket cash costs, is the final component of the synergies story, but a vital one. While gross synergies often capture headlines, net synergies, that is, gross synergies less CTA, are more important as they provide the basis for synergies sharing with customers. CTA represent the costs necessary to announce, approve, close, and integrate a transaction and are a fundamental element of the value equation. If CTA is not recognized, then synergies sharing will not be equitable between shareholders and customers, which will dampen industry enthusiasm for pursuing transactions.

CHAPTER 6

HURDLES AND OUTCOMES

Since 1995, utilities M&A transactions have had a favorable regulatory commission approval history, and most companies have been able to build a successful history of deal closes over these last 25 years. The nature and intensity of regulatory commission review has evolved and differed between the federal and state levels, with legislative activity reducing regulatory approval risk at the federal level, as well as increasing regulatory risk and delay at the state level.

When announced, utilities M&A transactions create dichotomous challenges strategically and financially. On the one hand, companies pursue mergers to advance market positioning, which is a strategic growth focus. But when they pursue M&A transactions, companies are also seeking to avoid any deterioration in financial integrity through deal structuring and financing or from the regulatory approval process. Sometimes, these dual goals clash and cause proposed transactions to be terminated due to an imbalance in proportional risk assumption or financial equity.

The U.S. utility industry has accomplished almost 100 transactions since the beginning of 1995. However, the number of CEO conversations and evaluated or attempted transactions probably exceeds the number of closed transactions by twice that amount—close observers in this time window would remark that "everybody's been talking, but not everyone's been listening."

In early times, it seemed that two to three of every five potential utility transactions would lose steam before serious board consideration or subsequent regulatory approval. This is a much better track record than for U.S. industry as a whole, with academic and consulting studies often citing that two of three, or three of four, proposed transactions fail.

In the early days of U.S. utility transactions, proposed or considered pursuits were often a reaction to other announced transactions—either concern over lost opportunity, option limitation, or independence risk. The small companies wanted to be left alone, mid-size companies knew they had to play, and large companies thought they were natural acquirors—but no one wanted to be in a position of having just a few options.

These abandoned pursuits (if they made it that far) were generally caused by some combination and weighting of premium difference (is it sufficient?), partner attractiveness (is it a fit?), regulatory challenges (can it get approved?), or social issues (are they acceptable?).

In some cases where missteps occurred with respect to target interest, pricing adequacy, or post-close leadership, these false starts were self-inflicted and usually linked to inadequate knowledge of target CEO and board of director deal sentiment, or a misread in the difference between early discussions and initial negotiations.

A few unlucky proposed combinations got caught between federal and state jurisdictional authorities and considerations. Other transactions found that CEO perspectives were not in harmony. Some deals simply created regulatory process risks that were viewed as unacceptable.

The risk of transaction non-approval due to unclear standards, at-odds jurisdictions, unknown outcomes, or indefinite timing caused many transactions to wither away since no obvious answers existed to identified impediments, or managements simply lost the energy to sustain the effort.

The hurdles to transaction close have always run through two groups: boards of directors and federal and state regulatory commissions, but their viewpoints are different. Boards are more concerned about company outcomes and shareholders, while state regulatory commissions focus on standards and customers. Good board work can avoid shareholder concerns, and smart executive engagement can minimize regulatory surprises. Shareholder risks seldom arise if investor sentiment is positive, so the primary focus of the following discussion is on regulatory risks.

Experience has been a sound teacher to U.S. utilities, but it has not replaced continuous management dialogue over how a potential transaction could be derailed. In most cases, management deliberation overwhelmingly focuses on regulatory approvals as the largest hurdle to overcome and a range of questions are usually asked:

- How do we sufficiently prepare the board of directors?
- Do the jurisdictions have established approval standards?
- Are there approval standard differences between affected jurisdictions?
- Have jurisdictions reviewed an approval filing in recent years?
- Have jurisdictions consistently applied their standards?
- Does the jurisdiction adequately recognize costs to achieve?

- Have jurisdictions been reasonable on shareholder treatment?
- Does the jurisdiction allow for sustained shareholder benefit?
- Can the timeline for approval be accelerated or managed?
- Are jurisdictions likely to obtain unfriendly external advisors?

If there is a single area where utility managements remain most concerned about the risks of execution, it is federal and state regulatory commission approvals. More than one management team have considered this part of the process to be the least transparent, least predictable, and least satisfying. Terms like "frustrating," "overreaching," "circus," "unpredictable," "unfriendly," and "political" characterize some of their sentiments after a deal finally received approval. Yet even with these memories, quite a few managements signed up to do another one, sometimes on several more occasions.

In bridging the gap between transaction announcement and close, utilities should start with the precedents that exist at the federal and state levels. But the uncertainty of evolving externalities, and the uniqueness of each transaction, continue to challenge the ability of companies to successfully read the direction of principles, priorities, and policies.

Board Readiness

Boards of directors play pivotal roles in the utility transaction evaluation and decision-making process. They certainly represent the interests of all shareholders in a fiduciary capacity, but also perform a role of strategic and financial guidance to management, which is especially meaningful for M&A transactions.

Given the *bet-the-company* nature of many transactions, and the usual cynicism over utility M&A activity among analysts and regulators, seasoned and sober perspective brought to transaction consideration by an independent board is a natural and critical management need. Too many moving pieces in a proposed transaction can go sideways, and sub-optimize future strategic and financial expectations, thus there is no substitute for sound board guidance.

When considering how companies prepared their boards for a potential transaction, Bill Lamb from Baker Botts remarked:

> In the mid-1990s, managements and boards were beginning to recognize that the potential for market competition or regulatory policy could cause more industry consolidation to occur. Management wanted their board to be ready for a potential transaction, since it had limited experience and, in most cases, no recent familiarity with utility transactions. We played a role in that preparation, leading board sessions through a range of issues like anti-takeover defense, merger agreements, shareholder rights, pooling accounting, PUHCA application, fiduciary duty, recent transactions, unsolicited offers, and state regulation.

Depending on when in history potential M&A transactions were presented for review and approval, boards could have been totally unfamiliar with utilities mergers and acquisitions, or they could have built a reservoir of experience from serial transactions conducted by their utility, or their own individual experience as corporate officers or advisors. This dichotomous level of experience presented a challenge to managements, particularly in the 1995-1999 period, when so many first-time combinations occurred for boards to deal with.

The composition of utility boards has always varied over time. In the early days, they represented a cross-section of large company, local business, and community experience, while today they are predominantly comprised of experienced private-sector or financial executives, many of them existing or retired CEOs (and some retired utility CEOs).

Gale Klappa from WEC Energy commented on ensuring his board of directors would be ready if and when a potential merger situation emerged:

> We spent time focusing our board on the broad context of potential deregulation and competition impacts, as well as regulation's role. As we developed a future view of our environment, the specific impacts of a merger became easier to see. We emphasized that any transaction had to be about increasing shareholder value, and deal pricing, synergy levels, asset mix, and regulatory outcomes were all linked. Comparing our current portfolio to the future market provided us an informed view of how to create value.

The level of experience in utilities M&A was naturally a gap in the early days of the modern era since there had been so few recent significant transactions in the decade prior to 1995. While some board members may have executed their own M&A transactions, the process, issues, and duration of utilities transactions are unique to this sector. Consequently, managements had to prepare their boards to address a potential transaction opportunity which could arise at any time as a buyer, seller, or partner.

When talking about board of directors preparation before a transaction was likely, Dick Kelly, formerly the CEO at Xcel Energy, remarked:

> In those days, boards had less M&A experience and a far more parochial view given their high local composition. This made them skeptical about mergers, even though we had recently done a small transaction. We spent a lot of time readying the board for a potential deal and used external advisors to support us in discussing industry direction, pricing trends, likely partners and competitors, and regulatory risks. We extended this model to include the board of our partner, so each had a common

perspective of the other, the process, and deal parameters. This served us well in creating a common view of the combined company and greater compatibility.

Typical board questions to address in an introductory session usually focus on the following:

- the utility transaction process
- the roles regulators play
- the length of the approval process
- the transparency of the approval process
- the ability to influence the regulatory process
- the potential value from combination
- the actions required if contacted by a suitor
- the readiness to undertake a transaction
- the typical utility transaction structure and pricing model
- the level of typical acquisition premiums
- the levers to avoid earnings dilution
- the impact of a deal on dividend policy
- the effect of a deal on strategy
- the wisdom of staying stand-alone

This education usually started with an investment bank (or several over time) providing a perspective on the utilities industry landscape and overview of the available partners, their financial positions, and relevant motivations of these "neighbors." The session provided introduction to utility transactions and was intended to open the eyes of the board and prepare them ahead of time for a possible eventuality. It also enabled the boards to see several investment bankers and gauge their capabilities, knowledge of their company circumstances, and ability to work with management and the board toward responsible shareholder outcomes.

Sometimes there were multiple preparatory sessions to allow for adequate dialogue and debate in an open information-sharing environment without the pressure of an actual event. When management and investment bank(s) were on the same page regarding the implications of the industry landscape and trends, then the board was well served by the time spent in understanding the drivers for the potential road ahead.

Beyond the investment banks, management usually held similar sessions with external counsel, particularly over governance responsibilities and regulatory processes. These sessions could be co-held with investment banks since there are obvious interface points related to decision roles, deal negotiations, and securities filings, among other areas.

The legal review addressed how a board should make decisions, the kind of factual and evaluative record needed to support decisions, and what a term sheet and purchase or merger agreement entails. This session also allowed regulatory counsels to educate the board on relevant regulatory commission standards and precedents, the nature of an approval filing, the potential responses from intervenors and staffs, and the typical decision-making process and timeline. This is an important step in the preparation process, as most board members do not have an appreciation for the extended schedule between merger or acquisition announcement and close.

In these preparatory sessions, management also engaged the board in dialogue about the benefits and risks of a transaction and the perspectives of management on attractive partners or targets, as well as potential regulatory outcomes and how other utilities handled prior transactions. Even if no potential transaction emerged in the near-term, a board is advantaged from this education and better prepared to quickly respond if the situation demands. It can also watch concurrent transactions and better understand the events and outcomes.

Jim Torgerson from AVANGRID at the time of the Iberdrola offer, addressed how he prepared his board of directors to consider an acquisition by an international entity:

> The board recognized smaller companies like UIL could be marginalized as companies around them grew larger. When Iberdrola emerged as an option, our board had never considered international activity. Many issues had to be evaluated, not the least of which related to how legislators and regulators would react since Iberdrola was headquartered in Spain and not known to them. The board needed to consider how a deal would affect local decision-making authority and how AVANGRID would be protected from unrelated events in other countries.

Of course, when board members are experienced with transactions, the nature of dialogue differs. It is less about core event education and readiness, and more about changes in the deal environment, detailed assessment of a partner or target, nuanced transaction structuring and pricing, and protection against topping bids and litigation. These are also topics covered as board maturity expands even without a transaction in front of the company.

The board becomes particularly engaged when critical social issues become topical before and during the negotiation of the merger agreement. These issues typically relate to headquarters location, CEO selection, CEO succession, board composition, key officer selection, integration lead(s) selection, new company name (if necessary), and related decision timing, among other areas. The CEOs lead the negotiation, but the boards are engaged every step of the way with their investment bankers and attorneys.

These issues reflect critical decisions that can set the transaction on a successful course or unwind it before it even gets started. Social issue disagreement is a frequent hurdle and a predominant cause of deal failures. If not adequately negotiated with input from both acquiror and acquiree, a lack of deference or trust can abruptly end a great deal for avoidable reasons. And since M&A discussions are grounded in clear communication, avoiding a situation in which the entities become two ships passing in the night is a predicate for getting to the succeeding steps of negotiation.

In a merger-of-equals situation, social issue discussion is paramount because premiums are lower, and the style of the transaction is intended to communicate equality, harmony, and shared perspectives. The acquiror CEO needs to be acutely aware of the position of his counterpart, who may be ceding leadership control, but not interested in looking like acquiree executive and company interests were inadequately protected.

Ideally, some of these issues, like naming of CEO and headquarters location, are agreed at the outset between the CEOs since they are a fundamental stage gate to further discussion. Unless agreed upon early, the danger increases that misimpressions are left over what was originally said versus originally heard.

In other cases, they persist until there is little remaining time to decide on the deal merits, and the risks of miscalculation or overreach manifest themselves in introducing unwanted issues to even the playing field at a late moment in the negotiating process.

If these critical decisions are not addressed in a timely manner, the board may need to signal to the CEO that a process pause may be appropriate to avoid deterioration in personal relationships, which is sometimes the critical element in accomplishing a deal that can be favorably viewed by key stakeholders. Personal trust between the CEOs is a prerequisite for any utility transfer of ownership to a successor.

While tendencies can emerge to aggressively negotiate everything, boards can be a stabilizing influence for CEOs with respect to constantly remembering the original rationale for the transaction. But do not expect the board to be the referee; its fiduciary duty is to shareholders, not the CEOs. And the CEOs get paid high compensation for a reason—to effectuate strategic outcomes for their stakeholders.

When a transaction is not a merger-of-equals and a solid control premium is clearly being offered, then the acquiring CEO has more influence over an outcome. Still, the acquiree CEO is generally more willing to avoid the appearance of seeking too many wins if it secures a high premium for shareholders. In this case, the acquiree CEO will seek to influence the outcomes that matter, such as executive management position consideration, local community presence, ongoing investment continuity, etc.

Boards experienced with merger transactions can pay significant dividends to the CEOs in providing valuable guidance and listening at the right moment of the deal process. On the other hand, inexperienced boards can leave the CEOs feeling deserted on an island without a place to turn, except to professional advisors. Fortunately, U.S. utilities today enjoy far more experienced boards than their predecessors did in the early days of the modern era of M&A.

Approval Standards

Utility mergers are the ultimate case of transactions being under a microscope. All aspects of the transaction receive public scrutiny and the approval filings receive layers of federal and state review and challenge. Simple shareholder voting is just one step in the process and, while consequential, only signals the process has been accepted to proceed.

In the early days of utility mergers, companies did not have full and complete guidance on what to file, what to emphasize, how to inform, what to avoid, or what to expect. The history of utility deals was largely unwritten, and what had previously occurred was not widely remembered or considered all that relevant. While merger standards generally existed, they were often crafted decades prior to address different needs and not revisited in that ensuing period. It would not be an overstatement that mid-1990s standards could be unspecific, unclear, and untested for the modern era of utility M&A.

Companies pursuing utility mergers have several review agencies to navigate at the federal and state levels for qualifying transactions. These include the FERC, SEC, DOJ/FTC, and NRC at the federal level and local regulatory commissions and agencies at the state level.

From an approval perspective, several stakeholders play a key role in affecting whether and how a proposed transaction moves to a closed transaction, with subtle and unsubtle differences in focus. While the number of reviewing federal or state agencies involved can seem burdensome, several have narrow responsibilities and/or fulfill administrative rather than evaluative roles.

- **FERC**: The agency approval focus is on ensuring effective functioning of wholesale markets and equitable access to supply. FERC merger intervention has diminished over time as RTOs/ISOs serve to enable market fairness, although FERC did add selected former SEC roles after PUHCA.

- **SEC**: The long-standing, highly proscriptive jurisdiction of the SEC inherent in PUHCA called for oversight of overlapping ownership, financing structures, business composition, territory contiguity, and affiliate relationships, but was transferred to FERC when PUHCA was terminated.

- **DOJ/FTC**: Mergers receive anti-trust review to ensure market power does not result from combinations. For utilities, focus centers on generation markets and electric and gas combinations, but utilities receive few *second requests*, that is, detailed questions.

- **State and local government**: The focus of these stakeholders typically extends to statewide and municipal impacts from a utility merger, particularly headquarters changes, job losses, economic development, and charitable contribution spend.

- **State agencies**: Utility regulatory commissions are the principal agency with merger standard application and conformance review of the public interest test, but environmental agencies also engage in compliance, risk, and outcome matters affected by the merger.

- **Shareholders**: Investors have direct approval authority over merger structure, impacts, and value outcomes through a formal proxy process where share voting is made. If shareholders do not approve a transaction, then remaining approvals are dead in the water.

- **Wall Street**: The broad investor community has no direct approval authority, but makes its presence felt through analyst opinions and rating agency commentary about credit quality and bond ratings, which influences shareholders and state regulatory commissions.

- **Intervenors**: Multiple entities participate to voice transaction concerns and provide extensive testimony on perceived merger flaws and public interest test shortcomings, though local union groups often back utilities if job commitments are satisfactory.

- **Customers**: The ultimate voice in a transaction is held by the group most affected if adverse impacts to prices, reliability, access, safety, and the local economy arise. If customers stand against a merger, it is difficult for state regulatory commissions to approve it.

- **Neighboring utilities**: Both friendly and competitive utilities maintain a close interest in announced transactions as they are concerned about how differently the combined company could operate and shift regional power market dynamics.

- **Bargaining units**: Most utilities have groups of corporate and operating employees that are members of local unions, which have a significant voice in shaping how mergers are structured to preserve existing agreements and favorable employee treatment.

Federal agencies all have standards or criteria they employ to assess whether a transaction that involves stock registration, market concentration, license transfer, or financial integration could have adverse impact to affected stakeholders. While the influence and control of these federal-level agencies was onerous in certain early transactions between 1995 and 1999, it has rationalized and clarified itself and is not as burdensome for current deals.

Despite the level of attention provided to transaction strategy, deal pricing, and shareholder approval, the state regulatory commission playing field is where the merger approval game is critically contested. FERC initially evaluated whether transactions were consistent with the public interest standard, but this was not well defined and centered on no harm to competition.

When asked about overall regulatory outcomes in prior industry merger approvals, Dick Kelly, formerly of Xcel Energy, commented:

> The standards, approaches, and personalities of each regulatory commission are different and that creates challenges to a multi-state utility. We viewed that early discussion to build buy-in would be valuable later and there was no disadvantage to engaging at the right time with regulators. In the early days of transactions, a 50-50 sharing of savings was common, although this changed over time as regulators focused on obtaining benefits earlier for customers than they were even produced.

States created or adopted their own versions of a public interest standard to use in reviewing utility mergers, such as a positive demonstration of benefit to customers, or, in the alternative, they were not adversely affected. Yet, the public interest is not consistently defined for application. It is uniquely defined by jurisdiction, and still subject to much interpretation.

The public interest standard has its genesis in late 18th-century England and was related to societal expectations for production, availability, and distribution of goods and services. This broad concept was applied to regulated businesses (radio and telecommunications) in the early 1920s and focused on the promotion of, or consistency with, local outcomes, whether tangible benefits, reduced risks, or increased general public good.

The positive showing test is the less widely adopted model by state regulatory jurisdictions compared to the no harm test in the U.S. For all practical purposes, however, the difference in real application today has become negligible. Even though the no harm test does not require tangible demonstration of customer benefit, regulatory commissions today still demand that customers directly benefit from synergies through rate credits or rate moratoriums—this provides the same effective end result whether merger benefits were originally quantified and filed or not.

Two state regulatory examples of public interest determination offer a glimpse into how unique merger approval standards can be—the Kansas Corporation Commission (KCC with a positive showing test) and the Massachusetts Department of Energy Resources (DOER with also a positive showing test).

The KCC updated its existing merger approval standards in 2016 prior to the Westar Energy–Great Plains Energy transaction in 2017, culminating in a comprehensive 12-element list for transaction evaluation in the context of two integrated utilities.[1] The KCC outlined the following criteria to determine whether a transaction would promote the public interest, including:

- **Financial condition**: comparison of pre- and post-financial condition of the two companies with and without a merger
- **Purchase price**: assessment of whether the purchase price is reasonable and how it compares to expected synergies
- **Quantifiable benefits**: evaluation of whether synergies arising from the transaction can be quantified
- **Premium to synergies**: determination whether total synergies justify a premium in excess of book value
- **Existing competition**: the avoidance of any deleterious impact to current markets and competition from the transaction
- **Environmental impacts**: assessment of any adverse effects to the future environment within the state from resource selection
- **State and local communities**: whether the transaction is beneficial to the various economies within the state and whether job dislocation may be harmful
- **Commission jurisdiction**: whether the transaction will preserve the ability of the KCC to continue to regulate and audit the companies
- **Shareholder impacts**: how existing shareholders may be positively or adversely affected by the transaction
- **Kansas energy resources**: whether the transaction maximizes existing energy resources within the state
- **Economic waste**: whether the transaction reduces the possibility of economic waste within the state
- **Public safety**: how the transaction has any effect on existing safety of property and/or persons within the state

The above list encompasses a wide range of financial, operational, customer, stakeholder, environmental, and public impact areas. The number and specificity of these criteria exceed many other state regulatory commissions, but in their expansiveness, provide regulated companies with discrete dimensions of transaction impacts to directly address in their merger approval filings.

Chairman Mark Ruelle at Evergy continued describing how he viewed regulatory outcomes from transactions:

> Regulators are interested in synergies as tangible benefits to customers. We are regulated in Missouri, but all state regulators take a "show me" the savings attitude. Regulators view customers as first-in-line for synergies and increasingly require immediate value for customers before synergies occur. This outcome disadvantages shareholders and we work to ensure they are compensated for the risks they assume. We know synergies are real, but a fair outcome is required, or utilities will not undertake transactions and customers will not receive benefits. Regulators have been tough, but the end result must be acceptable, evidenced by utilities having not stopped doing consolidating transactions.

The Massachusetts DOER updated its merger approval standards in 2011 to move from a no harm test for the proposed Northeast Utilities–NSTAR transaction and adopted a list of four primary areas of inquiry at a minimum, with ten sub-elements to be considered in the context of a distribution utility.[2] This standard allows for other elements to be evaluated or required as determined necessary by the DOER. These specific criteria include:

- **Rate changes**: the plan for how existing customer rate levels will be affected once the transaction is closed, like rate credits and rate case moratoriums

- **Service quality**: commitment to improvements in the level of local delivered service to communities and customers
- **System strategies**: range and sufficiency of programs to maintain and enhance the delivery system, such as renewables, energy efficiency, and electric transport
- **Net savings**: the reasonableness and sufficiency of quantified benefits that arise specifically from the transaction
- **Competitive effect**: the impact that combination could have on retail or wholesale competition in Massachusetts
- **Financial integrity**: consideration of the effects that combination could have on debt levels, cash flows, and credit ratings
- **Benefits distribution**: the level and rationale for how net savings (gross savings less CTA) are attributed to customers and shareholders
- **Societal costs**: the impacts to local communities and public from adverse transaction outcomes like, employee dislocation and environmental impacts
- **Economic development**: the impacts to the development of the state and local communities and preservation of local economic vitality
- **Merger alternatives**: comparison of available options to the parties and the trade-offs to the proposed transaction

These specific criteria reflect the issues of a transaction through the lens of Massachusetts regulators, just as their counterparts view them in other jurisdictions. Merger standards may sound the same, but they reflect the attendant policies in place in those states. Massachusetts, for example, specifically focused on renewables, energy efficiency, electric vehicles, hydroelectric, and other areas, not as germane to a typical transaction, but because the circumstances of their regulatory priorities and local energy supply sources made these issues pertinent.

Although the list is both narrower and different than in Kansas, the practicalities of any regulatory approval setting is that everything is in play for review when a merger approval transaction is before a state regulatory commission—new concerns enter each transaction because unique circumstances or intervenors make them issues. The challenge to utilities is to not allow uninvited guests into the proceeding who bring issues that have little to do with the transaction, or carry-over from recent rate cases.

Positive-showing state regulatory commission reviews typically are more contested than those in no harm states, not simply because the criteria are greater and more explicit, but because they can overlap and be more susceptible to ambiguity. Criteria utilized in a no harm state are broader and emphasize the most pivotal issues, sometimes in a general manner.

Even though the FERC has not taken an aggressive approach in recent merger approval processes, it did utilize a structured standard of the public interest that applies a no harm test. Generally, no harm tests address impacts to customer rates, system reliability, competitive dimensions, and capital structure and costs. The FERC adopted several specific attributes in its merger approval standard that were codified in Section 203 of the Federal Power Act.[3] These attributes allowed a determination of consistency with the public interest by addressing several merger concerns, including the following:

- the effect of the proposed on operating costs and rate levels
- the contemplated accounting treatment

- the reasonableness of the purchase price
- whether the acquiring utility has coerced the to-be-acquired utility into accepting the merger
- the effect of the proposed merger on the current competitive situation
- whether the proposed consolidation will impair existing regulation, either by the FERC or the appropriate state regulatory authority
- whether the merged companies can operate economically and efficiently as a single entity

No positive showing of merger benefits was required under FERC's public interest test, only a general showing of the general impacts on costs and rates. The no harm test applied a simpler framework for approval than others highlighted above, reflecting that FERC's interest was in avoiding adverse impacts rather than establishing a specific set of attributes that would require detailed demonstration of customer benefits, rate impacts, community implications, and risk avoidance.

The Ontario Energy Board (OEB) in Canada also follows a no harm test but further formalized its requirements. The OEB created a Handbook to Electricity Distributer and Transmitter Consolidations.[4] This document provides the general thinking of the OEB about mergers and is grounded in five objectives established by the OEB for execution of its duties:

- Protect the interests of consumer relative to prices and system reliability.
- Promote economic efficiency and cost effectiveness.
- Promote electricity efficiency and demand management.

- Facilitate implementation of a smart grid.
- Promote the adoption of renewable energy.

The OEB has crafted its no harm test to incorporate these guiding objectives for the agency into the evaluative framework it applies when presented with transactions. The OEB is seeking to identify whether any adverse outcomes could result from a merger transaction and considers two specific objectives:

- **Objective 1**—protect consumers with respect to price and the adequacy, reliability, and quality of electricity service. This element looks for demonstration that future costs will be lower than without the merger, although demonstration of this outcomes does not require a detailed review of future costs. In addition, the adequacy, reliability, and quality of service are to be guided by existing operating metrics, with an intent to encourage continuous improvement in the future.

- **Objective 2**—promote economic efficiency and cost-effectiveness and facilitate the maintenance of a financially viable electricity industry. This element looks at the expected financial capacity of the acquiring and/or combined entity and the financial impacts of the purchase price and future financing of costs associated with the transaction and integration of the combination.

These two examples of the no harm test demonstrate some difference in areas of attention, particularly between a province and a federal agency. More importantly they demonstrate a fundamental difference between a positive showing and a no harm test in establishing consistency with the public interest. A positive showing requires far more affirmative demonstration of the test and satisfaction and can include a broad mix of financial, operational, and environmental impacts. On the other hand, the no harm test addresses some of these same topics but is generally narrower and less prescriptive about quantitative demonstration since it focuses on potential adverse impacts.

When addressing how he viewed the regulatory process for deal approval, Steve Fleishman from Wolfe Research described his perspectives on their reviews and outcomes:

> The approval standards, approaches to merger application review, and quality of state regulatory agencies varies widely across the country. Timelines are longer than they need to be, common issues exist across states, though some are often narrow and state-specific, the ability to negotiate outcomes can be different, and equity in outcomes is unpredictable. All these factors create doubts about the ability of a company to successfully close a transaction.

Once a state regulatory commission investigation of a merger is docketed, the fun really begins. In addition to state regulatory commission internal staffs, the intervenor landscape is populated by representatives of consumers, industrial companies, state government, local municipalities, merchant associations, military, labor unions, trade associations, public interest groups, competitors, and a host of sometimes off-the-wall groups.

One of the curious, but entertaining, derivatives of a crowded intervenor list is how they behave. These intervenors seldom adopt fully consistent positions—rather, they are schizophrenic in their actions. Depending on the issue, they can be in lockstep, or totally unaligned, depending on their purpose in intervention, which is always self-interest.

The most ironic situation is when theoretically similar intervening parties take fundamentally and logically opposite positions on an issue. For example, merger synergies are front and center of every merger transaction. Some parties argue that the utilities are substantially inflating the claimed cost savings to sell the deal. The exact opposite position can be argued by another intervenor—that the synergies are deliberately understated to hide the ball and reduce sharing requirements.

Those are the moments during regulatory proceedings when watching cross-examination is worth the price of admission—unless you happen to be a utility legal representative charged with bringing rationality to the hearings and decision process. It is no wonder the tenure of regulatory commissioners on average is three and one-half years as they consistently have to gauge the temperature of hearings issues such as synergies. Are they too hot, too cold, or just right?

Even if the public interest test appears to be satisfied, that does not mean a transaction has smooth sailing to approval. The regulatory approval process can break down as other, less tangible issues enter the decision process. For example, the state regulatory commission perceives reputation shortcomings in the acquiror; doesn't particularly think the acquiror is the best option; has misgivings about state and local impacts; doesn't trust what it hears about financial commitment; or receives significant external pressure about the efficacy of the transaction.

Erle Nye, formerly of TXU, provided his perspective on how regulatory decisions affected the success of U.S. utility transactions:

> There is no substitute for strong regulatory relationships when a merger is pursued. Outcomes are better when your company is well run, has strong respect by your regulator, and your operating track record is commendable. Sometimes, the industry outsmarted itself by claiming high levels of synergies that simply encouraged regulators to take a bigger bite for customers. I believe regulators take more synergies for customers than justified, but they have a job to do too. I also believe that the risks that shareholders bear are not adequately recognized by

regulators, which can contribute to inequitable outcomes from the approval process.

Pursuing merger approval through its high and low points over an extended time period requires aptitude, fortitude, patience, and providence. Utility executive managements do not regularly train for mergers and related approval processes. Valuable regulatory capabilities are only gained through real-life experience.

Conditions and Commitments

The satisfaction of the public interest standard through the explicit tests referenced above is not the only critical element of obtaining approval of a merger. State regulatory commissions also frame a series of requirements for acceptance of the merger related to

Figure 21: Typical Conditions and Commitments

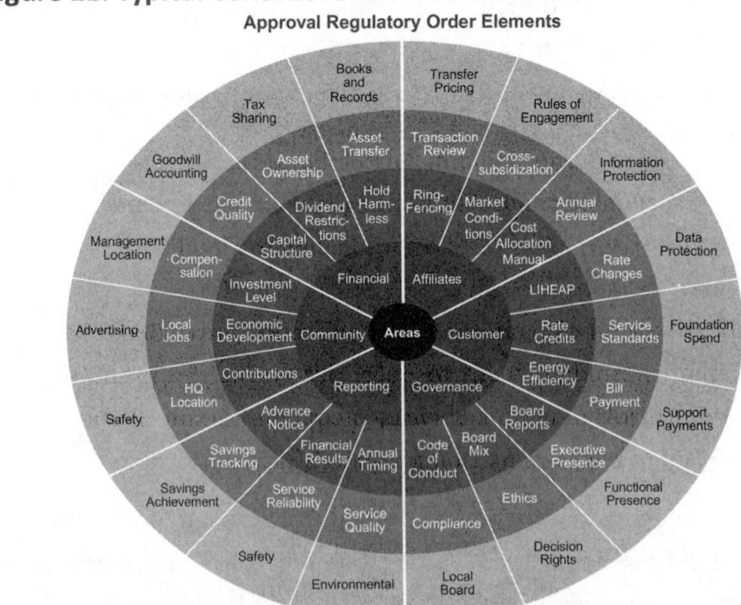

Sources: Illustrative view from state regulatory commissions orders

information reporting, compliance with proscriptions, standards of performance, capital investment, targeted expenditures, and support for policies.

These requirements frame the conditions and commitments that the combined company must agree to accept and apply after the close of the transaction. The conditions reflect state regulatory commission mandates that are often not negotiable, such as advance notice, hold harmless, code of conduct, ring-fencing, books and records, dividend restrictions, affiliated interest guidelines, and asset transfer, among many other areas—but they are not overly onerous.

Commitments are more formal and usually require specific agreement or action once the transaction is closed. Typical commitments address headquarters locations, credit ratings, service standards, economic development, energy efficiency, board composition, synergies tracking, and capital structure, with a broad range of additional requirements.

Many of these conditions and commitments relate to the normal course of business and are long-standing in utility operating jurisdictions. But a number specifically stem from the transaction itself and require specific attention from management at the close and thereafter. Most conditions and commitments established by regulatory commissions do not turn the business upside down—they can be lived with, even if a bit exasperating. More importantly, if a utility can point out that a condition or commitment is not workable, or is regressive, most state regulatory commissions will find a cure that is satisfactory to all parties.

An observed trend, however, is that the number of conditions and commitments seem to always grow as new ideas emerge or "most favored nations" approaches such as best-order elements across all jurisdictions are applied. For example, in the Duke Energy and Cinergy transaction the Kentucky Public Service Commission adopted approximately 40 conditions and commitments, while the North Carolina Public Utilities Commission adopted almost 120 requirements after several states had added to the list of original requirements and the State of North Carolina finally weighed in.

In a 2018 transaction between Great Plains Energy and Westar Energy, the Kansas Corporation Commission adopted just under 60 conditions and commitments, although many had sub-parts which increased the actual number of requirements.

Companies completing transactions in their jurisdictions should note that compliance with these conditions and commitments is not time-based. Many of the requirements are perpetual and comprise an ongoing standard of business conduct, and even those that appear temporary can have long windows for expected reporting or action.

For example, since the mid-2000s, the requirement to conduct regular synergies tracking, which can extend for years, became commonplace and was structured to provide for periodic reporting, which could be monthly, quarterly, or annually.

Synergies tracking was not a general requirement in most of the early transactions. The practice extends back into the 1980s with the PacifiCorp and Utah Power & Light transaction, but became more common as state regulatory commissions were interested both in targets being met and in ensuring that higher-than-target synergies capture could be identified and recognized as part of ongoing performance reporting or in subsequent rate cases.

Synergies tracking is not onerous, but often receives push-back from utilities as administratively cumbersome and unnecessary depending on the nature of the regulatory plan. State regulatory commission mandated tracking usually requires timely reporting on synergies attainment and CTA incurrence at a discrete level, for example, cost type, line item, and individual category.

For staffing reductions, this category is relatively easy since discrete position reductions from a merger typically occur at specified dates, or within time windows, and can be separated from all other additions and subtractions to the workforce by cause. In this case, the starting point staffing baseline is known, the targeted reductions are known, the targeted reduction timing is planned, and the actual reductions and timing can be identified from typical human resource separation activities such as severance actions, paycheck eliminations, and exit meetings.

Non-labor synergies are somewhat harder to determine as reductions are often fungible with other related expenditures. Cost avoidance or elimination actions, like a planned future expenditure such as a technology system being cancelled, or reduced directors resulting in foregone board payments, are permanently turned off and simple to identify, quantify, and report.

Operating cost reductions, for example, shareholder services, professional services, or benefits, are a little more of an art, as total costs are reduced, but not in as discrete a manner as avoidances. There will be a need to separate baseline cost elements and escalation from reductions due to consolidation or changed performance plans. In these cases, more description of process changes and cost impacts will be necessary.

The most complex synergies element for tracking is when economies of scale, that is, purchasing leverage, comes into play for third-party expenditures like insurance, materials, and contracts. These areas create unit cost differences which are harder to distinguish between quantity, prices, timing, and comparability of items. In these cases, more detailed decomposition of baselines, market changes, activity incidence, and decision drivers are necessary. While more complicated, tracking, outcome analysis, quantification, and reporting are still doable, even if requiring a little more digging to obtain necessary insights.

CTA is another tracking requirement, but it is simpler because it is largely front-end loaded and costs typically follow events (separations), payments (professional fees), expenses (carry-over insurance), or projects (system conversion). Each of these CTA types create a paper trail that can readily be determined from work orders, invoices, or disbursements.

Both synergies and CTA tracking typically last until steady state is achieved, which is between three and five years after close. The majority of CTA tracking is completed by the end of year three, although small amounts in each category may continue if third-party contracts or licenses are in play. While synergies continue into perpetuity, state regulatory commissions tend to be satisfied with prior reporting to date since the next rate case obscures the future distinction between synergies and the ongoing costs of the business.

Shareholder Risks

Merger transactions always bring into focus the tension related to providing fair and equitable outcomes for stakeholders from a combination. As foremost in regulators' minds as customers are, shareholders are just the opposite and too frequently become the forgotten party to a deal, despite the sustained financial support they provide and the risks they assume.

Adversarial parties to a merger approval process tend to ascribe a notion that shareholders are already compensated in a merger transaction through a merger premium received. For an acquiree, that is initially true, but for both the acquiror and acquiree long term, that is, the new company, it is not true unless specifically established in the regulatory approval order.

When shareholders support a transaction, they do so with the expectations that the outcome of the transaction will ultimately create accretion to earnings and share value in recompense for the absorption of financial costs and execution risks. Their approval of the transaction and the use of the balance sheet in cash, stock, or some combination of the two is tethered to the belief and trust that any short-term dilution will be replaced by greater earnings from synergies and enhanced strategic and financial positioning over the long term.

Shareholders directly face and accept numerous risks related to their shares in an acquiring company or as a result of a two-company merger situation. These risks are borne from the moment a merger announcement occurs, through the receipt of state regulatory commission approval and over a three-to-five-year window until post-close operations achieve steady state.

ANNOUNCEMENT PERIOD

With the announcement of a transaction, shareholders find themselves facing immediate risks. Investors will instantly react, rating agencies will quickly weigh in, and management can quickly become distracted. Much of the risk borne at this stage is externally driven and less controllable by management, with exception of how Wall Street perceives the purchase premium—too dilutive and it will be hard to shed that baggage. Thus, risks to shareholder value start with transaction disclosure and few are mitigated until much later in the merger approval cycle.

- **Pricing risk**: Shareholders depend on boards and managements being prudent stewards of the capital they have provided. If transaction pricing is disciplined, then shareholders can be more comfortable that earnings dilution can be mitigated or avoided. If pricing is aggressive, then shareholders witness future earnings dilution from new share issuance and future regulatory and management actions in the approval process become critical to mitigating these impacts.

- **Market risk**: The investment community immediately evaluates transaction pricing, structures, rationale, and actions, and reprices acquiring company stock the day of announcement. As a group, investors have good insight into management's ability to make good on initial commitments and produce favorable outcomes. They closely parse early management statements to develop a quick perspective on whether the industrial logic for a transaction is compelling and persuasive to hold the stock price.

- **Performance risk**: Investors know that managements become distracted once a transaction is announced and attention begins to turn outward. Managements also recognize that employees are immediately overcome with a mix of pride and dread once a deal is announced. Without careful and immediate attention to these outcomes, confidence in ongoing performance can be diluted and lead to further pricing pressure, which exacerbates shareholder value exposure.

APPROVAL PERIOD

Most transaction risk occurs during the extended time frame between approval filing and receipt of a commission order, when managements are at the mercy of a process driven by political appointments or public elections. These risks relate to how well management communicates customer benefits from the transaction, and how effectively they convince regulators that business risk is negligible. In this elapsed period, companies need to actively frame the context for regulatory outcomes, even if they are not the principal influencers of a decision.

- **Execution risk**: Most employees in the business are not affected by a transaction before it is approved, but a lapse in operational performance can cause a ripple effect back to regulators, which creates additional scrutiny on management's ability to effectively execute post-close. Shareholders count on management to continue to operate the business as planned and to avoid any drop-off in performance outcomes that can create short-term earnings difficulty or shake the confidence of regulators in management capabilities.

- **Regulatory risk**: From the moment a transaction goes public, management is overwhelmed to rapidly create its approval filings, build a persuasive storyline and rationale, satisfy all necessary data requests for the business, and persuasively position the transaction with stakeholders at multiple levels. Shareholders assume management is actively focused on ensuring regulators and intervenors have more information than they need to avoid protracting and complicating an already treacherous process.

- **Order risk**: Success in a regulatory order is characterized by no surprises, equitable outcomes, and tolerable requirements. Every action from announcement through order receipt has been directed toward prosecution of the filing and mitigation of outcome risk. Shareholders dissect the actions of regulators through the entire process and focus on whether schedule adherence, synergies acceptance, CTA recognition, synergies distribution, conformance actions, and approval conditions enable expectations.

POST-CLOSE PERIOD

Companies often take a huge sigh of relief once a transaction is approved, but this is both misguided and perilous. Absolutely nothing has occurred regarding how the combined companies will perform after the close—all that has been achieved is the right to pursue success. The hard work of ensuring a transaction results in attainment of management expectations has yet to start and may exist outside what planning has been completed. At this stage of the transaction life cycle, future success is entirely driven by management, with no other antagonists to blame.

- **Strategic risk**: While the business is integrating post-close, the internal management bandwidth to pursue parallel or entirely new strategic initiatives is usually diminished in the short term, which creates additional risks to long-term positioning. Shareholders rely on boards to continue to apply in-place governance processes to maintain sufficient focus on preserving future flexibility and supporting planned priorities, so long-term enterprise value is not foregone or diluted.

- **Financial risk**: Post-close requirements and constraints can have adverse impacts on balance sheet flexibility, credit quality, and earnings growth and quality. Shareholders continue to bear the risk of financial performance challenges, whether due to policy shifts, near-term rate credits, future rate cases, or market volatility. These risks to shareholders and the value of this group's shareholdings rise and fall with the capability of management to be effective stewards of capital.

- **Execution risk**: Much of the value from a transaction to customers and shareholders is linked to the level of merger synergies obtained. Values may have been attributed to these savings, but integration plans have been crafted and few synergies start immediately at close. The ability to capture and retain these synergies lies in management capabilities to follow the synergies delivery plan, as well as manage the business effectively through a multi-year period when cost savings are realized.

- **Market risk**: Inevitably the circumstances at the time of the announcement have changed by the close of the transaction and new risks to future earnings levels and certainty arise. Shareholders bear the same normal risks to their ownership as would occur without a merger; however, the dexterity of management to both integrate the business and reposition the enterprise for the future is a greater challenge than normally expected, thus risks to positioning are increased.

Shareholders provide the at-risk capital to enable transactions to occur and succeed. Consequently, they are entitled to reward for the risks assumed prior to close, as well as those faced post-close. If shareholders are not compensated for the strategic, financial, regulatory, execution, and value risks they have assumed, the value of their holdings will be permanently diluted and essentially transferred to customers.

Joe Sauvage from Citi provided insights on how regulation affects the dynamics of transactions:

> CEOs rely heavily on their counterpart's ability to deliver regulatory approval from another jurisdiction—it's just natural to expect local regulatory relationships to be stronger. But the financial stakes are getting continually higher, and customer benefits from rate credits, economic development, energy efficiency, and targeted demographic funding are having a high economic impact. Incidentally, it's funny how a despised utility can become beloved overnight when it may be acquired. This shift in attitude and requirements suggests it's important to be realistic and flexible about the costs to secure a transaction.

The simple concept that shareholder risk assumption requires specific recognition in regulatory decisions is often overlooked, if not argued as irrelevant and gratuitous. Fortunately, there is a decent track record of state regulatory commission cognizance of shareholder risk and adoption of treatments to mitigate these risks.

Synergies Distribution

For utility management, it is often hard to put its finger on the most difficult issue to address in fully satisfying the public interest standard. However, experience suggests the centerpiece to transaction success is negotiating an equitable distribution of merger synergies between shareholders and customers. This outcome determines the short- and long-term financial viability of the combining companies and success of a merger.

When utilities provide their estimates of synergies from consolidation, they provide a view of total available gross and net savings, that is, an all-in view of benefits, and a coincident view that recognizes the costs associated with enabling the merger to happen and customer benefits to be derived.

Some regulatory commissions take a myopic view of merger synergies and believe customers to be the rightful recipient of all benefits derived from the combination. Others take a view that most merger synergies should flow to the benefit of customers. But many state regulatory commissions rightly recognize merger synergies are not the sole province of either party. Joint entitlement to an equitable sharing of cost savings is smart policy and a justifiable outcome.

This last category of state regulatory commissions believe that an equitable outcome of a merger should reflect a plus or minus 50 percent distribution between shareholders and customers to encourage

Figure 22: Regulatory Synergies Distribution

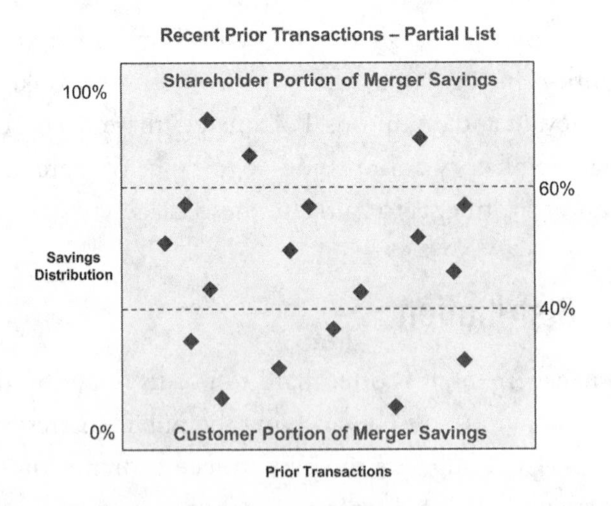

Source: Company filings; Strategy& (part of the PwC network)

industry consolidation and enhance effective operations and efficient costs. This approximately 50-50 split outcome has been achieved in a respectable number of transactions from 1995 to today.

Once the level of merger synergies is agreed upon, state regulatory commissions immediately turn to the question of how to pass savings along to customers, at what level, and how fast. Given how fast decision momentum can happen within a state regulatory commission, utilities need to have made their arguments for synergies sharing in their approval application filing. Hoping to begin to negotiate an outcome at a late juncture in a proceeding stacks the deck against the utility with predictably unwelcome results.

If synergies sharing was not requested at the outset, what responsibility does the state regulatory commission have to provide a separate award after the fact? The answer is obviously none, as regulators have no responsibility to provide an independent estimate or decision grant, which places shareholders at significant risk of being adversely treated.

Combining companies need to ensure that the following three specific decisions are addressed within the scope of their merger approval testimony to prepare for equitable synergies sharing:

- CTA needs to be offset against gross savings before addressing sharing distribution.
- Timing differences between synergies realization and CTA incurrence need to be recognized to reflect actual cash flows.
- Specific means by which to recognize synergies need to be defined.
    - **Net savings**: The amount of savings to be split between shareholders and customers is a table stake for decision-making. For example, if certain CTA items are excluded from consideration, the sharing result will be skewed toward customers.

- **Distribution timing**: *When* savings accrue is as important as *how much* is captured. For example, if proposed savings are distributed before actual realization, then customers are being subsidized by shareholders.

- **Pass-back methods**: The means adopted to flow net savings to customers affects the value of the distribution itself. For example, immediate credits provide a different form and level of benefit than a rate moratorium or an *as-earned* reduction,

For each dollar of CTA not recognized by regulatory commissions in defining relevant net savings, shareholder value is diminished because real out-of-pocket costs to execute the merger are not recognized. Numerous regulatory commissions disallow certain transaction or transition costs, for example, investment banker and professional service fees, and change-in-control costs because they believe they should be borne by shareholders. Other than the reality these costs are significant in value and convenient to disallow to reduce CTA, there is no legitimate reason not to recognize both, particularly if shareholders are not adequately compensated for risk in another form.

Transaction fees are a necessity as deals cannot be accomplished (and thus benefits cannot be realized) without their incurrence. Boards insist upon investment banker advice and Wall Street and shareholders would be surprised and quick to castigate or sue management if financial advisory activities were not undertaken to ensure appropriate deal pricing and thoroughly review a proposed transaction for fairness. And support in financial and tax matters is a natural need of management to assess and position a transaction, as well as protect both shareholders and customers from potentially harmful outcomes.

Similarly, change-in-control costs are simply one other dimension of executive compensation, though this is a zero-sum game. The only alternative is to increase the cash baseline or bonus compensation to reflect the market cost of executive attraction and retention, which essentially creates no net compensation difference if the objective is to retain intact the leadership team, with or without a transaction.

The timing of when net synergies are passed back to customers is particularly critical to determining equity in savings sharing. The cash flows for synergies and CTA move in opposite directions, that is, front-end loaded CTA often exceeds annual back-end loaded synergies. If state regulatory commissions insist on immediate rate credits to customers, these credits are paid from current earnings, not by the synergies realized.

This approach is confiscatory from shareholders since it requires the utility and its shareholders to incur a cost that would never have been realized absent the transaction, while the related benefits are still to be realized sometime in the future. If annual gross savings are offset exactly by net savings occurring in the same year as synergies are realized, then shareholders are not disadvantaged, nor are customers subsidized.

The methods used to share savings with customers have obviously different impacts to total value being distributed. An immediate rate credit generally has no linkage to any element of synergies realization because no net cost savings exist in year one. They are dwarfed by CTA and shareholders are disadvantaged immediately at close. But it is a convenient method for regulatory commissions to prove they are looking out for customers, even if its fairness is rightly disputed.

Rate moratoriums pose a different set of issues and these *stay-out* (agreement not to file rate cases) provisions reverse the flow of synergies; shareholders retain all cost savings until the next rate case when they flow to customers. This approach benefits shareholders for the fixed time frame of the rate moratorium, while leaving customers without near-term benefits.

Before moving past this synergies distribution discussion, it should be noted that the mechanics of synergies sharing are simple—either fix the annual dollar amount (a constant value), follow year-to-year net synergies attainment (a rising value), or establish an annual range of available synergies that reflects performance (a dynamic value).

When net synergies are measured, the mechanism to pass synergies to shareholders is to essentially create a *contra-cost*, which adds back the shareholder portion of the savings to O&M, thus only recognizing a partial cost reduction for customers in line with the intent of original sharing principles. Thus, when O&M costs are reduced by $1 million, customer charges would only be reduced by $500,000 (if 50 percent sharing), as the other $500,000 is preserved for shareholders as a contribution against earnings dilution or for earnings accretion. Thus, the customer rate reduction only reflects their portion of O&M reduction, that is, the flow through of $500,000.

Even with a multi-year retention of cost savings by shareholders, they are still disadvantaged because synergies ramp up to steady state through year three and rate moratoriums seldom last more than three-to-five years. On a present value basis, the perpetual pass-back of cost savings far exceeds the limited benefits to shareholders, which exacerbates the inequitable position of shareholders.

So, are there other ways utilities could fashion an approach that provides an alternative to the *bottom-up* approach to outcome measurement and reporting? Companies might seek to have the regulatory commission adopt an approach that simplifies the measurement of actual realized savings and allows for comparison of *before and after* adjusted costs. This approach is the O&M index and was used by both Entergy and Kansas Power & Light in earlier transactions with their regulatory commissions.[5]

The approach essentially looks at forecast O&M costs at the time of the merger (original forecast), less expected synergies (expected forecast), and compares that level to what has been achieved post-close (realized forecast) and extended into future years to derive how overall O&M costs have behaved.

Future costs are not precisely known, but are reflected in regular utility forecasts, and future synergies are also not precisely known, but are based on the detailed analyses underlying the original merger approval filing. Both forecast O&M and synergies are deescalated to allow values to be assessed in constant dollars to take inflation differences out of consideration.

Further, original, expected, and realized forecast O&M costs are adjusted for specific factors affecting cost incurrence that have nothing to do with the merger or are uncontrollable, but could impact the addressable cost baselines like transmission service for others, pensions, bad debts, mandated efficiency expenditures, unusual litigation costs, new programs, non-recurring expenses, and similar items.

Since merger synergies do not typically arise from the types of cost elements captured above, the baselines come closer to the affectable costs of the combined company and the pure results of actual synergies obtained, that is, unforeseen and unrelated costs are removed to create a consistent baseline for comparison.

The original forecast O&M costs are compared to the expected forecast O&M costs. To the extent the realized forecast O&M costs are higher than the adjusted forecast O&M costs even with expected synergies, then there has been a savings shortfall and the combining utilities may be at risk for recognizing full synergies expectations without adequate savings. To the extent the realized forecast O&M costs are less than the adjusted forecast O&M costs, then actual synergies realized are presumed to exceed expectations.

When realized synergies exceed expected synergies, then the combined company have fully met their synergies commitments and there is a surplus that can be further distributed to shareholders and customers in an equitable manner. That savings distribution would be agreed to prior to the conclusion of the merger approval process.

This O&M index approach obviates detailed synergies tracking and provides an incentive to the combined company to exceed expected cost savings and benefit from that outcome. The O&M index can be a useful tool to complement or substitute for other 50-50 sharing mechanisms and avoid extended tracking of actual accomplishment at a detailed synergies category level.

So, how should combining companies address the inequities that can result from an unbalanced and inequitable regulatory plan? The best guidance is what tends to work at all levels of business in general: keep it simple and treat shareholders and customers as partners.

The number one objective of combining companies is to complete a proposed transaction as rapidly as possible, which presupposes an equitable outcome as a foundation for that occurrence. The ability to successfully create and convince a regulatory commission of an elegant sharing distribution, with multiple pieces, is not a time-tested result. It is far better to rely on where industry precedent exists, based on a common acceptance that mergers will not happen without fair shareholder treatment, and customers cannot benefit if no merger occurs at all.

There is no substitute for the clear presentation of argument for an equitable synergies distribution that reflects the risks borne by shareholders, the level of net savings available, the timing to break-even between synergies and CTA, the methods to reflect synergies in rates, and the treatment of ongoing synergies after the initial period of the regulatory plan.

By and large, most state regulatory commissions understand the logic that customer benefits cannot be derived without acknowledging that risks are borne, and costs are incurred, to conceive and close a transaction. Fortunately, only a couple of state regulatory commissions act like there should be a free lunch and shareholders should just be happy with deal approval.

While state regulatory commission precedent is important, it can quickly change with elections, appointments, or other governmental or local sentiments. The merger approval application is the first and best chance to make the case for synergies distribution because this is when the opportunity to present a holistic and integrated argument for desired treatment most naturally exists. While regulatory lawyers may argue to wait on regulatory plan design until the direction of the case is known, this is a recipe for a poor but deserved outcome. No good has ever resulted from an approach that essentially offers to negotiate later.

The argument needs to be logically sound and empirically demonstrated. It starts with a recitation of the role played by shareholders and the risks they assume and finishes with the demonstration of how each of these two stakeholders are financially impacted by the proposed synergies distribution. Yes, defining guiding principles are stated, but no ambiguous philosophies and no hiding the ball on benefits distribution and values.

Most state regulatory commissions and utilities have little foresight about the long term, so architecting a life-of-business regulatory plan may be an exercise in futility. Again, it is probably better to directly focus on the first five years post-close with specificity, frame the compelling long-term equity argument, and then separately (and quickly) address the mechanics of long-term equity in a separate proceeding or the next rate case.

The regulatory plan should provide a holistic view of how all elements of the merger approval align and integrate public interest test conformance; risk recognition; synergies opportunities; CTA requirements; synergies sharing; conditions and commitments compliance; and synergies tracking and reporting.

In most transactions, both regulators and companies assume that at the end of a three-to-five-year regulatory plan period no further consideration of longer-term synergies treatment will happen. This is short-sighted and further exacerbates the confiscation of shareholder value.

Shareholders provide the front-end capital and bear the risks of transaction completion and post-close integration success until execution risks are fully compensated, related costs are recovered, and earnings are sustainably accretive. None of this happens in the first three-to-five years without specific regulatory treatment, and any shortfall—CTA recovery or accretion—is permanently lost if not addressed.

More importantly, while incremental value to customers continues into perpetuity in the form of lower costs, zero value attributes to shareholders after the end of the regulatory plan period. This asymmetrical outcome is inconsistent with long-standing regulatory principles of equitable treatment and no confiscation of shareholder value.

However, several ways to cure this inequity exist that allow shareholders to continue to share in merger benefits. First, a simple return on equity sharing band can be employed to set a range of financial performance. If companies earn above the midpoint of the range, then a portion of that amount could be recognized as earnings to be distributed to shareholders.

This distribution could be symmetrical, for example, 50-50, or asymmetrical, that is, 60 percent to customers and 40 percent to shareholders, or some other reasonable split, depending on the value gap that is embedded in the original regulatory plan—essentially shareholders earn out their dilution and risk absorption over a longer-period of time and are not foreclosed from this opportunity.

Another way to fix regulatory plan shortcomings to shareholders is to simply capitalize the future stream of synergies as a deferred asset and amortize a portion of this amount as a fixed offset (contra expense) to annual O&M. This treatment recognizes the ongoing value being produced by the company and funded by shareholders and creates certainty of equitable outcomes for shareholders.

Transaction Timelines

U.S. utilities merger transactions do not follow the path of industrial, financial, and consumer transactions which can be completed inside a calendar quarter, assuming no anti-trust issues or competitive bids emerge. Utilities deals can range anywhere from the 90-day *rocket docket* in Kentucky, to a year or more if multiple states are involved or the transaction has meaningful business challenges from a regulatory perspective, such as territory dispersion, wholesale markets, business diversity, nuclear licenses, or scale step-up.

The initial influence on the schedule is how long it takes the merging companies to file their merger approval application. The application includes both testimony and supporting detail surrounding merger rationale and benefits, as well as transaction structure, financial outcomes, accounting treatment, operational matters, synergies sources, affiliate interests, and customer impacts.

The general duration between merger announcement and application filing is within 60 days, with some as quick as within a month and others calibrated more closely to the expectation of the overall schedule, which could extend on average between eight and ten months.

Once the application is filed, a process ensues at the regulatory commission to establish an official schedule for discovery, hearings,

Figure 23: Regulatory Close Timelines

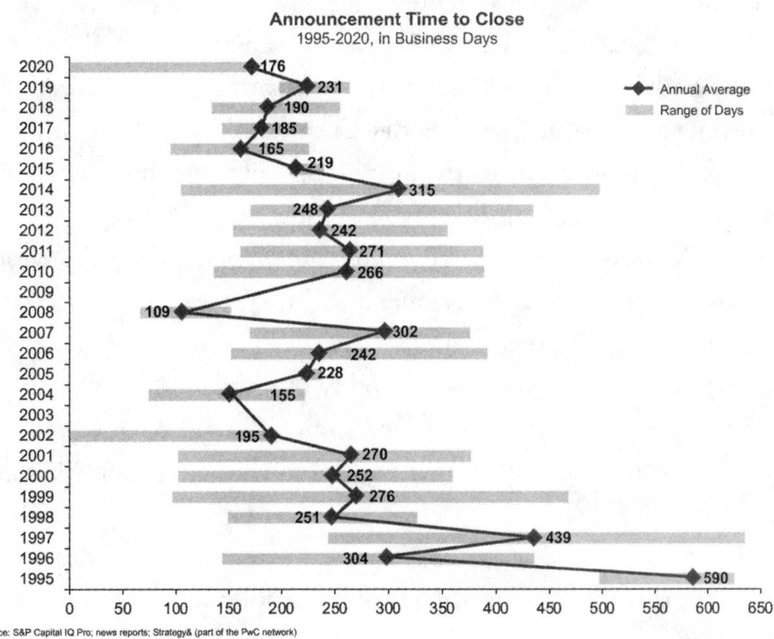

and deliberation to either conform to existing merger review statutes or reflect a negotiated time frame between the parties.

The track record of the U.S. utilities industry has been trending more favorably with respect to total elapsed timing from announcement to close from the early days of schedules that turned out to be unattainable and meaningless.

Transactions in the early days were hard to estimate, particularly if there were competing federal and state regulatory jurisdiction issues to resolve. Between 1995 and 1999, the average time to close was approximately 14–16 months (except for 1995 and 1996 vintage transactions, where 20+ months was not uncommon). As transactions were new to regulatory commissions and market power, convergence and PUHCA issues were heavily litigated.[6]

From 2000 to 2004, this time frame slightly declined as both companies and regulatory commissions became focused on avoiding open-ended merger reviews. In this time frame, the average duration was approximately 10–12 months, as a number of regulatory commissions had previously reviewed transactions and were familiar with the issues that warranted close review.[7]

During the 2005 and 2009 time frame, the nature of utilities transactions evolved, with both international buyers and financial sponsors becoming active as deal originators. Even with this added complexity, plus a few multi-state deals, the average approval timeline increased to approximately 15–18 months.[8]

The 2010 to 2014 period had fewer utilities industry transactions, although some of the larger ones in history occurred in this window. These larger transactions also caused some state legislatures and state regulatory commissions to modify their relevant statutes to provide for greater clarity on merger approval standards. Nonetheless, the average merger approval duration continued at approximately 15–18 months.[9]

In the final period of the 25-year modern era of utility M&A (2015 to 2020), the time frame for merger completion centered around

10-12 months, with some transactions approved within approximately eight to nine months, reflecting broad industry experience, serial acquirors, and experienced state regulatory commissions.[10]

From an observer's perspective, federal-level regulators were originally a principal causation for extended time frames for the reasons mentioned. State regulatory commissions have, on balance, been far quicker to process merger approval applications, even when multi-state jurisdictions have been involved. Companies have also gotten better at addressing merger approval standards and providing sufficient information to enable faster regulatory commission evaluation and decision-making.

While utility industry transactions take longer than is necessary, state regulatory commissions have not been an oppressive weight to merger approval. Statutes control timing in numerous states, while regulatory commission practices often influence the schedule for review and completion.

Several opportunities do exist for the utilities industry and regulatory commission to streamline overall merger review timing. First, companies can accelerate their approval application filing to 30 (or fewer) days by starting work pre-announcement if it appears purchase price negotiations are progressing well. Much information is readily available, and testimony can be drafted internally or with external support.

Second, companies and state regulators can work together to compress the time frame between approval application filing and setting the final procedural schedule to kick off merger evaluation, which can save weeks.

Finally, state regulators can be more prescriptive of the information to be provided in an approval application, much like they have established standard filing requirements in many states for rate cases. This effort would standardize the general requirements for filing and contextualize information needs beyond sometimes open-ended standards and ambiguous criteria. Each of these filing and timing enhancements could contribute to shrinking an elongated merger approval schedule without sacrificing the ability of regulators and intervenors to fully review a merger application.

Key Takeaways

There are no ends to the challenges that proposed transactions face in achieving deal success. Some are observable early, while others take time to appear. When deals do not get to the announcement stage, one or more of the following factors may be at the root of termination:

- Adequate pricing could never be reached.
- Social issues could not be agreed on.
- Financial outcomes risks could not be mitigated
- Perceived regulatory risks exceeded transaction benefits.
- Initial synergies were insufficient to justify the risks.
- A fair proportion of synergies retention could not be achieved.
- The integration of the companies was believed to be too long and disruptive to warrant the effort.

Most of the attention on transaction hurdles typically centers on the regulatory approval process—after all, there is nothing to talk about if a premium and structure could never be agreed on.

The ability to move transactions through the regulatory process in the early years of the modern era of utility M&A was challenged, mostly because federal and state regulators were in conflict over jurisdiction, facts, and mitigation steps. These regulatory agencies each wanted their requirements to prevail and utilities were caught between these two groups, which sometimes extended approval periods beyond two years, ultimately sinking the deals of their own weight. Standing back from the state regulatory commission approval process suggests there are several key elements to remember:

- A formal regulatory plan at announcement is a prerequisite. *Offering no plan leaves a critical vacuum that creates an open ask with no ceiling to regulators.*
- Synergies levels have little meaning for the business without the ability to retain a portion for shareholders. *Upfront focus on this issue is a table stake for success.*
- The regulatory plan needs both short- and long-term attention. *It is difficult to try and revisit long-term needs later when regulators have no incentive for consideration.*
- Shareholders bear transaction risks from announcement to through, and beyond, close. *Recognition and compensation of these risks is necessary for an equitable result.*
- Regulators frequently do not recognize transaction and change-in-control costs. *These costs are legitimate, but cannot be recovered if not asked and argued in the filing.*
- Regulators and intervenors are schizophrenic over same or related issues. *Synergies levels are suspect, even as significant costs to achieve receive little attention.*
- Regulators have been equitable with the sharing of synergies between shareholders and customers, *but 50-50 sharing requires more active and compelling argument each filing.*
- Rate moratoriums are a popular approach in a regulatory plan, *but continuing capital spend levels suggest earnings alternatives could achieve a similar multi-year outcome.*
- Regulatory conditions have a habit of growing over time and across jurisdictions. *Expect favored nation considerations to be applied.*

- Commitments to regulators offer attractive options for policy support that can create shareholder benefits. *Targeted investment is a positive tool for increasing deal value.*

In later years, a few transactions also had difficulties, particularly those involving financial sponsors or deals where cash flow and/or investment commitment vulnerability could exist from overpricing. However, state regulatory commissions generally provided a means to cure transaction weaknesses, through either re-hearings or re-trading the deal. Few deals in the last decade did not ultimately navigate the regulatory shoals, though for some the price of passage was steep.

The U.S. utilities industry has enjoyed great success in satisfying sometimes ambiguous standards on consistency or promotion of the public interest. Specific challenges to transaction structure, financial integrity, synergies levels, synergies sharing, and post-close risks continue to arise and can be vexing to solve, but the industry has found adequate ways to preserve deal viability in the face of these issues.

The FERC and SEC have not been impediments to completing transactions in the last 15 or more years, both preceding and following PUHCA repeal. State regulatory commissions occupy center stage on transaction approvals and will consider a broad range of issues, although the predominant focus is on financial stability, particularly in an all-cash deal with accompanying debt, and the level of supportable synergies and distribution between shareholders and customers.

Success in achieving merger close is more likely when utilities invest their front-end effort in building a compelling and persuasive case for the transaction complete with deep demonstration of rationale, benefits, impacts, and risks. The early start of this filing preparation and storyline also benefits companies by allowing the regulatory approval clock to start earlier.

But even a good case in the approval application for the transaction does not eliminate aggressive challenges from key intervenors and state regulatory commission staffs. These challenges are easy to predict. There will often not be enough synergies or synergies will be overstated. There will be too much debt or an overpriced premium, too little capital spend/unnecessary capital spend, etc., and can occur from either or both groups, sometimes in conflict with one another. In these cases, the good fight will include both rationale and empirics to carry the day in an acceptable manner to the combining companies.

U.S. utilities have been able to receive equitable deal approvals with many accomplishing 50-50 (or close) synergies sharing between shareholders and customers. Even though occasionally difficult to deal with, state regulatory commissions have acted responsibly and provided reasonable decision outcomes to preserve and balance the interests of both shareholders and customers. The open challenge to utilities now is to address how to preserve the benefits of realized synergies to shareholders for more than just a three-to-five-year period.

CHAPTER 7

SUCCESSFUL EXECUTION

The close of the merger is typically met with both celebration and relief after a concentrated effort to reach merger application approval. But as grueling as the application approval process has been after nine-to-twelve months of intense activity, the true success of the combined company now rests on how flawlessly the integration effort is executed.

To add a further dose of reality, at close the real integration work has yet to start. It may have been planned, but anticipated plans are *ex ante* and intended outcomes are *ex post*. The more sobering news is that the responsibility for the integration effort largely lies with leaders and individuals not always involved with the primary elements of the pre-announcement strategic, financial, operational, or regulatory evaluations.

As combining companies approach integration of stand-alone operations, they ask themselves several questions regarding how to think about integration as a post-announcement activity:

- When should integration planning be initiated?
- What should be the focus of integration?
- Who should be involved with integration planning?
- Should a steering committee be utilized?
- How are non-steering committee officers involved?
- How many stages comprise the integration process?
- How many different teams are required?
- How should team leaders and members be selected?
- How do we sustain a focus on business execution?
- How do we transition between pre- and post-close activities?

Notwithstanding receipt of the merger application approval, management needs to understand its next steps are pivotal to achieving the intended outcomes of the transaction. A convenient way of thinking about what needs to happen immediately post-close is to think of four *pillars* that usually closely framed the rationale for the transaction at its inception:

- **Strategic value**: how the transaction enables the combined company to create additional value sources and/or enhance existing sources within the scope of the current enterprise (e.g., new lines of business, platforms, partners, etc.)

- **Financial strength**: how the integrity of combined company finance metrics could be advantaged to provide additional flexibility, resilience, and capacity (e.g., capital structure, credit ratings, cash flows, etc.)

- **Operating prowess**: how the operations of the combined company could be enhanced through asset management, field productivity and technology capability improvement (e.g., capital investment, network delivery, work execution, etc.)

- **Market positioning**: how the offering portfolio and quality of customer relationships could be expanded and elevated from the transaction (e.g., product development, market channels, pricing innovation, etc.)

These *pillars* link an enterprise-level view of what the transaction is trying to accomplish, with the practicalities of designing an integration process that prioritizes the need for Day 1 readiness, functional alignment, and process assimilation in a post-close model.

The integration process is the linchpin between strategic vision, financial outcomes, operational expectations, and customer positioning underlying the original transaction, and the expectations for post-close benefits realization—market, economic, and performance.

Unless companies are serial acquirors, most first-time acquirors or partners vastly underestimate the complexity and rigor of integration. This process demands sustained and well-coordinated effort from companies and is generally not completed for at least three years. All the while, the business is expected to operate effectively in parallel to this effort.

Retired CEO Dick Kelly discussed how Xcel Energy approached integration of two combining companies:

> We recognized that two companies have two cultures, and it is difficult to embrace one another at the outset. Our message was to make the combined company the best we could be, not to use consensus to meet in the middle. We wanted the new company to not think mine versus yours, but to embrace the notion

the new company would be ours. This required personalized actions and we worked hard to be unbiased and quicker, better, faster, and uncompromising in our approach to positioning.

While job one of post-close companies is to keep the business running smoothly, job one-A is to ensure that the combined company is rapidly and effectively integrated and the promised deal value is realized. It needs to execute the transition stage with the same level of zeal and commitment it dedicates to ensuring high levels of day-to-day system reliability, service quality, and public safety.

A debate always ensues over the wisdom of creating a discrete integration structure or simply embedding these responsibilities with line management that ultimately needs to manage the outcomes from integration. Companies can choose to streamline and simplify integration leadership, but to make integration execution just another part of day-to-day operations is high risk and a recipe for sub-optimization of outcomes.

The reality of integration is there are no do-overs—you only get to integrate once, so do it well. A failure to conceive and execute a strong integration discipline substantially increases the likelihood of merger shortcomings or failures that cannot be recaptured, at least not without avoidable disruption.

Integration Execution

It does not take long for utility managements to recognize that integration execution is a tougher chore than expected, and more demanding of disciplined planning and rigorous accomplishment. After all, the first word in merger is "me," and people impacts dominate integration thinking and execution. Accordingly, experienced companies know that the integration planning process needs to start as soon after the merger announcement date as feasible, if not before, and experience suggests that three-to-four weeks is sufficient lead time to ready these efforts.

When talking about the importance of the integration process, Gale Klappa of WEC Energy suggested this process was vital to their merger success:

> While some companies believe their merger integration process yielded mixed results, I'm very happy with the results of ours. We start with several foundational elements: mission clarity, measurable objectives, and clear accountability. We focus on attaining results, even if it takes a little longer to realize them. We recognize that successful integration is not a sprint.

Utilities have three key milestones to focus their planning around: Day 1, Day 365, and long-lead-time target dates.

- **Day 1**: The first milestone is critical and signals the first day of combined company operations. At or by this date, the combined company needs to conduct all close activities, launch the enterprise, and initiate actual integration (versus only planning).

- **Day 365**: Actual integration activities begin immediately and extend through a series of targeted date stage gates. With the usual integration period extending three or more years, formal annual review enables recalibration and reprioritization of to-go activities.

- **Long lead time**: Many essential activities (e.g., technology applications) cannot be immediately integrated and require extended time frames for execution. The multi-year schedules of specific projects require extensive visibility and continuous management.

Six important activity areas also lead to fundamental outcomes of the process:

- Organization model
- Executive appointment
- Staffing finalization
- Process alignment
- System conversion
- Performance management

  - **Organizational model**: Downstream integration activities are grounded in how roles are designed, and interfaces established. This activity is partially accomplished by the close, but perhaps only through several levels of the model with more delineation to ensue.

  - **Executive appointment**: Organization design leads to leadership selection, which is necessary to drive integration after the close. These appointments are made prior to Day 1 through certain levels, and any carry-over dates need to be minimized.

  - **Staffing finalization**: The resources necessary to operate the business are established during integration planning. But if organizational model definition has not been thoroughly addressed, cascading roll-outs will impact other integration activities.

  - **Process alignment**: Creation of single process for the enterprise is necessary to allow work activities to be streamlined and consolidated. Since future resource-level changes are dependent on common process integration, synergies follow these activities:

- **System conversion**: Multiple activities exist across the enterprise and have integration schedules that can extend for three or more years. Each task is a unique project and is a fundamental predicate for common execution and resource optimization.

- **Performance management**: The business needs to be ready to operate as a single enterprise on Day 1, even as integration continues. Common metrics enable clear standards for achievement and are evaluated and designed prior to the close.

Each of these milestones and activities reflect critical undertakings necessary to enable future activities to be accomplished or outcomes to be realized.

Integration is an art, not a science, and is conceived based on current management philosophy or experience, and the recognition of the enormity of the challenge. Literally thousands of integration activities exist for management and their teams to execute within the general construct outlined above. And competing priorities and dependencies exist throughout the process and across functions.

Different integration models exist across the utilities industry: some very structured and meticulous, others focused on the vital few requirements of the business, and a few simply addressing selected enterprise-level activities and accepting stand-alone legacy companies.

The best model for a company depends on the point of view of management. If seamless operation is desired and robust synergies attainment is important, then full integration is the answer. If synergies are less critical and circumstances suggest a flexible operating model is appropriate, then an integration-lite approach may be the appropriate default. If a loose holding company model is to be adopted, then stand-alone operating companies may be ideal.

Each model may fit a particular fact pattern, but if combining companies are serious about building a portable platform for their next transaction and harvesting the benefits of standardization and simplification, then a model that leans toward full integration optimizes future positioning throughout the business.

When addressing how well prior merger integrations have been executed, Eversource Energy's Jim Judge explained:

> We have always achieved and exceeded our original expectations for synergies. We think we have a solid model to guide us and are very particular about the people we assign to lead and execute these processes. Our prior experience has benefited us by creating a platform we can rapidly adopt and extend from transaction to transaction that focuses on capturing value and returning that to both shareholders and customers. And we always stick to our plan.

Regardless of the overall integration philosophy and model adopted, management needs to understand the purpose of integration. It is not always just about operating model, synergies, and processes—consideration of how the transaction affects the strategic positioning of both the acquiror and acquiree as they exist today are equally important.

The typical integration effort focuses on both time frames and milestones, as well as activities and outcomes. Integration is also a logical process and follows a natural progression of stages that the combined company utilizes to position itself for succeeding activities within a structured timeline.

Integration needs to be thought of as a transitional process, but one where the time frame extends over multiple years, with not all affecting externalities visible. For some elements which emerge during integration planning, like regulatory application approval timing, the combining companies cannot control related outcomes and impacts.

Each stage of the integration process builds upon the previous one to allow for positioning, evaluation, formulation, and execution. And each stage of the integration effort directly addresses the factors that influence the future direction, structural alignment, performance model, and activity path to position the new company for success. The specific stages of integration each provide are a discrete element of the foundation for moving from two stand-alone companies to an integrated, combined company.

- **Strategic positioning**: A formative activity before integration begins is determining future business direction and priorities to drive a fundamental focus of the combined company. This early work addresses how the combination can create growth opportunities and priorities against which resources can be directed, and to align existing initiatives against other demands on the business.

- **Baseline development**: All integrations begin with establishing a clearly defined starting point for where the integration will begin, such as operating models, locations, organizations, staffing, technology platforms, and metrics, among other areas. This baselining effort is critical to ensuring a common set of facts and data points are made available to drive integration team review.

- **Target setting**: Generally, the initial synergies estimates provide the initial north star with respect to the level of value the combining companies seek to unlock through the transaction. However, savvy managements know that teams are extremely good at hitting specific targets and often consider the benefit of establishing stretch targets to provide additional uplift or a buffer to unexpected hurdles to original value estimates.

- **Current state**: Once the starting point is fleshed out, evaluating the stand-alone businesses and what exists, how it works, how well it is functioning, and what projects are underway is conducted to bring life to the baseline material. The result of this as-is review is to ensure integration teams fully understand how the current businesses exist—and are alike or different—before determining what they should look like together.

- **Future state**: The most important end product of the integration process is the definition of what the combined company will look like post-close and how long it will take to emerge at steady state. The gap from current to future state establishes just how complex the path will be to build and optimize the business and what level and timing of synergies is expected to be realized.

- **Execution roadmap**: Future state integration activities provide a picture of the new company and delineate what needs to be done, and in what sequence it will be undertaken. The path from the starting point to its logical conclusion is often not a straight line, and the roadmap needs to accommodate complexities, dependencies, surprises, workarounds, and CTA expenditure timing.

- **Activity close-out**: Integration completion activities typically cascade across different periods and through sequenced interfaces, hand-offs, and adoption milestones. Information technology conversion activities have the longest lead time to completion and are the most complex and critical path integration activities. It should be recognized that these close-outs are continuous and do not follow a regular cadence.

- **Results management**: Current state assessment and future state development activities are composed of 1,500-plus tasks—depending on the rigor of the integration philosophy—and the execution roadmap itself can exceed 4,000 discrete tasks given how many unique projects exist. Managing timely and thoughtful performance requires aggressive project management to ensure outcomes are produced and not diluted.

The above description represents a typical model for how integration processes can be structured and staged. There is no single approach that works best, but there are several attributes that need to be woven into any successful integration process.

Figure 24: Integration Attributes

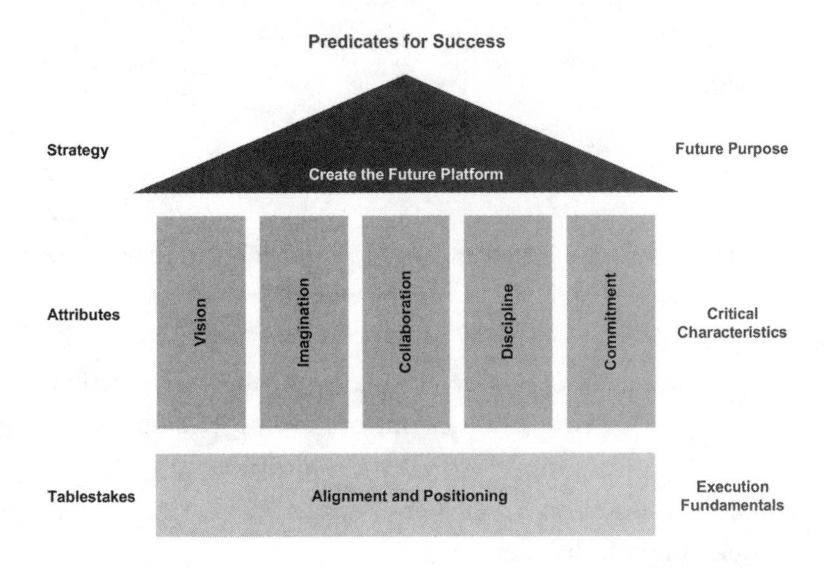

- **Vision**: Management of the combining companies need to take advantage of the transaction and use it to excite the organization about the future of the business and the optimization platform being created—direction, positioning, and value creation.

- **Imagination**: Integrations can fall short if they miss the opportunity to stretch how the business rethinks its future operating and delivery models and use the moment to reimagine themselves as a different company after close.

- **Collaboration**: Integration requires effective teaming to succeed, but real collaboration around shared principles, decision-making, and outcomes enables the results provided by the teams to successfully embed themselves into the business.

- **Discipline**: Companies can fall off track during integration planning since the process extends for 9-12 months from announcement to close and requires management to adopt formal governance structures and processes to ensure schedule compliance.

- **Commitment**: The extended pre-close integration readiness process can easily create *deal fatigue* within the combining companies, but management eyes need to be firmly on the multi-year post-close period when integration results are fully realized.

If combining companies can adopt the attributes above, they have a great chance of ensuring their integration process yields the type of strategic positioning, financial flexibility, operational synergies, technology innovation, and competitive prowess they believed was attainable through the merger.

Teaming Models

Successful merger integration requires coordination and collaboration among the hundreds of employees that are tasked with planning and executing the overall process. These employees typically represent all the affected areas of the business, including corporate headquarters, plant operations, field operations, back-office support, customer facing functions, and even non-regulated businesses, if they exist in both businesses.

Mark Ruelle of Evergy provided his insights on integration success:

> Integration requires early benchmarking and planning, then building targets into budgets to enable merger promises to be made manifest and results achieved. Naming an integration czar provides visible leadership so savings are realized. Teams are good at meeting targets, so we challenge ourselves to do better. How we address culture influences these outcomes, and we try to quickly move beyond "we and they" and strive for visible changes to the new company. Areas like investor relations take a day to reflect the new culture, but others more distant can take twenty years if not intentionally integrated. The more separated from shareholders, the longer it takes to achieve integration into a single, new culture.

Defining the number of integration teams is a first order of business once the leadership model, integration stages, and execution schedule are established across the overall integration process. Typically, teams are structured around functions, like Finance and Accounting, Supply Chain, Generation, Customer Experience, etc., with multiple sub-teams utilized that reflect significant activities or resource concentration within each function.

In addition to the vertical team structure, cross-business teams are also used to address activities affecting the entire enterprise, such as Information Technology, Facilities Management, and Human Resources. The purpose of these cross-business teams is different than the vertical teams. which focus on defining the future model for that function, for example, organization, process, and staffing. The cross-business teams address decisions that affect all vertical teams, such as technology application conversion, benefits and separation programs, risk management, and headquarters configuration.

Both types of integration teams can easily collectively number more than 300 full-time employees, with Information Technology requiring the highest concentration, depending on business scope and team construct. But these team resources can also be informally supported by dozens of additional employees on a part-time basis when specific expertise or surge support may be necessary.

With these multiple vertical and cross-business teams comes the need for a well-defined integration governance process. Integrations are led from the top of the organization, not the middle. Thus, a senior executive is typically charged to lead the process, although co-leads are not uncommon to preserve an equal voice in a merger-of-equals. Integration leadership has the responsibility to define a vision for integration outcomes, frame the integration schedule and stages, establish the guiding principles, determine value targets, manage day-to-day team execution and results, and resolve any issues that impeded the integration itself.

Managements face an immediate challenge in staffing these integration teams. Should teams be staffed with full-time employees, or should integration simply be part of the employees' ongoing work activity, just as most normal projects are? The choice made by management can significantly impact just how thorough and timely the integration process will be.

On the one hand, many organizations run lean and believe they do not have extra resources that can come off the bench to staff out a comprehensive and elongated integration process. Alternatively, managements also recognize that integration requirements are broad in nature, require subject matter experts, depend on collaborative analyses, and become more complex the closer to the close date.

This creates a classical trade-off—reducing stress to business-as-usual versus optimizing the effectiveness of integration and intended results. There is no substitute for full-time employees if management is committed to realizing the vision it established and fully capturing all identified benefits for the business. Said differently, jointly performing a full-time job and a demanding integration scope increases the likelihood of both gaps in regular work performance, as well as shortcomings to integration expectations.

Integration 2.0

Utilities are becoming more focused on building a portfolio of businesses that could exist within or outside the traditional business such as renewables, electric transport, and distributed energy resources management (DERMs). These businesses are intended to broaden the technology capabilities that utilities can bring to bear for their customers, as well as accelerate the availability of market offerings for these capabilities.

Some utilities seek to greenfield their own business start-ups or innovation centers, while others look to inorganic means to achieve market readiness more rapidly. If utilities do not have any form of non-traditional, competitive business in place, then accordingly the breadth of integration is narrow. Companies simply need to define how to bring the new business into the current enterprise portfolio in a non-destructive manner, avoid killing innovation, and refrain from layering excessive corporate costs on a small, nimble, competitive business. A more traditional acquisition of an entity that will expand an existing portfolio business—regulated or competitive—will naturally expand the integration scope.

In either case, the utility needs to avoid damaging the competitive business it acquired, which may still be in start-up mode with fragile earnings, competing in a tight margin business, used to running lean and leveraging constant creativity, and totally unfamiliar with how utilities think and act.

Consequently, a different model for non-regulated businesses needs to be utilized to preserve intrinsic and extrinsic value, sustain innovation momentum, retain critical capabilities, and enhance portfolio development in the acquired company or with a current competitive business in the acquiror. Companies need to think less about integration and more about configuration.

Figure 25: Integration – "Lite Approach"

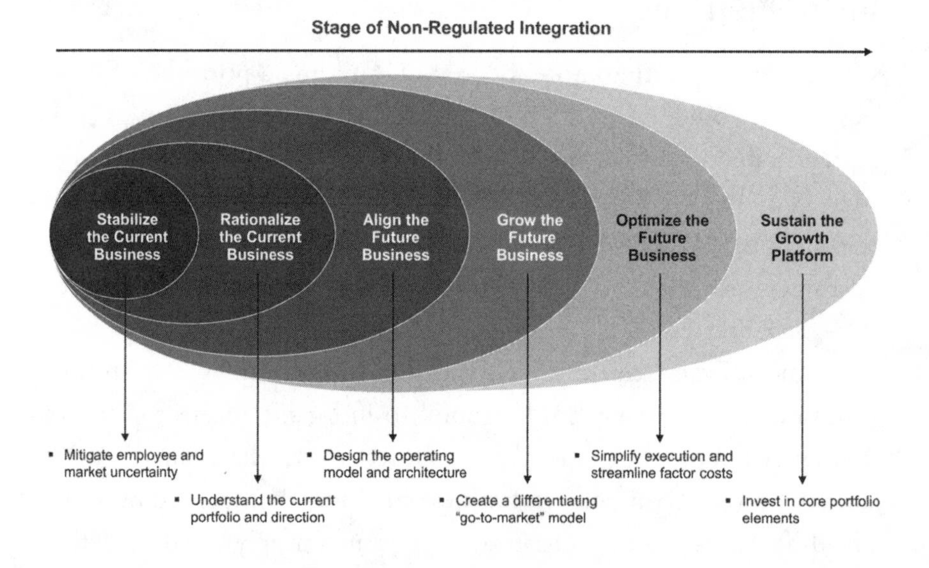

This model does not focus on comparison of processes and alignment of resources like the model described above, although limited features may still apply, like governance or financial management. Rather, it takes a more strategic approach intended to accelerate growth, build out the platform, enhance the go-to-market model, capture market share, and enhance market performance and profitability. This approach emphasizes how to position the acquired business for success, rather than standardize, streamline, or optimize traditional operations.

This approach focuses on working in *market time* since no merger approval process is required at a state regulatory commission for a competitive business. Expedited focus on the competitive businesses does not mean that companies can *gun jump* final approval, just that advanced readiness has its virtues. The approach also recognizes that the acquiree is competing among aggressive competitors and cannot be distracted from the market.

The first stage of this six-stage process focuses on stabilizing the business where it may be fragile to avoid disrupting the acquiree in the market, its employees, or its ongoing governance. The theme in this stage is to *do no harm* to the competitive business and ensure that key capabilities are secure, existing initiatives are continued, capital funding is available, and communication is supportive.

Typical cost synergies are not critical here, except where limited scale leverage, such as benefit programs, may be applicable, thus the focus is all about encouraging market expansion and revenue growth. If there are common businesses, such as in DERs or electric transport, then some traditional integration activities may apply, although the emphasis is still focused on market activities and success versus internally directed.

The second stage emphasizes rationalizing the business model, market presence, and infrastructure, not from a cost reduction perspective, but related to business simplification and margin enhancement to determine whether the current business is operating as it should. For example, technology start-ups often deploy their software engineering activities in a *virtual* manner where resources work from where they live, not where the business is located. These resources can be bi-coastal in clusters, or solo in local towns. Either way they work in an interconnected and collaborative manner.

Optimizing these distributed resources against the technology roadmap, product development plan, and market readiness, particularly when related competitive businesses may exist in the acquiror, can add productivity, effectiveness, and value across a portfolio. This stage also offers additional opportunity to the acquiror to do more in-depth due diligence and better understand the technology platform, related use cases, and customer positioning.

The third stage emphasizes *where and how* to align the businesses and how to bring them together for market success. This stage focuses on determining which model accelerates success and defining a future operating model and architecture for the business that enable seamless collaboration to occur, and the combined portfolio or entity to enjoy immediate competitive success in the market.

The fourth stage moves from stabilizing the business after close and rationalizing capabilities and resource elements to building alignment on the *go-to-market* strategy to both elevate future market positioning and high-grade offerings and customers in the market to determine how best to enhance the current market approach. This stage challenges the offering portfolio and identifies gaps to success and new revenue stream opportunities.

This is the most important stage of the configuration process for competitive businesses as it focuses on enhancing how the new business portfolio positions itself to capitalize on new capabilities and offerings to expand market reach and share. This stage also addresses where the businesses can be harmonized and what opportunities exist for margin uplift through bundling and pricing strategies.

The fifth stage focuses on moving the business forward from its current emphasis on market success, to the next level of competitiveness, like building a portable platform that can be extended across future acquisitions. This stage addresses both optimizing business portfolio margins, as well as identifying capabilities—technologies, processes, or people—to continue to elevate market competitiveness.

The final stage centers around *where and how* to grow and is about establishing going-forward priorities to expand the business scope, leverage the product platform, enhance offering attractiveness, leverage new market channels, establish a partner network, and embed a durable commercialization mindset to nurture and embed an aggressive market and value culture. In particular, the ability to fully address opportunities to cross-sell offerings is a focal point of two competitive businesses coming together.

This last stage links directly to the acquiror's thesis for original acquisition and leverages it as the starting point to perfect the future strategy and priorities for market growth, portfolio expansion, and market extension.

Post-Close Integration

Once the transaction receives approval, there is time for a quick celebration. Hundreds of thousands of hours have been expended by the integration teams to get to this point and companies are feeling satisfied with what they have accomplished.

The resources that executed integration planning and preparedness are feeling good as well, as they are looking forward to moving back into their original jobs and making actual integration the responsibility of someone else—the classic case of deal fatigue.

But then reality sinks in: nothing has actually been integrated by Day 1, and the real work is yet to begin. At this moment, management realizes it needs to have the overall organization take a deep breath, regather its energies, and begin the much harder task of actual integration as opposed to simple conceptualization and planning.

On adopting an integration model that produces and exceeds the expected result, Jim Judge from Eversource Energy gave additional insights:

> We want our whole team on board when we set out to integrate, particularly at the executive level. That is why we incorporate merger success directly into our rewards model. All our executives and key managers benefit when the enterprise is successful.

> We incorporate our merger outcomes directly into our Annual Incentive Plan and our Long-Term Incentive Plan so that we reinforce shared accountability for results.

In parallel, much of the organization thinks that the 9-12 months of preparation constituted the integration itself; while it was able to only observe the paper exercise, it never made the full connection that real integration could not be started before the close. Now the full organization needs to be reminded that the business must run seamlessly during actual integration, while short-term disruption occurs as organizations align, processes are modified, and technology conversions go through conversion.

Management's first challenge is how to fully execute the real integration—continue the integration teams as-is, modify them to fit-for-purpose, or devolve responsibilities to the operating businesses.

Surprisingly, there is much discussion about these choices at the executive level. A strong sentiment always exists that integration readiness is complete at Day 1, and the businesses or functions should drive integration from this point forward. This would align executive leadership roles with natural business execution, including integration responsibility.

But this point of view also ignores the reality that only organization models have been modified—process and technology change have months to years still to run. And the fact that technology conversion cannot be done by the businesses alone is often overlooked in the rush to get to steady state. Vertical functions have limited views into cross-business integration implications, if not closely aligned and interfaced through a natural and formal process.

Most managements come around to the approach that the enterprise benefits the most from high continuity in the integration teams. This approach also enables the collective management team to maintain line-of-sight into actual integration separately from regular operations.

An alternative model of devolving integration invites problems of second-guessing, backsliding, and delays if the actual integrators are different than the integration planners who conceived the architecture and planned the results of the integration. This approach essentially invites open second-guessing, which is anathema to an organization focused on effective execution.

Choosing to keep the original integration teams in place (with some realignment to reflect organizational modifications) helps management avoid unforced errors of pushing down actual integration prematurely. This choice also enables management to reduce the risks to integration and outcome realization known as the *four deadly sins*.

Figure 26: Four Deadly Integration Sins

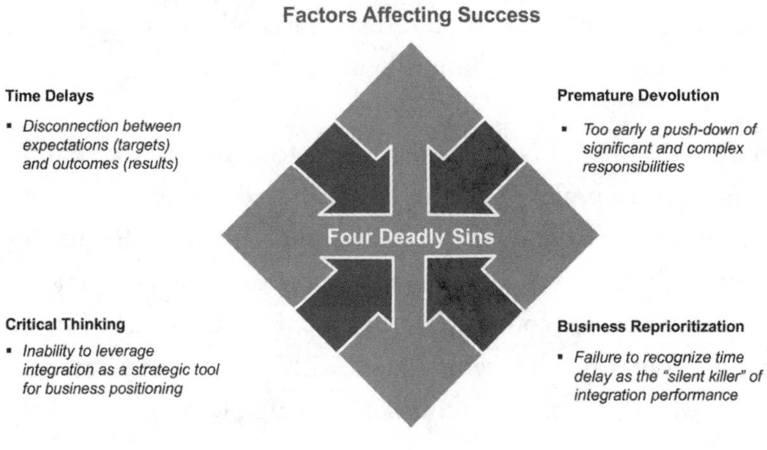

Factors Affecting Success

Time Delays
- *Disconnection between expectations (targets) and outcomes (results)*

Premature Devolution
- *Too early a push-down of significant and complex responsibilities*

Four Deadly Sins

Critical Thinking
- *Inability to leverage integration as a strategic tool for business positioning*

Business Reprioritization
- *Failure to recognize time delay as the "silent killer" of integration performance*

First, the most obvious integration sin is to allow time to become the *silent killer* of achieving integration outcomes by not following the timeline. If integration plans are not acted upon in the time frames as scheduled, then the risks of unwinding these outcomes occur. It is exceedingly difficult and rare for merging companies to successfully reengage later after the business cadence has become normalized.

Second, when post-close integration activities are pushed down within the business too soon, the ability to achieve planned outcomes is diminished. This occurs because it becomes easy to allow internal governance and execution processes to overwhelm integration leadership intentions. If operating management determines that risk of integration execution could have short-term adverse business outcomes, then these mindsets—right or wrong—are hard to change.

Third, a tendency exists after extended integration planning processes to assume that the post-close activity roadmap allows ongoing integration efforts to be a *color-by-numbers* exercise. While the roadmap lays out the activities, interdependencies, and cadence, the hard work of real integration lies in bringing the roadmap to life and managing through the challenges arising from complex actions, precedent activities, and unforeseen conflicts. And that all lies within the context of dealing with the "*me*" issues from the integration.

Finally, it can be easy for management to allow normal business operations, for example, regulatory decisions and customer actions, to rationalize new integration outcomes inconsistent with the intent of the original process. These unplanned surprises are unavoidable, but management can overcome their impacts by ensuring that targeted integration outcomes are embedded within overall performance incentives that encourage commitment to tangible results.

Addressing how well utilities have captured the value of scale through integration, Tom Fanning from Southern Company commented:

> The experience of U.S. utilities in capturing the value of scale is mixed—some companies created platforms to optimize how the business was operated. Others leaned into recognizing utilities are a local business and owning this kind of company necessitates

certain trade-offs between localization and optimization. When companies did not emphasize objectives like simplification, standardization, and optimization, it often was because they valued the positioning of their local brand differently than traditional holding companies where centralization dominated. Different success models exist, and distinctive choices can be adopted to accomplish specific ownership objectives.

Despite all the effort expended on developing the integration roadmap, future business success depends on effective ongoing management of the post-close process. Events as complex and interrelated as merger integration demand visible senior leadership of the process and alignment of the interests of the entire executive team.

Even with the potential for continued deal fatigue, the most successful integrations are achieved by treating this process as a critical enterprise effort with collective benefits for the ongoing business rather than simply a series of tasks with a defined end date and narrow beneficiaries. The most important outcome to be achieved is the seamless integration of the businesses in a manner that enables strategic, operational, and financial outcomes to be fully realized, even if under a slightly modified pace or sequence.

Like any undertaking of this scale, hands-on executive management of integration needs to occur throughout the life of roadmap execution. The easiest way to achieve this outcome is to continue the pre-close model of an integration czar who remains individually responsible for 360° process execution and outcome attainment. Rather than utilizing a selected steering committee within the executive team as during pre-close integration, the full executive team can now fulfill this role and enable broad visibility into all integration activities, issues, mitigations, and outcomes.

The ongoing management of the post-close integration process should use the same level of rigor as existed pre-close, and as expended on normal enterprise projects or programs. Milestone targets become even more important to hit as specific outcomes, like precedent tasks, link directly to broader goal attainment. But even more important is the level of tracking, measuring, and affirming that specific synergies and operational targets have been realized, and can be aligned to reduced budgets or higher earnings.

Although the impacts of integration are not equal throughout the entire business, adopting a means to align the interest of all executives can be beneficial to enterprise success. Smart companies recognize that shared ownership of post-close integration process outcomes enhances the ability to realize targeted expectations. This occurs because the interests of the many far exceed the value to a few, given the interrelated operating models existing within the business.

The simplest way to attain this shared ownership is to create specific metrics for integration success and incorporate these measures into the traditional short- and long-term incentive frameworks with a weighting to reinforce how critical integration outcomes are.

These measures could be tangible, like synergies levels and milestones, or less tangible and seek to evaluate the level of unintended disruption to the overall business from integration performance. Thus, shared outcomes where everyone has skin in the game can be a powerful tool to align the interests of all executive leadership. When all executives win together from integration success, then each executive wins individually as well—as does the full enterprise.

Just as it may be premature to devolve integration into the business after the close of the transaction, it can also be premature to dissolve these tight management processes too early. Long-lead items, such as customer information systems, extend at least three to four years, so it only increases performance risk to the business to weaken the nature and focus of ongoing roadmap management.

While some companies believe extending the formal integration management effort for one year only is appropriate, the truth is that almost none of the technology application conversion effort is completed in that time, and full execution risks remain for several years. It is far better to align formal integration management visibility for the life of roadmap execution than to allow these efforts to be lost within the day-to-day activities of ongoing business and functional performance.

Key Takeaways

Merger integration is a critical element of the transaction life cycle and proves out whether the original deal value can be produced, while it positions the combining companies for enhanced market position, effective operations execution, and continued business growth.

Even though integration is art rather than a science, a body of knowledge exists on how best to structure and execute the effort, as well as what problems to avoid through early recognition. Combining companies can leverage the experience of other utilities that have preceded them in transactions, or their own prior experience if they have already concluded one or more deals. These lessons are learned from the framework for continuous evolution of integration models:

- Integration only occurs after transaction close, *but its success is determined by how the time between announcement and close is effectively used.*

- Significant enterprise undertakings like integration require visible senior leadership. *The success of integration correlates highly with the level of executive in charge.*

- There is no such thing as a merger-of-equals between two companies. *Avoid over-rotating on achieving equality in how the integration process is designed.*

- Pre-filing synergies levels are estimated on narrow information. *Formal targets for integration results offer an ability to stretch early estimates and challenge the teams.*

- Talent for staffing out the integration teams should reflect dedicating the best resources the two companies have to offer, *not just those that are "around and available."*

- Time is the silent killer in an integration. *There is no room for decision delay or reconsideration of decisions already made that support a synchronized schedule.*

- Integration leadership and team leads are chartered to hold integration decision rights. *No need exists for uninvited guests and out-of-process management opinions.*

- Long-lead items in integration, particularly technology conversion, take on a life of their own. *Close attention needs to be paid to those areas where execution risk is critical.*

- Integration fatigue can drive integration leadership to prematurely devolve the process to line management. *No advantage evolves from providing less enterprise visibility.*

- Immediate codification of integration lessons learned provides high value. *Executive leadership has the role to fully document what worked and what didn't.*

With respect to integration success, management needs to get it right the first time. There are no second chances for integration. Not only is there no appetite within management to undertake a second effort (no matter how surgical), this action unwinds what has already been completed and creates disruption where none need occur.

The integration process is the linchpin between deal logic and value attainment. It is the critical element that distinguishes future enterprise success from a failed merger. There is no substitute for detailed planning of the integration process, and it needs to be done before execution can fruitfully occur. Planning on the fly creates avoidable risks and hamstrings integration success from the beginning.

My experience suggests a high correlation between the nature of integration planning and the actual results that are realized after close. On the one hand, it identifies the complexity and risks of under-estimating the complexity of integration, and on the other, it establishes the objectives, requirements, and options for how it can proceed and execution risks can be mitigated.

Getting the strategic and integration priorities properly aligned is particularly important since this process becomes the catalyst for achieving desired combined company positioning post-close. While integration is a tactical process, it is informed by the strategic priorities and intent of the enterprise, not the least of which is the mosaic for how the combined company is intended to look and operate going forward.

The integration process does not need to be elegant in design, it needs to be effective in execution. The more structured the integration process, the better the likely outcome, as well-defined purpose, principles, guidelines, requirements, activities, and deliverables set the stage for integration team understanding of how the results of their efforts will be incorporated into future enterprise execution.

Leading utilities will challenge their integration teams to exceed initial targets that may have already been identified, with synergies levels being the most common example. Management knows that a synergies estimate performed without full access to information and people will be inherently conservative or underdeveloped. Consequently, any initial estimates are often viewed as a *floor, not a ceiling*.

To challenge the integration teams to think more aggressively, managements may utilize stretch targets to push the teams beyond initial estimates. Depending on the circumstances of the combining companies, for example, proximity or composition, management may apply an upside challenge to the teams if they believe it may be attainable. Besides potentially adding upside to economic value, these additional synergies may provide a buffer against synergies shortfalls arising from changed assumptions or unforeseen impediments to organizational alignment or realizing market economies of scale.

A final activity for management to consider is codifying the entire effort it just executed in integration planning and through execution. Compiling a carefully considered lessons-learned document is an industry best practice and simplifies life for the combined company and integration leadership and teams the next time a transaction occurs. There is no need to reinvent the wheel for the next integration, even if it occurs after several years.

Two things management can count on are that the company would simply be lucky if many of the same people that executed integration planning and execution were still available to support the next effort, and that institutional memory fades fast.

Successful merger integration does not need to look exactly alike from one transaction to another. The underlying philosophies may align, but the relevant circumstances vary and dominant priorities may diverge. Nonetheless, if vision, imagination, collaboration, discipline, and commitment are kept in mind, the probability of a successful integration outcome will dramatically increase.

CHAPTER 8

RETURN TO RESTRUCTURING

The U.S. utility industry has undergone several waves of change over its history, particularly in the modern era of industry M&A. Market perspectives have evolved, strategies have shifted, risks have fluctuated, and externalities captured attention, and then dissipated.

Restructuring is a natural event for an industry in transition like U.S. utilities have been since 1995. Each era has followed its own drivers for portfolio rationalization and evolution of the business model. The first stage occurred when states mandated functional unbundling and business separation. The second stage occurred as U.S buyers of UK and Australian RECs sold their offshore investments, and marketing and trading units fell out of favor after Enron's collapse. The third stage reflected the increasing effect of climate change on power supply asset ownership.

Most time periods have been marked by assets either being in favor or disfavor, leading to shifts in continuing ownership sentiment among utilities. Examples include:

- **Stage 1:** market competition, generation carve-out, and gas convergence in the mid-1990s and leading up to 2000
- **Stage 2:** international expansion at the turn of the millennium, competitive business divestment, international exits around 2005, and build-out of renewables in 2010
- **Stage 3:** carbon reduction after 2015 and leading to heightened electrification focus in 2020

Now the industry is entering into a fourth stage which centers on further rationalization of natural gas businesses, remaining international assets, and competitive generation, all undertaken to create additional strategic advantage.

Externalities are creating different market expectations and tolerances for business and asset portfolio composition. As policies evolve to reflect the shifting sentiments of investors, lenders, regulators, and the public, the determination of which current businesses and assets reflect the right elements to hold for the future is subject to new interpretation.

Jeff Holzschuh from Morgan Stanley described some of the drivers for portfolio rationalization that is occurring:

> Utility restructuring is influenced by multiple factors, from high diversity in market multiples to under-valued assets to long-term asset value to specific state regulatory issues to lower risk tolerances to lower growth prospects. U.S. utilities generally are expecting 6-8 percent compound annual growth in earnings, so companies lagging this level have to ask themselves what they can do to shed businesses causing value destruction from those with higher recognized value in the market. We're seeing several U.S. companies restructure or trade their riskiest segments or assets to simplify the long-term business and position the remaining core for higher, more differentiated growth.

In particular, the financial community has shifted its views on what it considers to be core and on what it believes to be acceptable in a portfolio. Certain value chain elements, as well as certain asset classes, are no longer considered to be acceptable within a publicly traded utility. These externalities are leading to a reevaluation of portfolios by utilities, with the objective to reassess what fits and what doesn't against a future market and environmental context that is still forming. And these externalities are driving utilities toward meaningful action in response.

ESG Impetus

An emphasis on shrinking carbon emissions has been underway for decades across the globe and most industrial sectors. While actionable changes have not been uniformly accepted by all countries, like China, India, Russia, etc., most of the developed world has leaned in to environmental populism and taken a range of small to significant steps.

The focus on carbon emissions started at governmental levels, as most major policy shifts do. But when government actions start to move public sentiment in a similar direction, then even world-weary industries and jaded service providers get the message and begin to echo the emotional argument that underlies emerging policies.

Wall Street is no different, with the banking and financial communities actively engaging in the climate debate since 2008, when the first Carbon Principles were issued by the banking sector to guide lending to affected industries, like utilities, oil and gas, and transportation. These principles provided guidelines to institutions lending to carbon-intensive projects and a framework for project evaluation and public disclosure of climate risks.

While this prompted an important shift in environmental reporting when announced, these principles were still early in the financial community debate and more voluntary than mandated. But the genie was now out of the bottle within the financial community, and pronouncements continued to slowly cascade toward a real Wall Street revolution about carbon emissions.

In 2012, the next major event affecting Wall Street's climate views occurred with the formation of the U.S. Partnership for Renewable Energy, which brought the financial community together with the American Council on Renewable Energy (ACORE). This coalition focused on encouraging an all-the-above strategy on power supply, although this effort heavily focused on making renewable sources a mainstream choice for utilities over conventional fuels.

As momentum continued to build for action over succeeding years, leadership voices in the financial community—beyond just lending banks and ratings agencies—lent their stature to the need for more aggressive environmental stewardship. Other financial institutions also voiced their views on responding to the environmental challenges facing the industry and elevated the level of debate and degree of response on climate change.

For instance, Goldman Sachs publicized its priorities for environmental stewardship in 2019 and called active carbon emission reductions a smart business choice, with potential upside from market recognition and downside from failure to accept underlying predicates.[1] These priorities formally linked climate change actions to the broader topic of environmental, social, and governance (ESG) standards that were receiving active debate within the financial sector and the overall business community.

The Goldman Sachs release contained a bold call for $750 billion in available financing and advisory support to businesses emphasizing environmental stewardship and inclusive growth. This release also called for adoption of even more restrictive lending policies within the firm, although it did not call for an absolute abolition against fossil fuel lending. To put these and other pronouncements in perspective, it is estimated that almost $40 trillion in managed global investment will follow ESG principles by the end of 2021, and will rise to over one-third of all assets under management by 2025.[2]

To emphasize Wall Street's changing perspective, in 2020 the CEO of BlackRock, Inc., used his annual letter to clients and other CEOs to vocalize his concern over climate change and his commitment to sustainability.[3] In the letter, he communicated that BlackRock would reconsider its policies regarding investing in companies that held businesses or assets contributing to carbon emissions. And he called for other CEOs to embrace sustainability as a vital element of their business purpose.

In a follow-up letter to CEOs in 2021, the BlackRock CEO doubled down on his commitments and introduced further perspectives and tools he believed could be used to add transparency and clarity to environmental reporting and disclosure.[4] The CEO acknowledged the many other CEOs that had already committed to *net zero* greenhouse gas emissions (emissions offset by reductions) by 2050 and further asked them to commit to publicly disclosing and linking their strategy roadmaps to carbon neutrality.

BlackRock reinforced the pace of change and the level of sustained interest by noting that in 2020, almost $300 billion in sustainable products were invested in by mutual and exchange-traded funds, an almost 100 percent increase over 2019.[5] This level of activity echoed a survey conducted by Octopus Investment Limited in 2019 where investors disclosed the intent to divest almost $1 trillion in fossil fuel investments over 10 years and replace them with $650 billion of renewables.[6]

Tom Fanning of Southern Company discussed the wave of restructuring currently occurring and ESG's role:

> When segments or assets are divested, it suggests value levels have deteriorated, or have risen and it's time to release value. The former outcome indicates a company is dealing from weakness and something adversely shifted the risk and reward balance to where another owner makes more sense and capital can be redeployed to a higher purpose. The second outcome is classical portfolio

> theory and leverages the strength of historical stewardship to monetize value and recycle it to other segments for new value creation. ESG is a visible driver of portfolio rationalization more than value maturity. It's not a fad, it's a movement, and it has an outsized impact on future portfolio composition.

The events summarized above establish the intensity of financial community interest in environmental stewardship and the commitment institutions are making to a net zero outcome for greenhouse gases. The financial community is well aligned on climate change principles, and increasingly vocal regarding the investability of companies with significant carbon footprints and projects.

The culmination of these financial community proclamations is the intense interest in the level of carbon-emitting businesses or assets in company portfolios and the specificity and quality of the plans to achieve meaningful net zero targets in a reasonable time frame. The overall emphasis on ESG has furthered permeated other aspects of business and is becoming a litmus test on environmental stewardship and the commitment to responsible investing strategies.

Ratings agencies, insurance companies, investment banks, hedge funds, shareholder services firms, and investment funds have all joined in this economy-wide movement to evaluate the holdings of companies and commit to disposition of their current holding in these companies, as well as avoidance of future carbon-emitting investments.

CEO Tom Fanning from Southern Company continued his thoughts on assessing further restructuring:

> Sometimes, market perceptions cause the industry to move, like carbon response actions. Other times, malaise in other markets turn people in your direction, like European companies interested in U.S. renewables assets, or companies with large renewables positions. Over time, strategies tend to reallocate segments and assets to the best owners and realign risks between owners and buyers

to get the value equation right. Companies will continue to play a balance of offense (exercise options) and defense (rotate positions), as viable means of creative destruction of current businesses and revitalization of future portfolios.

Collectively, the trickle-down effect of these pronouncements has informed the analyst community about carbon responsibility and led to a clear determination that certain value chain elements such as fossil-fuel based assets no longer fit a responsible business portfolio, and should be divested, shuttered, or abandoned. In several cases, valuations have already reflected the composition of these assets and companies, with high carbon-emitting portions of portfolios suffering from valuation destruction in the public markets.

The sentiment and direction of the financial community are clear: dispose or de-risk businesses or assets that are not supportive of addressing climate change, or face a loss of investors and diminution of shareholder value. However, few pronouncements address just how rapidly desired consequences, like the timing of asset retirements and replacements or holdings dispositions, are expected to be executed within the U.S. or global utilities industry.

Joe Sauvage from Citi discussed how the difference in today's investors play into the actions taken by managements:

> Utilities investors are different today than in earlier years. In power, 30 percent of investors are active, passive investors comprise about 25 percent, retail investors amount to 20 percent, and the rest is made up of hedge funds and other financial entities. In earlier years, retail ownership was far higher and reflected more traditional utility investors. A major driver of investor shift is the presence of EFTs in the market, which create a different investment dynamic. Active investors have a unique profile, with 40 percent focusing on income, 25 percent on growth, and the remainder on value. Institutional investors have far less tolerance

for unique business models, which often means business rationalization forced by these activists.

The impact to U.S. utilities is further exacerbated by the actions of states or municipalities which extend the intent of policies referred to above into local decisions about where to invest and/or prohibitions against business expansion. These governmental responses have already surfaced in states like California and New York, as well as specific cities, like Los Angeles and Seattle. Natural gas has been the victim of these policies, with outright hostility toward core business functions in critical services like new connections.

While the die is not fully cast with respect to the timing and requirements of net zero outcomes, a picture has fast formed that decidedly shrinking tolerance for new carbon-emitting assets and more restrictions on continued carbon-emitting operations are the future for U.S. and global utilities, as well as all other industries.

Joe Sauvage from Citi commented on the nature of restructuring sentiment during 2020:

> Business model change is precipitated by business volatility. Today, investors are generally focused on 6 percent–8 percent earnings growth for U.S. utilities, and on business simplification. They like fully regulated business models, capable management, solid balance sheets, good growth, and being ESG-friendly. So far, owning gas has not been a real determinant of value, but that could change, and you can't ignore activist investors which prefer simplicity. What the "Street" thinks of you is important, and right now, there aren't a lot of utilities that need restructuring.

The sentiments and policies described above are already leading to broad reassessment of existing utility value chains and sober evaluation of the risks associated with non-core businesses and/or those that are a minority of the total value of the current portfolio.

Portfolio Rationalization

Given the proclivity of policy mandates and investor sentiment to rapidly shift without much lead time, utilities have become adept with handling changing market perspectives, albeit often after the handwriting is on the wall. Just as utility value chains have evolved through years of federal or state policy mandates, so too has portfolio composition been subject to internal reassessment of continuing market dimensions of business competitiveness and value.

It appears obvious that business rationalization is becoming increasingly driven by external market sentiment, rather than sober internal assessment of long-term portfolio value contribution. In the financial markets, simplicity is more highly valued than diversity, and in the governmental domain, small, new, and clean assets are more suitable than those large, old, legacy assets designed and built in a period where environmentalism was far less relevant.

Mark Ruelle of Evergy addressed the topic of restructuring currently being pursued by several U.S. utilities:

> Utility operating circumstances change over time. What was most valuable yesterday may not be viewed the same tomorrow. Non-regulated value propositions fluctuate based on who comes in and out of a value chain segment. Today, we see a heavy influence on carbon assets, driving certain asset class divestment and fundamentally challenging the value of a vertical, integrated utility structure. Traditional investors in utilities view capital investment as a structured, growing annuity, which is not always the case for non-regulated businesses. De-risking is fine, but understanding the compelling emotions for shifts, institutional attitudes, or pure circumstances is important.

When utilities pursue *carve-outs*, they have multiple options available to them: sale, sell-down, spin-out, and swap depending on their portfolio strength, market position, growth views, business performance, and risk tolerance. Whatever option prevails, management seeks to reduce value deterioration, capture upside value, or substantially de-risk the enterprise from continued ownership in its present form. Each option may apply, depending on how companies view their current and future market position.

- **Sale**: Most utilities faced with negative investor or regulatory sentiment ultimately turn to outright sale to cure financial and risk issues emanating from ownership. They also utilize the sale option when clear that the business or assets are of higher value to third parties than being retained. The benefit of a sale is that it provides a binary option to sellers—transfer the business or assets, if the price is right, or retain them if prices lag anticipated value over the long term.

- **Sell-down**: Utilities can also select a path that reduces their market exposure through partial sell-off of a business or assets, rather than complete divestment. Some optionality is also maintained under this model as utilities can determine how to best package the selected elements of the portfolio to optimize financial contribution. Under this option, management can evaluate how selected divestment compares to full ownership or full divestment and reserve the optionality of a multi-step process.

- **Spin-out**: When management believes that the business or assets have significant value, but may no longer be core to the primary business, then a full or partial public offering can prove to be an attractive option. This model allows management to capture full value for the carve-out business or assets, or to retain sufficient interest in the current business to both extract immediate value and optimize access to future value from the business or assets as they continue to mature and grow.

- **Swap**: A more difficult option to pursue relates to exchanging a business or assets with another entity for specific businesses or assets believed to be of equivalent or similar value and a better fit within the new portfolio. This model is complex to execute as identifying an alternative business or assets with equivalent value to the currently owned portfolio is a hard match and the dynamics of a swap are unusual in that a practical and effective alignment of a duality of interests is rare.

Carve-outs, which separate current parts of the business, have become a principal strategy for pursuing value realignment and high-grading the portfolio by subtraction or modification. By far, more businesses and assets are fully sold than are either partially sold, spun out, or swapped. The process is simpler, meaning the risk of transaction completion is substantially reduced.

But utility managements are not constrained by easy-to-execute market disposition models. Several utilities have previously been creative in fashioning models designed to optimize value to the seller in the form of partial sell-downs, spin-outs, and swaps. In the 2016–2017 period, *yieldcos*, that is, operating asset-based entities focused on investor cash flow, became a popular form of separating assets from the core business and focusing the market on an asset class viewed as strategically, financially, and environmentally attractive.

This vehicle structure is attractive to companies with growing renewable portfolios. Power purchase agreements (PPAs) have sufficient assets to create a sizable initial *drop-down* base, that is, separation and transfer of assets, and can continue to expand through additional asset contributions over time. The yieldco model separates less capital-intensive, higher cash flow assets from more capital-intensive, lower cash flow assets to produce more dividend income for shareholders.

In this stage of utility maturity, yieldcos are viewed as ESG-friendly investment vehicles because the underlying assets do not carry a carbon footprint and are particularly attractive in a low interest rate environment. NextEra Energy has created significant shareholder value through its yieldco, but scale matters, and few utilities have the enterprise capacity and portfolio characteristics to successfully execute this kind of strategic action.

In just the last 18-24 months, additional impetus has been driven by financial investors for utilities to further de-risk their businesses by streamlining the composition of the portfolio, that is, selling or carving out businesses believed to be inconsistent with or less consequential to the future profile and fortunes of utilities. These businesses include gas transmission, international networks, merchant power assets, energy service businesses, and retail entities.

Tom Fanning from Southern Company provided additional insight on why the industry is currently so active in restructuring and simplification:

> Value is a function of risk and reward, and portfolio rationalization and carve-outs signal a misallocation of risk presently exists. The utilities industry has had to face the fact it was not always the best steward of future value. Current segments or assets may be better owned by another party if ownership is not optimizing value. Companies and assets frequently changed hands and shifted value toward, or away from current owners, which added to, or shrank, scale.

Companies like Exelon, PSEG, DTE Energy, PPL, CenterPoint Energy, and Sempra Energy have all announced the intent to divest these types of businesses to simplify the legacy business, reduce non-utility market risks, reduce drags to earnings and valuation, monetize value, or redirect capital to provide financing flexibility or drive new growth. Some of these efforts have already been concluded.

The principal areas for disposition reflect businesses that at one time were viewed favorably by the market—merchant generation, midstream, international, retail—but have fallen out of favor as sentiment has turned to predictable earnings, balance sheet strength, cash flows, and lower business risk.

Each entity is pursuing a carve-out or strategic monetization event for their unique motivations, but they generally reflect investor messaging that the promise of these businesses is lagging expectations, or the risk associated with the businesses does not justify the returns and cash flows being generated.

- **Exelon**: The variability of competitive generation, particularly nuclear, and dependence on zero emission credits (ZECs) led to the move to split off its Exelon Generation portfolio of competitive nuclear, gas, renewable generation plants, and retail book. The early 2022 spin-out would leave Exelon as a pure T&D utility, with multi-state operations.

- **PSEG**: Competitive generation has been out of favor with the investment community and considered inconsistent with utility financial stability. PSEG initiated sale of its competitive generation portfolio and trading book in mid-2021 and, with the completion of its announced sale during 2021 or early 2022, would become a single-state T&D entity for the electric and gas sectors, with regulated nuclear plants.

- **DTE Energy**: The low growth rate and potential for the midstream gas transmission segment led DTE to decide to split off its pipeline segment into a separate unit. This spin-out in July 2021 leaves the remaining company as an integrated electric and gas utility with regulated power supply and T&D assets across both the electric and natural gas sectors.

- **PPL**: The company's UK electric network has long been subject to aggressive regulation and the investment community signaled it does not see sustainable value uplift from ongoing ownership. The sale of UK assets to NationalGrid was completed in mid-2021, while the purchase of The Narragansett Electric Company is expected to close in 2022.

- **CenterPoint Energy**: The jointly owned (with OGE Energy) pipeline business has been underperforming, with the investment community clamoring for disposition action by the owners. Midstream business (to Energy Transfer) and LDC asset sales in Arkansas and Oklahoma are completed, leaving a largely T&D business with limited generation assets in Indiana.

- **Sempra Energy**: Investment community sentiment for greater balance sheet strength led Sempra to initiate the sale of Peru and Chile assets and to sell a minority stake to KKR in Sempra Infrastructure Partners (renewables, natural gas, and LNG), which would then sit along side a U.S.-only T&D electric and natural gas utility in California and Texas.

The value of these business or asset carve-outs varies by entity, but individually they amount to several billion dollars. For example, Sempra Energy's sale of its South American businesses in Peru and Chile netted $5.8 billion in pre-tax cash and the sale of a minority interest in Sempra Infrastructure Partners will bring $3.4 billion in proceeds.[7]

The sale value of PPL's UK networks business brought gross cash proceeds of $10.2 billion to the parent, which enabled the simultaneous ability to acquire The Narragansett Electric Company. After this acquisition, the net proceeds are estimated to bring $6.4 billion in residual cash back across the pond to either reinvest in the business or purchase outstanding stock shares.[8]

PSEG's sale of its fossil fuel plants and solar resources is expected to provide more than $2 billion in after-tax proceeds when required regulatory approvals are received and assets are transferred.[9]

The future spin-off at Exelon will likely create value uplift, when executed, but it is difficult to speculate about prior to transaction execution or valuation. In any case, the previous or expected strategic moves by the companies above illustrate just how profound these carve-outs can be financially.

In a unique transaction for the U.S. utility industry, in early 2021 Duke Energy structured a partial sale of one of its principal operating utilities. This transaction allowed the company to monetize $2 billion in value from selling less than 20 percent of its Indiana utility business, and then deploy the proceeds toward a high and sustained level of capital investment plans, thus avoiding the need for near-term equity infusion.[10] The sell-down of its Indiana operations to GIC Private, a Singaporean sovereign wealth fund with substantial experience in investing in a wide variety of asset types, illustrates the creativity of financing models that is available to the U.S. utility industry. FirstEnergy has similarly announced its interest in assessing the potential value associated with a partial sell-down within its operating companies.

The business simplification and carve-out theme for selective assets has expanded to smaller operating properties as well. CenterPoint Energy has sold properties operating in Arkansas and Oklahoma to Summit Utilities (owned by JP Morgan Infrastructure Investments Fund), garnering a 30X earnings multiple and a price at 2.5X rate base, both extremely highly valued and illustrative of market robustness for digestible assets with good cash flows.

Based on these experiences, additional companies, like AEP, are evaluating carve-outs as well, which could potentially cover specific operating companies, portions of operating company ownership, and portions of operating businesses or assets.

Even though investor sentiment continuously shifts, the direction of travel over the last decade has been toward business simplification, financial flexibility, and de-risking the overall business. While the parameters of the future utilities industry are not fully understood in

2021, it is not likely that a turn-about in portfolio composition will occur and disrupt the momentum toward a narrower business profile and clearer business model.

The U.S. utilities sector has also been active in acquiring and disposing of non-regulated energy services businesses over the last five years. These businesses are vastly different than those that populated the utility industry when diversification of earnings was viewed as important and differentiating, from areas like insurance, trucking, trout farms, real estate, savings and loans, construction, sea transport, etc. While the broader scope of energy services is closely linked to the future core utility business, current portfolio holdings are relatively small compared to the asset-based businesses.

Companies like Edison International and Southern Company were first movers in acquiring energy services companies, like DERMs, energy management, solar financing, etc. In 2013, Edison International acquired companies or ownership positions in five entities, Optimum Energy (energy management software), SoCore Energy (rooftop solar installation), Delta Energy (energy consulting services), ENERActive Energy (energy efficiency), and Altenex (renewable energy procurement). Some of these positions have been unwound since original capital deployment.

Southern Company acquired PowerSecure for over $400 million in 2016.[11] PowerSecure provides energy efficiency and management products, infrastructure solutions, and distributed generation systems. Southern Company continues to leverage PowerSecure for its broad energy services capabilities, also adding Power Pro-Tech Services (distributed generation services) to complement PowerSecure in 2017.[12] Since the mid-2010s, other U.S. utilities such as Duke Energy, Exelon, and NationalGrid have also made investments or acquisitions of niche energy services or renewables-related businesses.

In the future, more companies will both buy and sell core-related businesses, like renewables, energy services, electric transport, and transactive energy, that are believed to be important to meeting the needs of customers and opening up new revenue streams. While these entities typically pale in scale to utilities, they are abundant, which makes for a greater ability for more companies to be investors, acquirors, portfolio builders, and/or portfolio optimizers.

As utilities search for more top-line revenue growth opportunities, rationalizing these types of entities as either established or start-up businesses will offer the potential to create a range of new channels to market to meet the growing demands of the new energy transition, or respond to adverse investor sentiment over business composition.

CHAPTER 9

FUTURE DIRECTION

The past 25 years have witnessed a robust movement from a highly fragmented electric and gas utilities sector to an industry characterized by high regional concentration, some super-regional footprints, and pockets of stand-alone independence. The pace of consolidation witnessed over the last 25 years was robust in certain periods, such as 1995-1999 (the high-water-mark years with 60 announced deals), but constrained during portions of the two recessionary periods between 2000-2004 and 2005-2009.[1]

There does not appear to be any reason for the U.S. utilities industry to not continue inorganic action among the 49 tradable companies standing during the first quarter of 2021, except the growing scarcity of available targets or partners, particularly those that have never completed a merger or acquisition within the industry.

Valuations of utilities have more than doubled over the last 10 years as high capital spend growth has been sustained and companies have become more adept at overall cost management. The level of U.S. utilities industry valuations, even with the 2020 year trailing prior period performance due to the pandemic and interest rate fears, is sufficiently strong enough to support more inorganic activity.

The majority of companies have done at least one merger or acquisition, so they understand the nature of the market, requirements of the process, and the results that can be achieved. Companies that have yet to undertake a transaction are often small and less likely to be acquirors given the dispersion of suitable candidates and close affiliation with local communities. But some observers believe this may have less impact than perceived.

Bill Lamb from Baker Botts directly addressed this thought:

> Companies reach a stage in their life cycle where they are willing to consider a change to the status quo, and it seems we are still in that cycle today. Small companies have capital needs, mid-sized companies seek growth, and large companies look to capitalize on the value of scale. Most companies recognize that scale has value, particularly in the form of a stronger balance sheet during sustained capital investment. Today, boards are more open to mergers than in earlier periods, particularly as shareholder value receives so much attention.

At the end of 2020, 17 U.S. utilities maintained a market capitalization above $20 billion, or about 33 percent of the total sector, which gives an indication of the capital firepower that can be brought to bear for M&A. At the same time, 20 U.S. utilities have market capitalizations fewer than $5 billion, suggesting there are numerous roll-up opportunities available. This valuation disparity has created a barbell effect on the industry, meaning there is similar heavy weighting between the largest and smallest market capitalization groups, with a thinned-out middle. There are 13 companies (here including AVANGRID, which is not wholly tradable) between $10 billion and $20 billion.

Figure 27: Market Capitalization Distribution

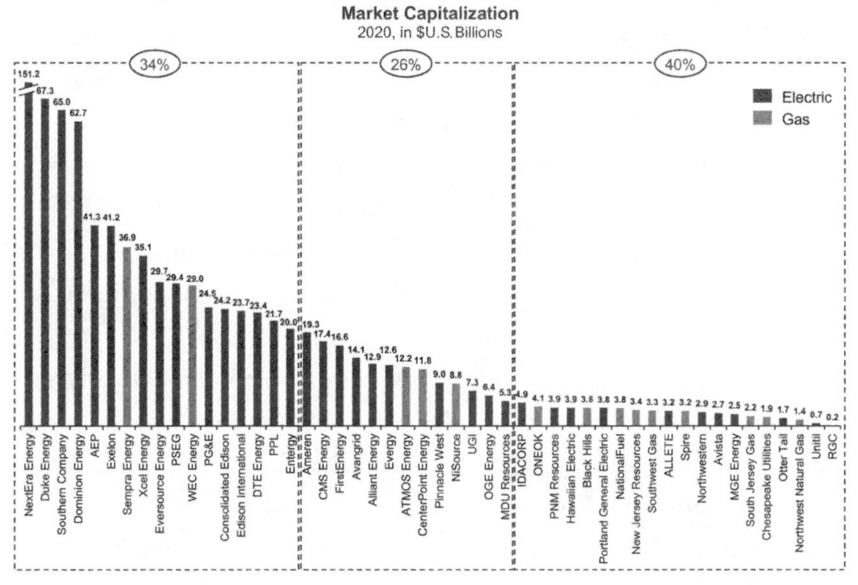

With this dispersion, it is easy to see how smaller companies could combine to gain scale and improve competitiveness, medium companies could combine to build necessary scale to compete with most of the larger utilities, and the largest utilities could pursue creation of a mega-utility or roll-up companies that fit geographically or compositionally, or that provide unique market or asset access.

Utility consolidation has been both popular and advantageous, not just because it is strategically logical and proven beneficial to customers, but because financial markets, competitive pressures, and fundamental economics support these actions. U.S. utilities have demonstrated they can capture estimated synergies, build balance sheets, and maintain lower rates to customers through transactions, when successfully executed. The financial markets are deeply experienced with transactions and sensitive to the long-term value of smart strategic actions taken by a utility.

Steve Fleishman of Wolfe Research provided a Wall Street view on future consolidation:

> I believe the opportunity for consolidation remains as underlying conditions still support it: the industry is still fragmented; high variability exists in scale, financial position, and costs; companies better understand how to gain merger approvals; and capital costs remain low. I believe deals will return to low premiums to preserve value and will probably bias toward larger deals to capture more synergies and value. LDCs as a group may lead the roll-up of smaller competitors since electric and combination companies are wary of adding gas system assets in the current ESG environment.

The clear consensus among the CEOs and professional advisors interviewed is that U.S. utility M&A has not yet seen its peak, with continued opportunity for both traditional and non-traditional transactions for pursuit. However, there is less consensus on what future utility industry M&A (or strategic events) will look like, whether utilities will always be the acquirors, or how other forms of value capture may be designed.

As Jim Judge from Eversource Energy noted about U.S. utility consolidation:

> There are still numerous consolidation options, so traditional deals are likely to continue. As the base of utility companies further shrinks, regulators will continue to assess all aspects of transactions to ensure that the attention of the acquiror to effective operations is not diminished. Whether deals are large or small, the same issues are important to regulators. As transactions get bigger and companies expand their reach, regulators could become concerned about potential diseconomies of scale depending on how local cost levels are affected.

In general, the CEOs and professional advisors agree they do not see prohibitive constraints to building larger-scale companies that grow to a level too big to regulate, at least not right now. And they generally do not believe diseconomies of scale are likely to be created as utilities grow in scale, because regulators will be keen to address any inkling that adverse customer economics could be an outcome during the approval process. However, what is "too big" or "too complex" is in the eye of the beholder and political decisions are often at odds with practical economic logic, so no real empiric or legislative guidance yet exists to apply to questions about scale limits.

Mark Ruelle from Evergy further commented on the topic of scale:

> The utility industry has improved at recognizing the value of scale and understanding being too small can have serious disadvantages. I used to think potential diseconomies of scale could occur, but I now believe that companies are more sophisticated in how they organize and operate, and regulators are more capable at sorting through complexity.

And Gale Klappa from WEC Energy noted:

> Looking forward, there doesn't appear to be a real constraint on deal size; even mega-deals can get done if companies are thoughtful about the scale issues that will emerge.

Most observers believe the overall U.S. utilities industry has been enhanced as a result of the swing from fragmentation to consolidation. Advisors have recognized that companies have not just grown, but strengthened, and have been able to develop the kinds of capabilities that will prove valuable in a more competitive market. Financial markets have observed that utilities have sustained capital programs and dividend payouts that continue to fuel growth and make the sector attractive to external investment. And regulators have noticed that utilities have successfully delivered on their commitments, particularly with respect to lower or flatter rates, sustained capital programs, and high-quality service delivery.

Importantly, U.S. utilities have been successful at identified synergies realization, rewarding shareholders, and enabling customers to benefit through continued distribution of these synergies once the transaction is closed and into perpetuity. These outcomes contribute to the perception within the utilities industry that consolidation, if done smartly, can provide impetus for future growth.

Erle Nye, formerly of TXU, commented on drivers for consolidation occurrence and success:

> Consolidation continues because the industry is still too fragmented and offers real value capture potential when companies combine, particularly when performance disparity exists. Opportunities still exist for rational management to take out the excess in companies and use operational excellence to drive efficiency and value. Achieving this outcome can be tempered by the complexity of the situation, and getting it done is harder than it looks, but it can be aided by simplifying operating model and structure.

Pure shareholder value empirics are difficult to assess because the discrete effects of the economy, market sentiment, regulation, and policy on the sector as a whole or utilities individually is difficult to accurately ascertain. But empirics, like earnings per share (which have generally grown on a sustained basis by 4 percent to 6 percent, absent recessions), are not the only measure to use in judging the success of a merger to a company. Other factors, like strategic position, agenda success, scale level, investment continuity, brand value, capital access, dividend security, and business risk, are also indicators that reflect how investors and regulators view transaction logic and results.

Potential Paths

The history of U.S. utility M&A has been centered on traditional company-to-company combinations more than elegantly structured products of strategic and financial engineering. But while the current population of U.S. utility M&A targets is still rich, that does not mean the direction of future transactions could not extend beyond traditional parameters, structures, and targets, particularly if disruptions occur in the economy or in policy.

Regarding the future direction of U.S. utilities mergers, Jeff Holzschuh from Morgan Stanley commented:

> The utilities sector is in a transition that is redefining the overall energy industry—what it owns, how it deploys capital, how it addresses externalities, and other matters. The universe of options is smaller, but the implications of option selection can have an outsized impact on the business. Companies are revisiting how to view risk and reward and readdressing whether opportunities exist to recycle capital away from out-of-favor segments and assets, toward investments that offer more cash, better returns, and less risk. Third-party capital sources like sovereign wealth funds and SPACs are aggressively seeking places to place investment, and utilities may be an attractive destination.

A range of M&A paths are available to U.S. utilities for inorganically growing the business or unlocking constrained value through restructuring. Some options may be business-as-usual; certain options may be determined unrealistic to pursue; and other options may currently seem unlikely to be available or worth considering. But the point is the U.S. utilities industry has multiple alternatives that could present themselves in the future if it is willing to open the aperture on the *art of the possible*.

The first element to consider is from where the impetus for potential future transactions will be driven. Will it be because the industrial logic for combination is so compelling? Will it come because an unexpected "bluebird" flew in the window and offered itself? Will the stars finally align to turn a spurned offer into a reality? Or will unexpected circumstances arise that present a once-in-a-career opportunity that cannot be ignored?

Remember, transactions do not only occur because a hard-fought courtship was successful. Many prior transactions that occurred were opportunistic and more the result of good fortune than good planning. Yet, it takes all manner of transactions to help consolidate an industry, and future M&A activity will likely arise from both a natural underlying logic, as well as sources and directions that were unforeseen.

Few would argue that mergers and acquisitions will continue at the same annual pace of two to three per year as they have for the last several years. Some may argue that the pace will increase due to scarcity, market-positioning drivers, and strong currency values. Most would not proffer that the pace of utility industry M&A will decline, either by mandate or by circumstance. But an interesting question is presented regarding whether the nature of inorganic activity will parallel that seen in recent years, or become more reflective of bespoke utility beliefs, strategies, priorities, and choices, and become less frequent.

On the future direction of U.S. utility M&A, Joe Sauvage from Citi explained:

> I expect it to continue—even with fewer partners still available—because companies remain interested in more scale and higher growth, even though they have to be pickier than in prior periods. Utilities are now wrestling with the question of whether integration is more valuable than specialization. Selection of the right choice will depend on how companies see the future utilities landscape playing out and whether they can afford to spend development dollars on low-contribution businesses in the near term. Regulatory diversity may also matter, and real success may turn on the presence of good regulation, or the ability to turn bad regulation into the opposite.

The range of M&A potential opportunity types for U.S. utilities is summarized below. The discussion is not exhaustive, as permutations of a particular inorganic event style are always possible, but it does reflect potential transaction pursuits that are both traditional and non-traditional, low and high complexity, small and large in scale, and asset- and services-based.

CONVENTIONAL MODELS

The most common types of inorganic activity to be seen in the future are likely to be conventional transactions, such as straight mergers or acquisitions between two utilities. These mergers-of-equals, modified mergers-of-equals, or outright acquisitions demonstrate the available deal structure, as well as the nature of the underlying strategy. The types of conventional transactions the industry may pursue include:

- **Mergers**: Companies will always seek friendly transactions within the sector, particularly mergers-of-equals which can leverage low premiums, to minimize market and regulatory concerns about financial stress and future operating performance.

- **Acquisitions**: Mid-sized and large companies may feel that outright acquisition, with a moderate to high premium, is preferred to searching for a selective merger-of-equals partner and paying a low offer premium.

- **Mega-deals**: Multiple utilities have market capitalizations above $20 billion, so combinations of any two of these companies will easily create another, or larger, mega-utility positioned to influence the new energy transition.

- **Roll-ups**: The number of companies with fewer than $10 billion in market capitalization provides sellers with ample opportunity for buyer interest, and buyers with sufficient targets to style acceptable transactions with attractive entities.

- **Segments**: Trading, fossil fuel, midstream, and retail businesses have declined in favor due to carbon emission and business risk aversion and provide an opportunity to buy or sell these segments in a manner to optimize proceeds and value to the owner.

- **Portfolios**: Coal, and even gas assets, are presently in disfavor with investors and offer the potential to high-grade existing portfolios, to both reduce financial risk, as well as align assets to policy preferences and regulatory mandates.

- **Financial sponsors**: Although the number of entities owning utilities is limited, infrastructure funds have maintained a constant presence in U.S. utility M&A and offer a potential alternative to utility acquirors through preservation of a separate identity.

- **Internationals**: While several foreign acquirors currently own U.S. companies, with some owning multiple entities, there are several other well-heeled potential acquirors that have previously indicated interest in entering the country.

UNCONVENTIONAL MODELS

The range of unconventional transactions is broad and diverse. These types of transactions will not involve all utilities but can be executed to achieve specific objectives and/or take advantage of opportunities not considered to be mainstream across the entire sector. The types of transactions that could be considered unconventional and available to the U.S. industry include:

- **Hostiles**: Unfulfilled interest in certain companies can cause acquirors to use an unsolicited offer as a means of addressing a reluctant target, even though these types of transactions have a dismal record of regulatory approval and close.

- **Three ways**: Given the number of under $20 billion utilities, the fastest way to scale may be to find two small and/or mid-sized partners to bring a compatible set of assets and positioning to accelerate readiness for the new energy transition.

- **Water**: Several investor-owned utilities have already acquired publicly traded or publicly owned water companies because the profile of these entities parallels the requirements for successful infrastructure operations that is core to many utilities.

- **Property sales**: Many situations exist where companies maintain a local presence in remote areas of their territory that are adjacent to another proximate company better suited to absorb or fit the property within its operating system.

- **Minority sell-offs**: The recent Duke Energy–GIC Private Limited transaction illustrates an opportunity to monetize value within a selling company, plus use the proceeds to avoid a need for additional equity to support capital investment.

- **Minority buy-ins**: Utilities may find a shortage in funding capability exists in smaller or troubled entities and be in position to address these needs in a friendly manner by securing minority ownership, much like existed in Europe for decades.

- **SPACs**: A Special Purpose Acquisition Company (SPAC) model has emerged as an acquisition vehicle for investors to use to enable participation in the new energy transition in a more passive manner than through a typical transaction.

- **Energy services**: The nature of capabilities needed to be successful in the new energy transition requires a different set of competencies, experiences, and offerings than utilities have provided in the past, which targeted non-regulated entities can offer.

- **Federal agencies**: It is not beyond possibility that a federal-level Power Marketing Administration (PMA), like TVA, could be sold whole, or in part, to support a reduction in the level of debt at the federal level and offer new market entry potential.

- **State agencies**: Like the federal PMA opportunity, an even greater potential exists for a state to seek to monetize existing power authorities, like that considered in South Carolina, to allow the net proceeds to be deployed for broader purposes.

- **Municipals**: Cities typically rely on their owned utilities to support the general fund in these municipalities and, like federal and state entities, could find that co-investment or outright sale could offer funding support to cash-strapped entities.

- **Operating agreements**: Utilities may find the opportunity to offer targeted, or a range of full-cost, services to public power entities to leverage available expertise or scale, or co-partner with these entities to enable local asset performance improvement.

As described, multiple alternatives exist for utilities to transact as either buyers or sellers. The choices to be pursued depend on the starting point of each company and their perspective on the future direction of the new energy transition. It is still likely that bulking up competitive scale will be a path almost universally followed in the U.S. utility industry, but it is also true that high-grading the current portfolio will receive attention to minimize business risk and unlock unrealized value within the business.

Based on trends over 2020–2021, business simplification and portfolio monetization will be consistent themes for utility managements to address. Several companies have already taken steps to not just shed less integrated, out-of-favor businesses, but also to transfer smaller, dispersed, or underperforming properties to either adjacent buyers or financial sponsors. Companies like CenterPoint Energy, NiSource, Xcel Energy, AES, AVANGRID, or Dominion Energy, among others, could choose to leverage a current seller's market for properties.

In addition, all utilities could seek to replicate the Duke Energy–GIP monetization transaction as a means to raise additional capital and avoid the need to issue additional common equity to fund future capital investment and growth.

Path Considerations

The U.S. utilities industry is steadily recovering from disappointing stock index results relative to the overall stock market in 2020. Although now improving, relative stock performance was almost 20 percent lower than the broad market, causing company P/E multiples and market capitalizations to drop and creating more relative separation between individual companies, depending on earnings results and portfolio composition.[2]

The relative disparity in individual company stock valuations may create market opportunities for successful target pursuit, but this can also reflect out-of-favor portfolio dimensions that could handicap an acquiring company's currency. Consequently, utilities are focused on avoiding actions that could undermine current acquiror valuations and create an avoidable impediment to future market participation and post-close success.

When weighing whether, where, and how to pursue a potential transaction, U.S. utilities need to consider several key questions that define the decision-making baseline for identifying, qualifying, and assessing potential M&A directions and implications. These questions include several front-end qualifiers to address before proceeding with serious pursuit of a transaction with a target, particularly if it is a large or complex transaction.

How does the potential transaction create strategic advantage? Can the transaction be efficiently financed? How can potential value be created from the transaction? Is the transaction regulatory review environment complicated to navigate? Does pursuit of the transaction increase the risk profile of the business? Each of these inquiries are singularly important factors to consider, and collectively frame the challenge of successfully pursuing and executing a potential transaction.

Transaction styles are likely to take many different forms in the future because the breadth of available options is so diverse. And with 33 tradable electrics and 16 LDCs, the number of options in each scale class, that is, mega-companies, mid-sized companies, and small utilities, are equally diverse, and reflect unique market positioning, financial situation, and transaction motivation.

Each of these scale classes have different motivations for consolidation, with mega-companies seeking to gain strategic scale and market positioning, in areas like market access, financial flexibility, portfolio balance, customer touchpoints, and reduced business risk. These classes also include mid-sized companies seeking sufficient scale to maintain adequate future market significance in an industry where the largest utilities continue to become bigger through organic or inorganic means. Included as well are the smallest utilities seeking to gain additional relevance in a bifurcated sector where scale and presence are required to maintain an adequate voice in industry matters, particularly the new energy transition.

With a remaining tradable electric and LDC universe numbering 49 utilities, there are ample targets for utilities of all sizes seeking inorganic growth. But when there are 17 tradable U.S. utilities with market capitalization above $20 billion (and two others just under this limit), 12 utilities (excluding AVANGRID, which is majority-owned by Iberdrola) with market capitalization between $5 billion and $20 billion, and 20 utilities with market capitalization under $5 billion, the transaction mindsets of each class, as well any utility within that class, can be dramatically divergent.[3]

Consequently, there may be a convergence in philosophies emerging among utilities. In the last third of the 25 years of the modern era of utility M&A, financial characteristics of transactions have centered more on disciplined bidding than in earlier years when markets for transactions were frothy, competitive, and driven by a desire to prevail. These financial characteristics, as well as others related to style, premium, value, regulation, and risks, are pushing utility M&A activity in a more conservative direction.

Styles and Premiums

Utilities have generally believed that merger-of-equals transactions were the most desirable because they were easier to do. They require lower market premiums, have less balance sheet and cash flow stress, are more comfortable for executives to accept, and are more attractive to regulators. But merger-of-equals partners (reflecting single-digit premiums) are harder to find since the smaller utility generally likes to be compensated for its loss of identity, independence, and perhaps leadership role. And they are harder to seamlessly integrate if a best-of-both mindset exists that sub-optimizes the nature of the operating model and the level of synergies to be attained.

If they have a choice, most utilities would obviously prefer to pay a lower market premium, which could lead to certain earnings accretion, even if synergies are constrained by an operating model design that leaves existing businesses largely intact. But that option does not always present itself, as the price of identity and independence are often high.

Modified mergers-of-equals have often been a default substitute, but this style has its drawbacks as well, with premiums ranging between 10 percent and 20 percent, leading to more financial stress and greater pressure on synergies realization, though fewer accommodations need to be made with respect to social issues.

Dick Kelly from Xcel Energy commented about future deals:

> Transactions are likely to be straight acquisitions—mergers-of-equals don't really exist, so why pretend they do. Even small deals take the same amount of time as larger ones, so mega-deals will be even more complicated and challenging to complete, particularly if multi-state and concentrated.

Gale Klappa of WEC Energy further stated:

> In my view, acquisitions with high premiums are not likely to be as prevalent anymore. A new era is emerging, and takeover level premiums can handicap a company for years.

Outright acquisitions may seem the simplest to design to execute since a control premium above 20 percent is established and the acquiror is able to drive all decisions affecting the combined company and avoid typical merger-of-equals disagreements that lead to extended timelines, lower synergies, and bruised executive feelings. On the other hand, outright acquisitions require a full control premium, create greater financial stress, and attract more regulatory scrutiny.

To be sure, the style of a utility transaction will depend on the circumstances prevailing at the time of the deal, irrespective of management preferences. If a target is a coveted entity to include within the acquirors portfolio, then management may not feel so constrained about the premium level to be offered, or it may not have a choice if it seeks to be the selected suitor. Alternatively, two combining companies know that the fewer impediments to success that are negotiated into a merger agreement—such as the premium level—the more likely the strategic and financial success of the proposed transaction.

Value Formulas

Several takeaways from prior transactions have been discussed, shedding light on how utilities have previously fared regarding the breadth of value sources and how they have performed relative to expected value creation. Utility transaction outcomes have been mixed in fully recognizing the value of scale when considering a transaction, with companies often being too myopic on reflecting this critical outcome to the strategic positioning of the combined company post-consolidation.

Utility managements have directly focused on capturing the most direct and tangible benefits from a transaction through integration of the two companies—cost synergies from consolidation, whether at the corporate center, operations support, or operating plants and field operations. However, as illustrated in **Figure 16**, potential value extends well beyond this single element of cost reduction and into strategic advancement and tangible market appreciation.

Gale Klappa of WEC Energy believes the search for lower operating costs will continue to be a driver for consolidation:

> Revenues have not been growing lately, which places some companies in the position of emphasizing sustained reduction in cost levels and rationalization of the business, even as the low-hanging fruit has been harvested.

The concentrated focus on cost synergies over other potential enterprise areas like multiple expansion, capital investment, revenue enhancement, portfolio composition, and strategic positioning is often the product of some combination of limited business insight at the time, priority of short-term outcomes, unclear strategic priorities, and undefined aspirations for the post-close combined company.

These additional value areas are likely to receive elevated attention in future transactions as the scale of companies increase from consolidation, particularly among mega-utilities. Cost synergies are critical to gaining regulatory approval, distributing benefits to customers, and rewarding shareholders for the risks they have assumed, but are just one element of future value that flows from scale. As the new energy transition accelerates and raises the visibility of utility positioning, heightened attention will also flow to the thoughtfulness and differentiation of strategies and the quality of management in conceiving and capturing all value sources.

U.S. utilities possess an enviable record of capturing identified synergies, as compared to other sectors of American industry. Primarily pursuing costs versus creating new revenue sources accounts for most of that performance difference. But utility managements have been effective at displaying an integration discipline that starts with detailed Day 1 readiness, and ends with full synergies attainment, even if synergies are realized over several years post-close. This characteristic has served utility managements well and enabled them to produce the earnings accretion they expected to solidify financial position.

The future value formula will be multi layered and comprised of discrete elements like identified synergies, which creates the floor for value, and extend into both specific sources like capital investment, capital structure, and revenues, as well as more strategic elements like portfolio composition, growth strategies, premium differentiation, and platform architecture. These are the elements that will transform synergies outcomes beyond annual earnings considerations to permanent strategic advantage from the value of scale.

Utilities will need to nurture, develop, and embed the necessary capabilities to support identifying and evaluating the value of scale since they extend beyond conventional thinking about transactions and the normal course of business. These capabilities will include attributes like imagination, which defines the scope and range of future aspirations, and platform thinking, which establishes the sustainable operating model for converting single company positioning into multi-company advantage.

These capabilities will also include a *market-back* orientation that defines solutions outcomes and revenue offerings from the perspective of the future customer. And these new capabilities will be grounded in the discipline of strategic innovation, which underpins how companies will move from operationalization of technologies to commercialization of solutions.

Approval Timelines

The experience of the U.S. utilities industry has been improving over the modern era of utility M&A from 14 to 16 months on average in the early years (1995–1999) to 10 to 12 months on average during the last time period (2015–2020), which also saw more recent transaction approvals drop to between eight and nine months. This reduction in duration is the product of increased regulator transaction familiarity, improved approval application content, and less contentious combinations. This shortened approval duration period is a welcome outcome, but not one entirely within continued utility control.

Unlike rate cases, most states do not have a time certain by which a merger approval application decision must be delivered. Specific state timelines can be a function of prior precedent, current case load and general visibility, and complexity of the transaction itself. Utilities can work to shorten the average decision time frame, but they need to be creative and adaptive to accomplish this objective.

For starters, combining utilities need to start earlier in preparing the merger approval application, even as certain specific decisions, facts, and actions are still being negotiated or defined. Plenty of prior transaction examples exist, specifically in the jurisdictions where the combined companies will be filing, to provide a roadmap to follow, if one does not exist internally, and a head start.

More importantly, companies need to start framing the key elements of the merger approval application in tandem with the merger agreement itself, since the application will rely on many passages and elements to describe the parameters of the transaction. Even if all areas of the merger agreement are not known prior to closing, many elements of the merger approval application can still benefit from early incorporation of what is known.

Most merger approval applications tend to be filed between 45 and 60 days post-announcement, with a few standouts completed in fewer than 30 days. With many companies having experience with merger approval applications before their regulating jurisdictions, and some serial acquirors having multiple experiences before these same regulators, the precedents, principles, and parameters affecting ultimate regulatory outcomes are well known. With an early start, companies could shorten the filing timeline to between 20 and 30 days without sacrificing content completeness, standards conformance, or argument effectiveness.

In tandem, combining utilities should begin to think about how to educate the state regulatory commissions and Wall Street about the rationale and contours of the transaction. Day-of-announcement presentations are a primary vehicle, but these are subject to how prepared management is to address more than the combination rationale, transaction parameters, and expected timelines. Many recent presentations have been devoid of key details about the regulatory standards, precedent timelines, strategic advantages, synergies composition, and regulatory plan, among other areas.

State regulatory commissions are particularly keen to understand the parameters of the proposed regulatory plan, for example, how and when customers will receive benefits, how shareholders will be treated, how future rate cases and benefits sharing could be structured, etc., to identify a few key considerations. It should be accepted that regulatory scrutiny over customer benefits, public interest standards, and financial and operational risks will be front-and-center in the minds of regulators, and that their scrutiny will grow in breadth after every transaction.

The benefit of early discussion with state regulatory commissioners is not to just inform them of the nature of the forthcoming regulatory approval application and regulatory plan, but also to gauge the reception to the key elements of the filing and the critical question of synergies handling. Unfortunately, no amount of dialogue will cause the state regulatory commission to commit itself to any specific action at this point, or even to a general path forward.

But that is not the intent of an early sit-down with regulators. The purposes here are to position the preferred path forward, test the efficacy of the critical dimension of synergies sharing, allay concerns the state regulatory commission may have about the transaction, and identify potential areas where the merger approval application may need to be fortified precedentially, factually, and persuasively.

If pre-filing effort is expended to understand any regulatory impediments and communicate to the state regulatory commission that the merger approval application will satisfy their policy and evidentiary needs, then perhaps a faster regulatory schedule can be obtained, which will accelerate benefits to customers and shareholders.

Future View

Since the population of potential targets is sufficient to satisfy the strategic growth needs of all basic types and scale classes of U.S. utilities, it is likely that industry M&A will continue to be viewed as a fundamental means to create value. However, with only 49 tradable utilities to choose among and many companies hungry for growth, it should be expected that buyers will be judicious in evaluating which entities to prioritize, and sellers will be cautious in deciding which suitors provide the best long-term outcome for shareholders and customers.

There are no fundamental impediments to continued U.S. utilities consolidation: an industry-wide track record of successful deal approval exists; regulators have largely provided equitable outcomes in approval proceedings; companies have captured expected synergies and other benefits for customers and shareholders; and managements have digested mergers or acquisitions without creating excessive disruption to longer-term strategies or short-term operations.

This does not mean there will not be naysayers to the wisdom of utilities pursuing M&A. To the contrary, state regulatory commission staffs and intervenors and their consultants can be resourceful in painting a picture of why consolidation is an unnecessary and gratuitous adventure, does not yield the benefits expected, and creates avoidable risks to customers. And no number of prior transactions will make these concerns disappear.

But U.S. utilities understand the nature of the regulatory process and have proven effective in demonstrating conformance with approval standards and tests, presenting and supporting compelling rationales for consolidation, preserving or improving credit ratings, identifying and quantifying meaningful cost savings for customers, reporting positive results on synergies attainment, sustaining capital investment for system growth and reliability, and delivering high-quality service to customers.

The potential for further consolidation will not be constrained because of actual or perceived shortcomings in utility industry M&A performance. Rather, this experience will buttress the perspective of management on adopting M&A as a core strategy element and serve as a catalyst for more combinations. Any slowdown in U.S. utility M&A will likely reflect temporary macro-economic factors that affect capital access, interest rates, financial liquidity, and/or overall market risks, or major shifts in federal and state energy policies.

There are sufficient inorganic opportunities for almost any utility in the U.S. to avail themselves. These opportunities obviously range across every scale class, whether electrics or LDCs, and provide a menu of possibilities depending on the size of the initiating or acquiring utility. For perspective, the range of scale differences among electrics is dramatic, with a $150 billion spread between the largest (NextEra Energy) and smallest (Unitil Corp.) entities.[4] And for LDCs, the spread is approximately $36 billion between the largest (Sempra Energy) and smallest (RGC Resources) companies, and particularly large within a small peer set.[5]

Among the small electrics, the largest concentration of these companies exists in the upper Midwest and Mountain regions, and for LDCs in the mid-Atlantic and Midwest regions. For moderate-sized companies, concentration is highest for the electric sector between the Gulf of Mexico and the Great Lakes, with only a couple of LDCs in this size range. Of course, the electric mega-companies generally possess a super-regional footprint and their currency travels without borders, but few large LDCs exist, with both also owning large electric operating companies.

As illustrated in **Figure 10**, geographical separation does not inhibit M&A activity, and step-out transactions across regions have consistently occurred in both the electric and LDC sectors. Given the current regional reach among the 49 tradable U.S. utilities, it is likely that regional and super-regional transactions will be unavoidable.

A few companies may see themselves as only likely to do a single merger or acquisition because they would seek to combine with another large entity to create a mega-utility with one action. Others may see themselves pursuing a roll-up strategy designed to create a larger integrated regional presence through acquisition of multiple companies within or proximate to the territory. For electrics, numerous candidates populate the center of the U.S. and could expand the size of all scale classes of companies. This roll-up approach could be particularly viable with respect to LDCs along the East Coast or Northeast, where several acquirors and acquirees reside.

Simply because of the prior track record of utility M&A, it should be expected that simpler, rather than more elegant and complex, transactions will be the priority for pursuit. Whether these pursued M&A transactions are styled as mergers or acquisitions will depend on the market circumstances prevailing at the time and the relative scale of the seller and buyer.

For numerous reasons, utilities may still prefer a merger approach since it brings the potential benefit of a lower premium, is more financially attractive to Wall Street, and is more socially acceptable with regulators and local governments.

But this virtue may be its biggest shortcoming as well. Too low a premium can attract other suitors that believe they can provide a superior premium and total offer to the acquiree's shareholders. This undercuts the transaction and offer strategy of the seller and buyer, which believe the long-term strategic and financial benefits of the transaction are better served through focusing on sustained growth and valuation rise over short-term gratification from an elevated premium.

Consequently, utilities may be persuaded that the smartest strategy for combination may be an outright acquisition, using financial discipline (and persuasive demonstration of outcomes) to avoid high premiums that undercut the short- and long-term financial viability of the combined company, which then can adversely affect the viability of the core strategies of the business.

Clearly, any auction that is used as the vehicle for sale will generally result in an acquisition of the company that is offered. It is more likely that a higher acquisition premium will result, particularly if the auction is well subscribed and multiple bidders are in play.

Restructuring will happen when circumstances support a shift in portfolio composition due to changed market sentiment and different perceptions about the value of keeping the portfolio intact versus selling pieces to buyers, which can create more value with them than the incumbent owner.

As Steve Fleishman from Wolfe Research commented:

> Companies are using property sell-downs to raise capital as an alternative to selling equity and selling off subsidiaries where the strategic fit and financial returns are no longer obvious.

The six current restructuring situations provide a model for outcomes under a range of market disposition approaches. Select segment or asset portfolio rebalancing is likely to continue over the next few years given Wall Street's emphasis on ESG goals and the general federal and state policy direction against fossil-based fuels in either electrics or LDCs.

The U.S. utility industry is attractive to numerous investor classes, such as international utilities, private equity, infrastructure funds, pension funds, and possibly even SPACs. All these investors could have an interest in elements of the 49 tradable companies, or portions of their portfolios.

International utilities are natural acquirors of U.S. utilities, and six utilities have entered the U.S. and demonstrated their willingness to enter the market on multiple occasions, with four owners extending their presence once initial presence has been achieved. The logical international buyers are well capitalized, with adequate capital scale and access to pursue most U.S. utilities, if so inclined. But the concern to be addressed will be whether they will choose to do so.

Bill Lamb from Baker Botts offered his perspective on the potential for international acquirors to be active in the future:

> I don't see international companies being overly active because it's a hard sell for a company of that nature in a local regulatory environment.

Steve Fleishman from Wolfe Research weighed in with a different perspective:

More unique transactions are possible, like international entities reentering the US in the pursuit of stable returns and renewables assets.

The arguments for international entry are clear: highly transparent legal model, stable governmental policies, higher earned return potential than many alternatives, workable regulatory environment, and growing energy use. Yet, arguments exist for international entities avoiding the U.S. as well. Utility valuations are relatively high, competition for attractive companies can be expected, and local governments can be aggressive over conditions and commitments required to close a transaction.

The arguments for international acquirors pursuing future U.S. utilities transactions outweigh those against participation, but this comparison does not mean that these entities will choose to test the market again. Given the search for growth among international buyers, it is more likely that one or more new entities will seek to enter the U.S. utilities market, and international players with existing presence will seek to expand, particularly given the operating models that the Canadian, Spanish, and UK companies have adopted thus far.

The CEOs and professional advisors generally believe that financial sponsors, particularly infrastructure funds with long time horizons, will remain interested in the U.S. utilities sector. These entities have lower return thresholds and are viewed more favorably by local governments and regulators than private equity.

Pension funds have been active investors with infrastructure funds because they share a similar investment strategy and profile, that is, long-term holds, passive management, and reasonable, stable return expectations. They already have ownership in U.S. utilities like Puget Energy and Oncor and have been successful at simultaneously growing their investments and delivering on commitments to boards of directors, regulators, and customers.

Bill Lamb from Baker Botts opined:

> Pension funds have been active investors and owners in Canada and bring an attractive profile match to a utility situation—deep capital and long-term hold perspective to an entity with sustained capital deployment for growth and solid returns compared to a normal investment portfolio. State regulators are familiar with infrastructure funds, and this type of investor may be even more appealing.

Erle Nye, former TXU CEO, also addressed international and financial sponsor buyers in the U.S.:

> I don't expect to see new international players, but I believe financial sponsors will still be with us.

While infrastructure funds have had difficulty in finding opportunities for acquisition within the U.S., they have maintained an active, visible profile. And they benefit from utilities already observing and understanding their ownership models. Related to small utilities, which happen to fit the investment capital scale sweet spot for these long-horizon funds and often syndicate to reduce capital exposure, 20 opportunities exist among electrics and LDCs with market capitalizations under $5 billion. That is a target-rich environment for a financial sponsor in the right place, with the right pitch, at the right time.

Unique Events

Pure vanilla transactions have always been the staple of the U.S. utilities industry, with few deals requiring exotic structures or dependent events, such as merge and spin, or immediate subsidiary divestment. Utility deal contours and structures have been simple and predictable.

Numerous other types of opportunities exist in the market today to drive unique transactions or extend M&A into adjacent sectors. A dozen discrete, unconventional transaction types were described that could be considered by utilities. Several are not likely to emerge in the short term, but many others could occur and provide a different avenue to inorganic growth.

Hostile offers have been few and far between in the U.S. utilities industry, and largely unsuccessful as well. More than a dozen hostile offers have been attempted to date, with only two progressing to actual close.

These hostile offers have encountered difficulty in reaching a successful conclusion because they initially involve a willing buyer but an unwilling seller. Most recipients of an unsolicited offer to shareholders or a bear hug to a board of directors are surprised and angered by this type of move by an acquiror trying to win their favor and acquiescence. Hostile offers also create immediate disfavor among many key stakeholders, for example, principally the board of directors, CEO, and executive management, and then local government and state government officials, regulators, unions, editorial boards, and employees, among other groups.

Even if the hostile offeror finally obtains a supportive shareholder vote, usually by sweetening the offer price, that does not solve regulatory issues that typically emerge. Regulators remain concerned about the levels of the premium, the financial stress created by the offer price, the ability to commit to sustained capital spend, and the continued focus to service delivery, among other issues.

While hostile offers may move through an initial shareholder approval or proxy solicitation stage gate, they generally bog down at the regulatory level and do not receive regulatory approval, at least without satisfying regulatory requirements, some of which can be onerous.

Full unsolicited offers to potential acquirees are less likely to be utilized in the future because of their track record. However, less hostile tactics, which provide more compelling strategic logic, use more constructive language, and are less alienating, may well find their way into the approaches selected to enter meaningful discussion with targets, particularly given the dichotomy in industry scale composition.

While hostile or unsolicited offers may continue in a softer form, such as not immediately employing proxy solicitations directed at shareholders, they are most likely to occur when a specific set of circumstances are present, such as financially or operationally vulnerable targets, sympathetic regulators, and weakened managements.

Much of the U.S. utilities industry views itself as possessing a core competence of operating local electric and LDC infrastructure businesses. A few utilities have already concluded these competencies are extendible to the water segment, for example, Eversource Energy and Northwest Natural Gas, and more are likely to follow this path, particularly where smaller-scale companies can offer seamless operations and friendly collaboration to municipalities.

Steve Fleishman from Wolfe Research notes:

> Water acquisitions by electric and/or gas companies could occur since they are infrastructure businesses, which is a core competence for these utilities.

This thought has been mentioned by other CEOs over time, though little action to date has followed such musings.

There are fewer than ten publicly traded water companies, with one, American Water, dwarfing the other individual entities. Conversely, there are more than 50,000 community water systems within the U.S. that could offer buying opportunity, although outside the major metropolitan areas the majority are short on customer numbers (less attractive), while long on required capital investment (more attractive).

It is the need for additional capital that makes a sale of the water system attractive to municipalities, and it is the regulatory policy of several states to allow fair value rate base to reflect acquisition values in future rates. Notwithstanding these promising conditions, these transactions still have issues to solve related to tax basis and public sentiment.

Several U.S. utilities would welcome the chance to assume the roles and acquire the assets of PMAs, state agencies, or large municipal systems, but transactions of this type are situational, which means they first require a recognized need for sale, a firm decision by a public owner to sell their system or assets, and face a protracted financial negotiation over structuring the transaction and normalizing differences in financing costs between an investor-owned utility and a public power entity, specifically the impact to customer rates. This is a deterrent to most investor-owned utilities that do not like to initiate processes that could take years to resolve.

The uncertainties over the sale of a PMA, state agency, or municipal system far exceed those related to conventional investor-owned utilities, as federal government agencies and Congress, multiple levels of state and local government, and municipal mayors, city councils, and consumer groups will all weigh in on the advisability, risks, and costs associated with these kinds of dispositions. Investor-owned utilities are hard-pressed to be active drivers of these types of transaction and are highly dependent on other catalysts for action in the public sector.

Other lower-profile inorganic actions could be taken by U.S. utilities, but they are not likely to attract much notice or create large strategic or financial impact. These include actions such as property sales or swaps and operating agreements. Sale of discrete properties should be simple to accomplish, but tax basis issues and valuations seem to create higher hurdles than necessary.

Similarly, operating agreements make a great deal of sense in selected situations such as state agency or municipal system operations settings, but are not usually front-of-mind for either of these two types of owners and operators, nor between utilities. Pride of ownership is certainly a challenge to overcome, as is mistrust of intentions and commitments by an unaffiliated operator.

However, these types of public power entities typically maintain aged workforces facing heavy retirements, which create near-term experience and capabilities gaps that may not be closed from within the current owner and open the door to investor-owned utilities.

In these cases, state agencies and municipalities may be more incentivized to consider an alternative source of expertise or capital through a sale or contractual arrangement, much like LIPA executed with KeySpan and PSEG in the past. Dick Kelly from Xcel Energy believes there are opportunities for U.S. utilities:

> I've always thought that investor-owned utilities could play a larger role with municipalities, particularly ones that are cash constrained and have high and sustained capital investment needs.

With the new energy transition pushing U.S. utilities toward cleaner assets and new technologies requirements, companies are recognizing that the core knowledge and operating capabilities of the past do not fully satisfy a different nature of customer needs. Rather than core infrastructure design and operations, utilities now need to be actively engaged with customers about technology development, adoption, and deployment; device interconnection; system monitoring, analytics, and control; demand flexibility; and behind-the-meter application and device installation and management.

These are capabilities that the utilities industry has not needed to focus on in the past and that are now enabled by new technologies being brought to market for utilities and their customers. The U.S. utilities industry can obtain these capabilities through technology acquisition, licensing, or subscription, or through acquisition of the providers of these technologies and services.

Most current providers of these technologies and capabilities are either subsidiaries of OEMs or start-ups, and few are publicly traded entities of scale. The logic for acquisition is not just that utilities themselves have a need for the kinds of capabilities these start-up entities bring to bear to support local operations, but that these services are germane to many individual residential, commercial, and industrial customers and disintermediation by a third party through direct access diminishes the value of the utility to its customers.

Utilities still need to move past operationalizing technologies to commercializing capabilities, products, and services for customers, and ownership of these solutions providers offers the ability to preserve customer relationships and create new value from these interfaces and touchpoints.

These types of inorganic actions usually align with the non-regulated business, which has traditionally been more asset versus technology and solutions oriented. But these capabilities to better serve customers are enabled through start-ups and align directly with where the new energy transition is leading U.S. utilities and should be considered as core to the future utility offering portfolio, not a high-risk, unrelated investment.

Non-traditional M&A opportunities in the emerging energy services space could create smaller, but more plentiful options. These types of businesses may capture market attention because of their uniqueness, as well as signal a vision of what the new energy transition will look like and how utilities can position themselves to avoid disintermediation and commercialize offerings for broad customer bases. For mega-companies with more than five million customers, the current and addressable customer bases can be large enough to create a scalable platform beyond the current territory to proximate public power and other utilities.

Outcome Risks

U.S. utilities will continue to utilize M&A as an element of their growth strategies—there is just no substitute when sustained organic customer demand growth is generally around one percent and sustained capital investment cannot be presumed to be a permanent annuity.

The universe of inorganic utilities options will remain robust for at least the next five years, or until prior transactions dramatically reset the playing field and limit the attractiveness of available options. Pursuit of M&A will not get any easier, particularly as scale, reach, and impact dimensions continue to evolve.

Managements continue to focus on synergies capture, which provides for lower costs than would have been realized in the absence of the transaction and can offset normal escalation for a couple of years. Utilities have been adept at controlling costs in general, with many companies holding O&M cost growth below the rate of annual inflation.

Intervenors in utility M&A proceedings like to talk about diseconomies of scale, but this has not been an outcome for U.S. utilities to date. The focus of management provides additional confidence that O&M costs are not adversely affected just because companies became larger. Dick Kelly from Xcel Energy suggests:

> There may be a ceiling on being too big, but no one has found it yet.

If utilities thoughtfully consider the value of scale before announcement and during the transaction integration process, and design operating models that emphasize optimization of the combined business, then the potential risk of diseconomies of scale rapidly dissipates.

Even when utilities successfully control costs, effectively integrate acquisitions, and grow earnings at reasonable levels, this does not mean they can avoid interest from either other utilities or types of investors. Other utilities may admire the success of the company and see it as an attractive partner. But other investor types, like activists, may see additional value that is not being captured or created and believe they can "help" the company elevate its performance or accelerate its growth.

Activist investors bring compelling discipline to capturing shareholder value and fashion their business model around challenging management norms and behaviors. This type of investor often looks to leverage several complementary strategies when entering an investment with a U.S. utility, including evaluating whether the current strategy is clear and aggressive; challenging the fit of current segments and assets with the current business; comparing relative financial and operating performance with peers to identify additional value opportunities; and assessing the full enterprise value against what may be attainable in the market if the business was sold.

Mark Ruelle of Evergy remarked:

> Activist investors are a market fixture, and they can serve a purpose. We have worked directly with a firm and were not afraid of taking a second look at our business. We had the option of selling or improving, but the results at the time indicated the better path being a stand-alone plan.

Activist investors in the U.S. utilities industry are not atypical. They have made visible investment in more than a dozen companies and pursued the strategies mentioned above. Sometimes they have been successful at obtaining management commitment to directly address O&M levels, and in other cases secured an enhanced level of capital investment. Other times, they pushed companies to auction themselves in the market to test value, while in others they have helped a company to rationalize its business composition through divestment.

Even if a utility executes a smart M&A transaction or strategic plan, it does not mean the activist investor cannot find a reason to believe it can extract even greater value through management engagement or board of directors representation. In the future world of activist investors, utility managements will need to consider not just the perceptions of current shareholders, but the perspectives of potential future investors which are armed with significant capital resources and aggressive executives and advisors.

In the next era of utility M&A, certain companies will unavoidably face the challenge that large scale brings to the regulatory environment. For mega-utilities, regulators will be assessing whether adverse circumstances—market, financial, or operational—could emerge when two large entities combine to create an entity above $100 billion in market capitalization. For moderately sized companies, regulators will be interested in whether the combined company has the capability to manage a substantially enlarged business when levels double from $20 billion to more than $40 billion in market capitalization. As Erle Nye, formerly of TXU, reflected on deal-making:

> Regardless of who the acquirors are, my advice is if you can't walk away from the deal if you need to, then don't do it.

Regulators will explore the concept of scale from a different angle than utilities, which look at scale as a beneficial outcome to drive competitiveness and flexibility. The opposite view will receive attention from regulators, that is, asking whether this larger scale makes the new company less stable, nimble, economic, capable, or responsive.

Smart utilities will need to address these concerns in their regulatory approval flings, particularly those creating or extending mega-utilities. Companies will need to directly address what will be the not-so-subtle elephant in the room, and particularize the benefits of scale, not just with platitudes, but with empirics. Whether they address this topic from an offensive or defensive perspective will influence whether they can take the high ground on the issue or be forced to rebut assertions after the fact.

Final Thoughts

U.S. utilities are poised to continue their surge in overall growth for the foreseeable short term because they have been effective financial stewards and capital investment growth is expected to stay close to current levels for the next several years. But for the longer term, no crystal balls exist to accurately predict what the future will hold as the new energy transition takes hold.

Consequently, utilities need to utilize every tool they have to ensure that they can sustain growth, including aspirational vision, compelling strategies, strong management, aggressive cost control, high capital investment levels, reasonable dividend policies, responsive regulatory results, and multiple inorganic options—particularly M&A.

When Ed Tirello forecast the U.S. utilities industry could shrink from over 150 companies in 1987 to about 50 in five years, he was not incorrect about the outcome, just its timing. It took until 2020 for the combined electric and LDC sectors to reach this level and electrics, which were substantially larger as a group than LDCs, did not reach this level until 2013, distilling from about 100 companies in 1995.[6]

Perhaps a more relevant view of the future could be framed around the ultimate size of the utilities industry, such as how far it could shrink through M&A. Plenty of head room exists for further contraction, and with only two to three transactions per year, it could reach below 40 well within five years. Could this pace continue? Certainly, but sooner or later the universe of attractive utilities will shrink, and companies can only grow so large before policies could reverse and an AT&T-like divestment could occur.

While there is no known limit to industry scale—either how big a company or how small the industry—somewhere in the future the industry will find those limits and a new era of restructuring could again be a topic of discussion.

NOTES

Chapter 1: A Fragmented Industry

1. "Emergence of Electrical Utilities in America," Smithsonian Institution; Encyclopedia.com, February 2021 Update.
2. "Annual Retail Electricity Sales, Monthly Energy Review," U.S. Department of Energy, Energy Information Administration, January 2021.
3. "Emergence," Encyclopedia.com.
4. "2020 Statistical Report; National Rural Electric Cooperatives Association," Edison Electric Institute; "America's Electric Cooperatives Fact Sheet," Energy Information Administration website; American Public Power Association, 2019.
5. "Water and Wastewater Systems Sector," Department of Homeland Security, Cybersecurity & Infrastructure Security Agency, 2021.
6. Hyman, Leonard S. *America's Electric Utilities: Past, Present and Future, Public Utility Reports* (1988), 74.
7. Hawes, Douglas W. *Utility Holding Companies: A Modern View of the Business, Financial, SEC, Corporate Law, Tax and Accounting Aspects of their Establishment, Operation, Regulation and Role in Diversification* (Release 2) (Clark and Boardman, August 1986).
8. "24th Annual Report of the Securities and Exchange Commission" (Securities and Exchange Commission, June 1958), 107-23.
9. "Fifth Annual Report of the Securities and Exchange Commission" (Securities and Exchange Commission, June 1939), 63-68.
10. "Public Utility Holding Company Act of 1935," Wikipedia.
11. "Public Utility Holding Company Act of 1935: 1932-1992," Energy Information Administration (January 1993).
12. Various news reports.

Chapter 2: Natural Opportunities

1. "Stock Performance Data," Edison Electric Institute (February 2021).
2. "The History of Electricity Restructuring in California," Center for the Study of Electricity Markets, pp. 6-8 (May 2002).
3. "Stock Performance," Edison.
4. "Stock Performance," Edison.
5. S&P Capital IO Pro.
6. S&P.
7. "Stock Performance," Edison.
8. "Stock Performance," Edison.
9. "Stock Performance," Edison.
10. S&P.
11. S&P; "Stock Performance," Edison.
12. S&P; "Stock Performance," Edison.
13. S&P.
14. Company websites.
15. Company websites.
16. Company website.
17. Company website.
18. Company website.
19. Company website.
20. "Water Market USA," *Water Intelligence* (May 27, 2009).
21. S&P.
22. "Her Majesty's Treasury: Implementing Privatisation: The UK Experience" (1998).
23. "Knowledge at Wharton: Private Equity Firms Discover Electricity – and Lead the Charge for Energy Investment" (April 2007).
24. "Merger and Acquisition Announcements 2020," Edison Electric Institute; "Completed Mergers, Acquisitions, and Deals 2009," American Gas Association, various news reports.
25. "Merger and Acquisition," Edison.
26. "Completed Mergers," American Gas Association; reports.
27. "Merger and Acquisition," Edison.
28. "Completed Mergers," American Gas Association; reports.
29. "Merger and Acquisition," Edison.
30. "Merger and Acquisition," Edison.

Chapter 3: Modern Era of M&A (1995–2020)

1. Ray, Dennis, Stevenson, Rodney, Thompson, Howard, "Electric Utility Mergers and Regulatory Policy" (University of Wisconsin, Schiffman, Roger, National Regulatory Research Institute, NRRI 92-12).
2. "Stock Performance," Edison.
3. "2019 Financial Review," Edison; "Completed Mergers," American Gas Association; reports.
4. "2019 Financial," Edison; "Completed Mergers," American Gas Association; reports.
5. "2019 Financial," Edison; "Completed Mergers," American Gas Association; reports.
6. "Stock Performance," Edison.
7. "2019 Financial," Edison; "Completed Mergers," American Gas Association; reports.
8. "2019 Financial," Edison; "Completed Mergers," American Gas Association; reports.
9. "2019 Financial," Edison; "Completed Mergers," American Gas Association; reports.
10. "2019 Financial," Edison; "Completed Mergers," American Gas Association; reports.
11. "2019 Financial," Edison; "Completed Mergers," American Gas Association; reports.
12. "PSC Unanimously Rejects BBI Buyout of Northwestern" (May 23, 2007).
13. "Stock Performance," Edison.
14. "2019 Financial," Edison; "Completed Mergers," American Gas Association; reports.
15. "2019 Financial" Edison; "Completed Mergers," American Gas Association; various news reports.
16. "2019 Financial," Edison; "Completed Mergers," American Gas Association; reports.
17. "Stock Performance," Edison.
18. "Stock Performance," Edison.
19. "2019 Financial," Edison; "Completed Mergers," American Gas Association; reports.
20. "2019 Financial," Edison; "Completed Mergers," American Gas Association; reports.
21. "2019 Financial," Edison; "Completed Mergers," American Gas Association; reports.
22. "Industry Capital Expenditures," Edison Electric Institute (2021).
23. "Stock Performance," Edison.

24. "Industry Capital Expenditures," Edison Electric Institute; S&P Capital IQ Pro.
25. "2019 Financial," Edison; "Completed Mergers," American Gas Association; reports.
26. "Stock Performance," Edison.
27. "2019 Financial" Edison; "Completed Mergers," American Gas Association; reports.
28. "2019 Financial" Edison; "Completed Mergers," American Gas Association; reports.

Chapter 4: Maverick Actions

1. S&P Capital IQ Pro; various news reports.
2. Various news reports.

Chapter 5: Value Sources

1. "Testimony of Thomas J. Flaherty Before the Kansas Corporation Commission," Company filings; Strategy& (part of the PwC Network).

Chapter 6: Hurdles and Outcomes

1. "The State Corporation Commission of the State of Kansas: In the Matter of the Joint Application of Great Plains Energy Incorporated, Kansas City Power & Light Company and Westar Energy, Inc. for the Acquisition of Westar Energy, Inc. by Great Plains Energy Incorporated, Final Order" (April 2017): 3-5.
2. "The Commonwealth of Massachusetts: Department of Public Utilities, Joint Application for the Merger Between NSTAR and Northeast Utilities, Final Order" (April 2013): 29-31.
3. Moot, John S. "A New FERC Policy for Electric Utility Mergers," *Energy Law Journal* Volume 17 (1996).
4. "Handbook to Distributer and Transmitter Consolidations," Ontario Energy Board (January 2016).
5. "The State Corporation Commission of the State of Kansas: In the Matter of the Joint Application of Kansas Power and Light Company, KCA Corporation and Kansas Gas and Electric Company for Approval of All Classes of the Capital Stock of Kansas Gas and Electric by KCA Corporation, Final Order" (November 1991): 65-77.
6. "Merger and Acquisition," Edison; "Completed Mergers," American Gas Association; reports.
7. "Merger and Acquisition," Edison; "Completed Mergers," American Gas Association; reports.
8. "Merger and Acquisition," Edison; "Completed Mergers," American Gas Association; reports.

9. "Merger and Acquisition," Edison; "Completed Mergers," American Gas Association; reports.
10. "Merger and Acquisition," Edison; "Completed Mergers," American Gas Association; reports.

Chapter 8: Return to Restructuring

1. Solomon, David, "Goldman Sachs Commercially-Driven Plan for Sustainability," *Financial Times*, December 15, 2019.
2. "ESG Assets May Hit $53 trillion by 2025," *Bloomberg Intelligence*, February 23, 2021.
3. "CEO Larry Fink's 2020 Letter to CEOs, The Fundamental Reshaping of Finance," BlackRock: January 2020.
4. "CEO Larry Fink's Letter to CEOs, The Global Transition to a Net Zero Economy," BlackRock: January 2021.
5. "CEO Larry Fink," BlackRock.
6. "The Great Transition: Opening the Renewables Floodgate," *Octopus Investment Limited*: October 2019.
7. "Sempra Completes Sale of Assets in South America," *San Diego Union-Tribune*: June 24, 2020.
8. "Strategic Repositioning of PPL Corporation," PPL Presentation to Analysts: March 18, 2021.
9. "PSEG Agrees to Sell PSEG Fossil Generating Portfolio to ArcLight Capital," Press Release: PSEG Newsroom: August 12, 2021.
10. "Duke Energy Partners with GIC to Secure Minority Investment in Duke Energy Indiana," Press Release: *Duke Energy News Center*: January 28, 2021.
11. "Southern Company to Acquire PowerSecure International, Inc.," Press Release: *Southern Company News*: February 24, 2016.
12. "PowerSecure Expands Distributed Infrastructure capabilities with Acquisition of Power Pro-Tech Services," Press Release: *PowerSecure News*: April 7, 2017.

Chapter 9: Future Direction

1. "Merger and Acquisition," Edison; "Completed Mergers," American Gas Association; various news reports.
2. "The Fleishman Daily," Wolfe Research: March 26, 2021.
3. "Stock Performance," Edison; S&P.
4. "Stock Performance," Edison.
5. S&P.
6. "2019 Financial Review," Edison; S&P.

INDEX

Figures are indicated by an italicized *f* following a page number.

A

B

C

D

E

F

G

H

I

J

K

L

M

N

O

P

Q

R

S

T

U

V

W

X

Y

ABOUT THE AUTHOR

THOMAS J. FLAHERTY, a retired senior partner from Strategy&, enjoyed a global consulting career spanning over forty-five years, leading utilities consulting practices at several top-tier firms. Focusing on all sectors of the utilities industry, he specialized in corporate strategy, mergers and acquisitions, business models, organization architecture, and innovation.

The early 1990s triggered policy, regulatory, and economic factors to enable market competition, driving utilities to seek greater scale within a highly fragmented sector. Mr. Flaherty led hundreds of merger and acquisition analyses for clients, including the vast majority of U.S. utilities stock transactions, and deals in multiple global regions. These transactions transformed the U.S. power and gas sectors, resulting in consolidation of the industry from approximately 150 tradable companies in 1995 to fewer than 50 today.

His recognized expertise in synergies quantification, regulatory strategy, and post-close integration led to testimony before twenty-five federal and state regulatory agencies, and frequent articles on mergers and acquisitions.